Our Children, Our Future

THE CHINMAYA WAY

ॐ

Tejomayananda
7.7.2013

Published by

Chinmaya Mission West
P.O. Box 129, Piercy, CA 95587 U.S.A.
Tel: (707) 247-3488
Email: publications@chinmayamission.org
Website: www.chinmayamission.org

First Edition: May 2013, 5,000 copies

Gratitude and prostrations to Pūjya Guruji for his love and blessings.

Grateful prostrations to Swami Nikhilananda for his inspiration and guidance.

Grateful acknowledgment to the Ācāryas and all contributors from Bala Vihars worldwide — to the sevaks and students whose inspired experiences have created this book.

Many thanks to CM Delhi, Anjali Singh, Chinmaya Archives, Tapovan Prasad, CCMT Publications, Chinmaya Kalpanam, Chinmaya Mission (West) News. Special thanks to Sangeeta Chadha for her invaluable support.

Author

Parveen Bahl

Project Coordinator

Kalpana Vaswani

Content, Edit, and Design Support

Kumkum Bhatia and Sharda Chawla

Support by the Mananam team

Swami Shantananda, Margaret Dukes, David Dukes, Neena Dev,
Rudite Emir, Br. Eric, Rashmi Mehrotra, Arun Mehrotra, and Aarthi Ramalingam.
Special thanks to Padmashree Rao, the Mananam (Bala Vihar) liaison, for her advice and assistance.

Illustrations, Design, and Layout by

Nidhi Wadhwa and the Blue Fish Designs team

Printed by

Silverpoint Press Pvt. Ltd., India

Library of Congress Control Number: 2012953222

ISBN: 978-1-60827-011-8

THE mananam SERIES

CHINMAYA BIRTH CENTENARY CELEBRATION SERIES

Our Children, Our Future

THE CHINMAYA WAY

CHINMAYA PUBLICATIONS
CHINMAYA MISSION WEST PUBLICATIONS DIVISION

IT IS IMPORTANT TO PROVIDE CHILDREN A CHEERFUL ATMOSPHERE OF AFFECTION AND TENDERNESS. TOUCH THE CHILDREN. TELL THEM THAT YOU LOVE THEM, THAT THEY ARE BEAUTIFUL, INTELLIGENT AND GOOD. LET CHILDREN SEE THAT YOU ARE VERY EAGER TO BE HELPFUL. THESE CAN VERY QUICKLY IMPRESS THEM AND SINK INTO THEIR PERSONALITY. A NOBLE CHARACTER IS THUS EASILY FORMED.

| SWAMI CHINMAYANANDA |

ॐ

Foreword

A person completes his education successfully, and is happy.... He gets a job, earns his first pay, and is very happy.... He gets married... and is very, very happy! But the greatest joy comes when he is blessed with a child. Most married couples desire a child - a good child. 'Good' is meant to indicate a physically normal and intellectually healthy child who will be successful, gives joy to others, and does not cause any trouble to the parents. Children enter this world through a natural process, but to *make them good children* is a great responsibility.

If parents want the child to be good, they must do something about it. Nothing happens automatically. Other than rare saintly exceptions, children need support and guidance. To nurture children, help them reach their potential and become great is the primary responsibility and role of parents. But how good or great they become will depend on *how* they are groomed. That is the key. Of course, children are born with their own karma, but despite this, we can mold their present and shape their future.

In olden times, when children studied in gurukulas, the teacher did all the grooming. Later, in joint families, traditions were imbibed through a process of osmosis. Today, the gurukula system is no longer prevalent, and joint families are fading away. Everybody is busy. In this environment, the responsibility of spiritual organizations becomes greater. Being a part of society, they have certain obligations toward the well-being of its members.

What is Chinmaya Bala Vihar? It is a program for children between the ages of three and seventeen years, held once a week for one-and-a-half hours in different homes. In case of a large attendance, a school or community space is rented to hold the classes. Typically, a Bala Vihar class follows a certain structure. The first few minutes are devoted to prayer. Then the children sing bhajans or songs, after which they learn stories from our epics and are acquainted with inspiring historical figures. They learn about festivals and understand the symbolism behind Hindu gods. The class could comprise quizzes, puzzles, and games. It concludes with a prayer.

All the activities in a Bala Vihar class or camp are specially designed for children. The primary aim is to teach children to look at life as a game. Further, they must understand that even though life is viewed as a sport, every sport has rules, and discipline is important; just because it's a game, it does not mean we can skip the rules.

Arts and crafts, music, dance, and dramatics are taught at Bala Vihar camps. Children learn and are slowly inspired through all these activities. Often, many Indian parents living abroad worry, "How will our children learn about our culture and values?" In fact, Bala Vihar children invariably end up knowing more about the epics, saṁskāras, festivals, and customs than their parents!

The purpose of Bala Vihar is to help children learn about values in an enjoyable atmosphere. Experience shows that children love attending Bala Vihar classes when teachers are good and teach well. Hence teaching should be in such a way that children effortlessly imbibe the knowledge: *To shine like the sun, and to delight like the moon.*

"Shining like the sun" means that children have to achieve brilliant success in their own lives. But their success – like the moon – must delight others, and elevate the mind. Success that makes everybody miserable is not success. Individual success is great, but it should not overwhelm others.

Look at Chinmaya Mission's mission statement. It says: *To provide to everyone, from any background, the wisdom of Vedānta and the practical means for their spiritual growth and happiness, enabling them to become positive contributors to society.*

Inherent in this mission statement are two factors: The first is our own growth, and the second is service to others. Therefore, right from childhood, Bala Vihar must ensure that these two objectives are fulfilled.

Bala Vihar helps children to grow. As a gardener helps to grow a plant by tending and nurturing it, we facilitate the growth of children through the various activities of Bala Vihar. One young lady told me, "The greatest gift that our parents gave us in our childhood was taking us to Chinmaya Bala Vihar."

Many children, having gone through Bala Vihar, have moved on to Yuva Kendra. We even have Ācāryas in the Mission who have been with us right from Bala Vihar. So, the sevaks conducting Bala Vihar have to be clear about the vision behind the classes, their purpose, what to teach and how to teach it. It is not just about telling a story. It is about inculcating values. The story should flow effortlessly, almost as if the teacher has not taught, but the child has learned. The moral should come directly from the child.

For example, if we ask a child, "Do you love your birthday?" Most children would reply in the affirmative.

We can then ask, "Why do you love it?"

The child will answer, "Because of the gifts and the feeling of being special."

At this stage we can ask, "When you get a gift from someone, you say thank you to that person. Now suppose someone presents you a golden ring, then you say thank you, and feel very happy. But who gave you the finger and the hand?"

The child will say, "God!"

"Have you said 'thank you' to God?" we ask. The child will answer in the negative. Slowly, through this process, the perception of the children changes; they become aware that their bodies themselves are a wealth that they possess. More importantly, they realize that they can live without the ring and a host of other things, but not without the body. When their attention is captured, they are quick to understand, and then they themselves provide the answers.

Chinmaya Mission has created a formal syllabus to assist the sevaks and sevikās with ideas on running a Bala Vihar class. In addition, a huge volume of material, including CDs of bhajans and chanted Sanskrit ślokas, and a wide variety of storybooks, is also available to supplement the syllabus. Our vision for Bala Vihar remains strong, and it is my very great wish that this program is replicated in all our mission centers.

In India, Chinmaya Mission has more than eighty schools (Chinmaya Vidyalayas) with the complete infrastructure of classrooms. These remain unused on Sundays. So, I suggest that every Sunday the school premises be used for Sunday Bala Vihar.

With dedicated parents, sevaks, and sevikās working together in growing facilities worldwide, the Bala Vihar program promises to make a difference in every child's life through the joyful teaching-learning process. I remember a beautiful statement made by the great Rabindranath Tagore:

> *The birth of every child shows that God has not lost faith in man yet, because God feels that this child is going to make the difference!*

Tejomayananda

Swami Tejomayananda
Head, Chinmaya Mission Worldwide

Contents

Preface

Who would have imagined that one thought in the mind of Pujya Gurudev, would in a short span of time, metamorphose into a magnificent movement with a worldwide presence? *Our Children, Our Future – The Chinmaya Way* is a tribute to this phenomenon – Bala Vihar.

A miracle has been and is unfolding before our very eyes. And writing about a miracle can only be another miracle. How this book happened is just that – a series of wonders. The placement of every word, thought and incident is here, because it was meant to be so; part of a design, which evolved. The content for the book, the photographs and the team that worked on it – all arrived when they had to, not before not after.

It came together as an offering of love from Bala Vihar beneficiaries – sevaks, parents and children. Their voices bring alive the glory of Gurudev's vision – our gratitude to them for their wholehearted participation.

Thousands of lives have been transformed through the experience of Bala Vihar. As a tribute to this wisdom, the five parts of the book, answer questions on different aspects of Bala Vihar: What? Why? How? When and Where? Who?

The book is offered at the feet of Pujya Gurudev Swami Chinmayananda, through the hands of Pujya Guruji Swami Tejomayananda.

Part 1

The What

Part 1

The What

I Mold the Child, Mold the Future

Pujya Gurudev's vision — Imparting right values from early childhood

II Rooted in Time

The story of Bhakta Prahlāda — The Purānic inspiration for Bala Vihar

III The Play Unfolds

A glimpse into the world of Bala Vihar — The learning and the fun

IV The Vision Translated

The objective of Bala Vihar — Guruji's words of guidance

I

Mold the Child, Mold the Future

The pair of deep-set eyes belonging to Pujya Gurudev Swami Chinmayananda could cut through the shroud of time and gaze into the mystery of creation.... At will, they could twinkle merrily or shine with piercing intent, penetrating deep into the issues of approaching times....

Even as he worked with focus in the world of that day, his concern for future generations was etched in every plan he proposed, and indeed in every activity he undertook.

Tuned to the oncoming vistas, he knew that special training was the need of the hour. Only a protective armor could safeguard the children of the future so that they could live meaningful lives. The shield had to be shaped from the wisdom of the past and strengthened by the culture of their ancestors. The efforts to reach out to the children had to be in harmony with their physical, emotional, intellectual, and spiritual needs — in consonance with nature!

Time was insistent, and a solution had to be found. Fearlessly, Pujya Gurudev responded with a clarion call....

MOLD THE CHILD,
MOLD THE FUTURE.

His appeal to empower the child and build an inspired future resounded far and wide...roaring in some places, and whispering in others.

A collective response to his plea arose from the hearts of parents apprehensive about the future of their children. Gurudev appropriately named it and behold...

• Bala Vihar was Born! •

Gurudev spoke from many a raised platform, addressing the call of the future. Concerned parents and sensitive volunteers hung onto his every word, not just because of his charismatic persona but also because of the relevance of his message. Everyday his words brought new meaning into their lives, and what was more, despite the changing times, they remain ever fresh and pertinent in any situation...

A Reverie...

Grey-haired Shanti, with her hair coiled into a low bun, was biding time in her garden. A soft breeze wafted through the verandah as she waited for her daughter-in-law Shraddha and grandson Gopal to accompany her to the Guru Pūrnimā celebration at the Delhi Chinmaya Mission. Indeed it was a special day.... She was filled with gratitude for her Guru. Her meeting with him had changed not only the complexion of her life, but that of her whole family!

As if from nowhere, a host of memories crowded in. They jostled with each other for a chance to be heard. How had her transformation begun? What was the vision that drew her? How did it permeate her life? How did it affect her children? Even on this very day, how was it shaping her future?

Questions about life as seen from a wider perspective had initiated a search for a path that would give her the answers she sought. It started when she was a young mother concerned about her children growing up in an atmosphere that had witnessed rapid change and was not always in keeping with universally accepted norms. The balancing act of her motherly role vis-à-vis the peer influence on her children weighed on her mind. She had stepped into a new phase of life, and desired that its demands be met.

When the desire is sincere, the universe conspires to fulfill it. And so, a series of seeming coincidences later, an altered direction of life brought her to where she was now.

Shanti's memories carried her to a particular day in 1987, when Swami Chinmayananda spoke to a gathering of teachers and parents at the Jamnabai Narsee School in Mumbai. She had arrived there, a concerned parent, with a desire to know how she should raise her children. Would she find the answers in this forum? Was a sannyāsī competent to advise on the delicate issue of raising children? Curiosity had brought her thus far, and bursting with questions, she was willing to give the Swami a hearing. "In all fairness," she thought, "He does have a powerful presence...."

On the stage, Swami Chinmayananda adjusted the microphone and began his address. Shanti had no choice; without her knowledge, without her consent, stealthily, her transformation had begun....

Gurudev spoke eloquently, and with passion. Step by step, he presented a vision for the future education and training of children:

When we say that today's world is to be the future world, it means that today's people and their contribution is what will mold the world, its ways, and its life in the future. Today's adults will not remain and survive in the future, but the expectation is that today's children will survive. Naturally, therefore, if the present children are molded in their attitudes, in their values, in their ideas, and in their ideals, we can logically expect a better and more organized world of tomorrow, and achieve the design for the world that we hope for at this moment.

This future design cannot come in our own lifetime; it needs a long period of time for the changes to come about. Change it will, but the kind of change will be determined by the moral fiber of the growing generation. Therefore, when we say that today's children are our future, we mean that we must strive right now to mold the children to think correctly, to judge rightly, and to have the heroism to live up to those convictions.

All progressive countries in the world are such because their progress is guided by, decided by, thought of by, and planned by the intellectuals of their generation.

Since the 1950s, India has grappled with problems of changing social values, degradation of morals, and other social and psycho-social issues. There was little to strike hope in the hearts of the traditionally inclined. Situations could not be wished away or changed in the twinkling of an eye. Change has its own pace. Even so, a fresh beginning had to be made. Without taking the first step, the goal would always stay at a distance. Cognizant of this, Gurudev offered a solution:

We cannot come out of it immediately — it is not overnight that things happen. It is not a revolution that we are thinking of, but an evolution of a country's culture, its social status, and its individual character. It is a slow process. So if the future is to be bright, we have to mold our children to think — not in our pattern, which is disastrous, as we have already seen — but in a new pattern, with a new inspiration, and with a new vision in their minds.

Everybody will accept the idea that our children are our future. But we have yet to realize the implication of this, and to start thinking about it. This understanding cannot happen just because some textbooks have been changed, or because a lot of blabbering is going on in the newspapers and television about value-based educational systems that should start in the country! Mere talk is not sufficient — it will not help. Children do not learn from books...

...Shanti, a professor of child psychology, knew that children learned from diverse circumstances and the people to whom they were exposed. Modern science is just waking up to the reality of the importance of prenatal education, a fact well known to the ṛṣīs of yore. Unfortunately, the West had to authenticate even the age-old Vedic wisdom. Indians were just not convinced about the ancient wealth that was theirs for the asking! Focusing on the current parenting scene, Gurudev remarked....

Our children are our future, and mothers are the ones who mold children. In order to do this, a mother has to spend extra energy, and this is the most expensive gift we can give to our children — our time.

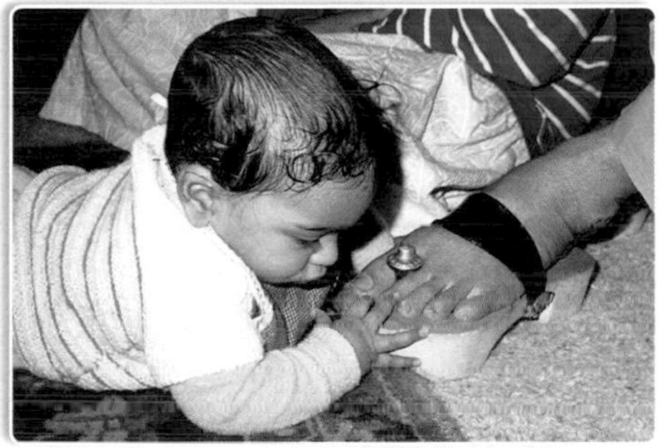

But what is the prenatal education that mothers are giving to their children today — films, videos, those stupid books? These are the ideals we are feeding the children, and when they come out as demons, we say, "the children have gone astray!" We don't understand what has happened to the world! It is our mistake!

Yet one little child can change the entire history of the country. This is how all great men of the past were made — a Shivaji, an Einstein, a Tagore, or a Mahatma Gandhi. From their childhood onward, their mothers inculcated noble ideas into them. If you read their autobiographies, they all openly declare that if they achieved success and greatness, they are indebted to their mothers!

It is always the mother at home who imparts values and ideals to the child, who molds the mental thinking of the child.

You may not like what I am saying, but I am on a platform where truth is to be brought out. Nobody else will do it because they all want a vote! I do not want a vote! I do not want anything from you.

Gurudev understood the critical role assigned to womankind. He knew that once the woman of the family is convinced of the value of the scriptural teaching, the whole family is secure. He wanted women to be aware of their important role in the larger scheme of life:

The mother can impart the soft values. She gives the child the ideals of charity, goodness, tenderness, affection, and forgiveness. She never imparts values by giving the child a discourse, but through her life she demonstrates these ideals, and the child sees it — these ideals become embedded in the child.

When mothers lose touch with the spiritual values of the country, and the adults' lives become loose and unethical, then their children's lives will also be degraded.

When the same children become youngsters, they start looking around and find that the values they have been given are hollow, empty, and lonely. They don't feel satisfied, and they don't have the right mental discrimination to think correctly. They want to escape. And how do they escape? Through alcohol and drugs! Are parents then not directly responsible for driving away their youngsters to these ruinous, suicidal escapisms? You think on this.

I am not accusing you though. I can't accuse because you never meant it! There is no motive behind your thoughtlessness, but it has created this aberration in our society.

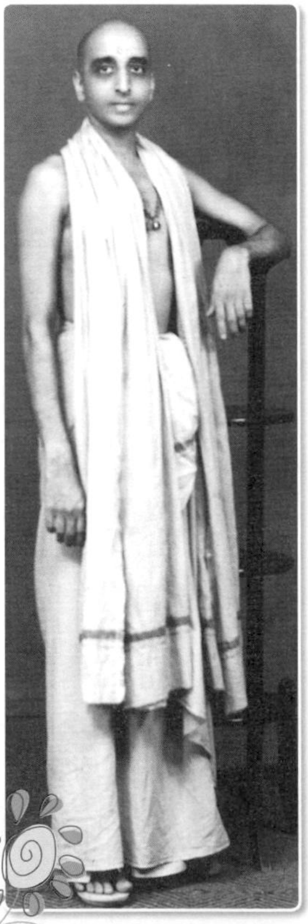

...Shanti was struck by the deep compassion with which Gurudev completely exonerated women from the guilt pangs that they often experience. His message was not to blame, but to redress erroneous thinking. To benefit generations of parents and teachers, he unveiled his vision for children. He proclaimed....

To return high ideals to society, the obvious choice is to learn the scriptures and Indian culture. And through these, we can impart values to our children, and give them a healthy foundation upon which they can build their life.

In the old story of the *Rāmāyaṇa*, we see greater and nobler values being demonstrated. These are the values that we silently and expectantly hope for in the youth of today. And we are charmed by it because it belongs to the very heart of our country. So it is not so difficult to impart these ideas to our children.

When we sit down and try to analyze how to remold and recast the future, we see that it is through the child of today that we beget the leaders of tomorrow. *But, we must supply them with the vision.*

Only when a plant is young and we sincerely care for it, can we train it to grow straight. A plant can be trained, but not a tree. If the tree has a bend, it has a bend — full stop! Then, we can only trim the branches but not the trunk.

...While he spoke, Shanti's mind marveled: "How true are his words, visually profound, and yet so simple. An aware person alone can train young minds to equip them with the necessary strength to face life's challenges. Swamiji wants us to accept the existing ground realities, for only then will we direct the mind to search for a solution."....

Gurudev continued to outline a course of action, envisioning a special breed of teachers to impart this training. It was important for teachers to expand their own vision and to holistically understand the intrinsic nature of a child:

- All schools must start a program to give special training to teachers in how they may, whenever possible in their classrooms, make the children understand that there is an unseen hand that molds the affairs of the entire universe. Why are you afraid to have such programs? Christian churches can do it; Islam is doing it in their schools. How is it that Hindus alone cannot do it?

We have to bring back the system, which is healthy, which in our neglect, we have thrown away. In addition to this, we must also teach the children to have the courage and heroism to live up to these values and convictions. This is very important.

It is not that we actually have no intellectuals. To only be eloquent in coffeehouses, restaurants, and so on, but not where it matters because we are afraid to stand against the tide — this is not intellectualism at all! We must have the courage to declare our values at the right places, at the right time, and to the government if necessary, with logical reasoning, how the present policies are wrong. Think. A real intellectual cannot keep quiet when he sees injustice, and he doesn't care what the consequences are!

▲ GURUDEV AS A BALA VIHAR SEVAK

Therefore, we must teach our children not only to have right values and convictions, but also to have the heroism to live up to them. If this kind of training can be imparted to even one child, we will have shaped a better future.

We have to take responsibility for molding and beautifying the child, prepare him to face the world of the future. It is a tremendous responsibility. The remedy is with us.

... Shanti was bowled over by this appeal to her innate wisdom. Impressed by the fact that she was not being coerced into any cult, her intellect paused to consider.... Gurudev had presented facts and left the choice to the judgment of the listener.

Not one to let grass grow under her feet on any venture that touched her heart, Shanti began to learn about the activities of Chinmaya Mission. She was fascinated by the immense possibilities presented specially by Bala Vihar (BV), the children's movement. This opened avenues not only for children, but also for the volunteers who served them.

The sound of a car horn signaled the arrival of Shraddha and the imp Gopal. This brought Shanti's reverie to an end. With an anticipative smile she walked to the car. And no sooner had she opened the door, a bundle of energy dragged her in. Excitement oozing from every pore, she was greeted with Gopal's impatient chatter, "Dādī, dādī! You promised. You promised to tell me the story of Prahlāda! Please! Please! Can you do it now?"**....**

Bala Perspectives

Dear God, I did not think that blue and orange was such a good combination till I saw the sunset you made last week. Keep it up! — a BV child.

II

Rooted in Time

"Prahlāda, Prahlāda.... Let's play!" called the friends of the little prince, Bhakta Prahlāda. "Our teachers have gone out!"

"No, my friends, let's not waste this time. We should use every moment in remembering and loving God.... Let's chant His name," replied Prahlāda.

"But why must we chant the Lord's name?" asked one friend.

Prahlāda answered, "When we chant His name, we surrender our mind to Him. He purifies it and gives it back to us."

Prahlāda's playmates asked again: "But what's the hurry? Why do we need to do that now?"

"Friends!" began Bhakta Prahlāda, in all earnestness, "Human birth is difficult to attain, for only in this birth can we gain the ultimate goal of life. Life is short and unpredictable. There is no way of knowing when it may end. So the search should begin early. We should not depend on youth, or old age to start. It is best to start now, in childhood itself."

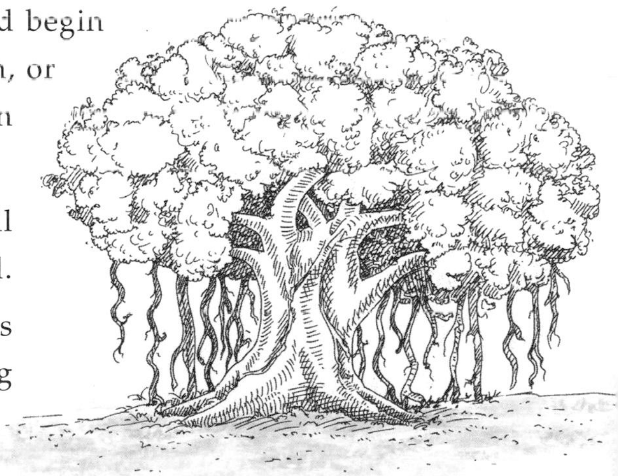

"Prahlāda, wait. Who told you all these things?" wondered another friend.

"I learned these things when I was in my mother's womb. My father, King

Hiraṇyakaśyapu, went to the forest to perform austerities, and Devarṣi Nārada took my mother to an āśrama...."

...Gopal listened wide-eyed and enthralled, as Shanti recounted his favorite story. While Gopal let his boyish imagination fly into a mythological landscape, Shanti's memories led her to Gurudev's masterly story-telling of this same story. She remembered how he termed Prahlāda's story as Devarṣi Nārada's experiment in prenatal education! He had said....

When the demon king Hiraṇyakaśyapu went to do austerities in the forest, Indra (the king of the gods) took the opportunity to do an experiment. He felt that if even one Hiraṇyakaśyapu was too great a threat to the good values of life, what would happen if every child growing up in that land wanted to become another Hiraṇyakaśyapu! Therefore he collected all the pregnant ladies and took them to heaven, where he hoped the children could be molded in a new atmosphere to become better people. The genes had become so bad that they had to be revitalized!

At this time, Devarṣi Nārada came along, and he wanted to try his own experiment. He requested to be given only one specimen — one pregnant lady — the queen of Hiraṇyakaśyapu.

Devarṣi Nārada took the queen to an āśrama where she listened to the discourses of Vedānta day in and day out. She herself may have understood very little, but because she was exposed to Vedāntic ideas for the last three months of her pregnancy, the child within her was remolded — not outside, but in the mother's womb, akin to a prenatal education — and it is this child who became the great Prahlāda.

Nobody taught Prahlāda these ideals in the world, but he was convinced of the higher values of life. His father wanted him to become another demonic Hiraṇyakaśyapu, but because of the prenatal spiritual training, this solitary little boy stood against the entire materialistic culture that had developed in the country at the time. Prahlāda brought his country back to the healthier and eternal values of Upaniṣads.

...Shanti was prompted out of her nostalgia by Gopal, "Dādī, tell me, how did Prahlāda make all his friends sing, 'Om namo nārāyanaya?' Did they get into trouble for following Prahlāda?" he asked. Going back to the story Shanti turned his question into a teachable moment....

Prahlāda reminded his friends, "My dear friends, because we're young, it is easy for us to tune ourselves to God. See, how easily you believe in my words! So let's not wait. It is wrong to think that our younger days are for enjoyment and when older, we will somehow turn toward God. Training in the spiritual way of living must begin early. We must engage in devotional service from childhood itself. This is our highest duty."

"Yes, yes! We understand," his friends agreed. "We will do what you say, Prahlāda."

The children chanted in chorus:

Om namo nārāyanaya, Om namo nārāyanaya
Om namo nārāyanaya, Om namo nārāyanaya ....

(Story from the *Bhāgawat Mahā Purāṇa*, Canto 7.)

Prahlāda taught his friends the wisdom that he had gained in his mother's womb. And it was only through his efforts that an entire generation of asuras was transformed.

...As Shanti completed the story – of how often and dramatically the Lord had saved Prahlāda from his father's varied and wicked attempts to kill him, a thought flashed....

THAT COULD HAVE BEEN THE FIRST BALA VIHAR CLASS!
AND BHAKTA PRAHLĀDA, THE VERY FIRST BALA VIHAR SEVAK!

From Puranas to Pujya Gurudev

With a vision born of a timeless conviction, very similar to that of Prahlāda, Pujya Gurudev Swami Chinmayananda inspired the modern day Bala Vihar (BV). Like Bhakta Prahlāda, Gurudev understood the need for children to connect with the Supreme at an early age. He also knew that for achieving success in the outer world, they require a strong value system strengthened by discipline. For only then would they be able to work fearlessly in the world outside, while remaining rooted and peaceful within.

▲ GURUDEV POSES WITH THE TROUPE FROM CHEMBUR (BV AND YUVA KENDRA MEMBERS) AFTER 'BHAKTA PRAHALAD' - A MEGA DANCE-DRAMA PRODUCTION

Gurudev often said: *"Culture can never be taught, it can only be caught!"* Therefore, he gathered the core values from the scriptures and packaged them into BV. He encouraged the use of innovative methods to create an interest in the minds of children, giving it a new look just as Prahlāda had done, ages before, for his friends.

Pujya Gurudev's main concern was that children must be given the right saṁskāras (good values) at the right time. He explained how these values should be inculcated in children:

> When the child has crawled out of infancy and reached sufficient proficiency to move about, watch, and observe, the child is now fit for self-education. The child's endless wonderment at things, the steady sense of inquisitiveness, and the silent but very thoughtful attention to everything said and done around it in the world, the experiments with love, affection, anger, jealousy, covetousness, instincts of acquisition, grabbing, fighting, kindness — the entire gamut of emotional life — is the next stage. During this time, education starts; and this highly impressive period is the most crucial time in building up the child's entire future.
>
> At this juncture, the main study is from example; the child imitates all the elders in the immediate world. Parents, servants, maids, neighbors, their children, and visitors — from everyone the child picks up traits, habits, words, ideas, dress habits, and even their accent and inflections of speech. The child is never tired of observing around him and learning from everyone and from every situation.

Gurudev knew from his own childhood experience that self-education had to begin in the tender years of infancy. So he set about opening the doors to a worldwide classroom filled with love, laughter, and learning —

• BALA VIHAR! •

Bala Perspectives

A BV teacher was telling the children, "Prayer is not begging. So we must avoid asking God, 'Give me this. Give me that.'" A child raised his hand and asked, "Teacher, is it ok if my friend asks on my behalf and I ask on his behalf?"

III

The Play Unfolds

BALA = Children **VIHAR = Recreation**

BalaVihar (BV) is a place where children learn values while having fun. The concept of BV took shape from the vision that Pujya Gurudev had for the well-being of future generations. He declared:

- *Children are not vessels to be filled, but lamps to be lit.* Children are the architects of the future world. They are the builders of humanity. The seeds of spiritual values should be sown in young hearts and the condition should be made favorable for their sprouting and steady growth by the exercise of proper control and discipline. Cared for with the warmth of love and affection, such a tree shall blossom forth flowers of Brotherhood, Universal Love, Peace, Bliss, Beauty and Perfection.

So what happens in a typical BV classroom, which holds the promise of Gurudev's words? A flashback to Chembur, Mumbai, in 1976, holds the answer.

...Memories are often like never-ending scarves that a magician keeps pulling out of his big hat. Drawn into a chain of recollections, Shanti in retrospect could clearly see — the first in the series of coincidences that brought BV gradually into focus for her....

Back in 1976, Shanti was invited by her cousin to accompany her to the tenth anniversary celebrations of BV Chembur. Shanti's cousin was all keyed up and excited about helping in the play, so Shanti willingly accompanied her to the event.

What struck Shanti was the enthusiasm in the air. It was infectious. Her cousin said that the play was conceptualized by Nirmala Chellam, a founding BV sevikā. Shanti sat in the audience and watched the sequence....

The curtain lifts to show seventeen-year-old Shyamala Acharya surrounded by students of her BV class. Two children, accompanied by their parents, walk onto the stage, as though looking for something.

Parent: We were looking for a BV class. Do you know where it is held?

Sevikā: (*responds confidently*) Hari Om! This is a BV class. How can I help you?

Parents: (*Introducing themselves, the couple expresses a desire to know more.*) Who are you, and what happens in this class? Who are all these children?

Sevikā: (*brimming with confidence*) Sir, I am a sevikā and this is a BV class run by the Chinmaya Mission. We meet once a week, on Sundays at a fixed time. These classes provide a platform where children learn the value of values, and gain insights into their Indian culture, in an environment of love and fun. This leads them to a better understanding of the world and themselves.

The unique aspect of the program is that the teachers (sevaks) are all volunteers. They deeply revere Gurudev's vision of BV and cement their commitment by offering their services, for its fulfilment.

Parents: Amazing what inspiration does! Where are these classes held and what is their duration?

Sevikā: The groups vary in numbers - ranging from four or five children up to twenty or twenty-five children.

Smaller classes are most often conducted in homes of devotees. Larger numbers are accommodated in Chinmaya

Mission centers or in rented premises, such as schools, community halls, temples, and churches.

The class normally lasts for ninety minutes and follows a fixed schedule. Please join us today to get an understanding of the program. As we go along, I will explain to you why we do what we do.

The couple, along with their children, joins the outer periphery of the circle and the class commences:

Together, everyone chants 'OM' three times.

Sevikā: Before commencing the class, let us invoke the blessings of Lord Gaṇeśa, the remover of obstacles. Who wants to lead the prayer today?

A little boy raises his hand and excitedly says. "Dīdī me! Dīdī me!" The sevikā smiles and nods encouragingly. As he chants, "Eka dantaṁ...," everyone joins in. Then, the children invoke Sarasvatī Devi, the Goddess of Knowledge, and the Guru, whose Grace enables the connection to the Supreme.

Sevikā: Dear children, I am so glad that you have come today. I will be even happier to see you every Sunday. Regularity is very important.

She takes a roll-call and each one answers with "Hari Om."

Sevikā: Children, let us learn the Dhyāna śloka of the *Bhagavad gītā*, the queen among scriptures. Have you seen that picture of Lord Kṛṣṇa and Arjuna on the beautiful chariot?

Some children raise their hands and nod. The younger enthusiasts point to the picture and speak all together.

Child 1: Yes. Yes. We know Kṛṣṇa, the butter thief!

Child 2: I know Arjuna, he was a very brave prince.

Child 3: Look, look... Arjuna and Kṛṣṇa are sitting on the chariot!

Hearing the cacophony of excited voices, the adults share smiles.

Sevikā: As you grow, you will understand the message of the *Gītā* and try to live the *Gītā* way of life.

The sevikā chants one verse, "Om pārthāya pratibodhitāṁ...," the children repeat.

Sevikā: Children, what wonderful chanting! Now, story time. Who wants to hear a story?

The children shift gears and there is palpable excitement as they ready themselves for the story.

The sevika tells a story about Kṛṣṇa stealing butter from the gopīs.

Sevikā: (*Turning to the parents*) In this class, we share stories from the *Rāmāyaṇa*, the *Mahābhārata*, or the *Pañcatantra*. We also talk about the lives of saints, and other great devotees of the Lord who lived the eternal, universal values of Sanātana Dharma.

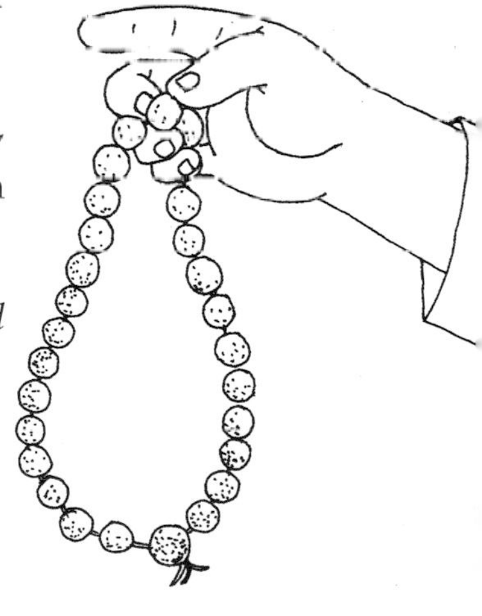

Sevikā: How many of you enjoy making things out of clay, colored paper, strings, and beads?

(*To the parents*) Through games, arts, and crafts, children learn the subtle art of concentration and develop the spirit of teamwork.

The children demonstrate a simple activity and hold up small japa-mālās for the audience to see.

Sevikā: Wow, that is excellent! Now, let us sing a bhajan.

Everyone sings with joyful abandon, "Śri rāma jaya rāma jaya jaya rāma..."

Sevikā: (*To the parents*) In every class, we recite the Chinmaya Mission pledge. Penned by our founder and Guru, Swami Chinmayananda it connects us to this great organization. And through an unshakeable foundation it: "keeps us on the path of virtue, courage, and wisdom!"

The children recite the pledge.

Sevikā: Time to bid farewell to the Lord and seek His blessings so that the light with which we see His face may dwell always in our hearts.

She leads and the children join, "Om jaya jagadīśa hare..."

Sevikā: My dear children, you were so good today while I attended to our visitors! So now it is time for prasāda! (She passes around little packets of prasāda.) What better way to end the class than with a sweetened tongue — to spread the message of love! See you next Sunday! Hari Om!

Chattering happily the children leave the class, eating from their respective prasāda packets. The couple is clearly impressed and wants to know more.

Parent: Is there anything else that happens in BV?

Sevikā: Yes, indeed, we have special events that include:

Celebrating Festivals

We celebrate Śivarātrī, Janmāṣṭamī, Dusserā, Divālī, Holī, and other festivals. The children learn about the reason for celebration and the parents join in the fun.

Mātṛ Pūjā

An especially poignant BV tradition that both mothers and children look forward to is the Mātṛ Pūjā, where the children, through a simple ritual, worship their mothers and receive their blessings.

Graduation Day

Graduation Day is an annual feature, when the class graduating to the next level, Chinmaya Yuva Kendra (CHYK), offers thanks for what they have gained from the devoted service of their sevaks. They promise to live the values that they have learned over the years in BV. In some centers this moving ceremony is often part of an annual all-day event.

Summer Camps

An extended BV experience happens during the Summer Camps. These vary in their duration from one week to three weeks and provide booster doses of inspiration. They offer time for bonding — among the sevaks and also among the children; eagerly awaited, they are channels for action oriented fun activities!

GĪTĀ CHANTING COMPETITIONS

And, the star activity of BV is the annual *Gītā* Chanting Competitions, that happen world wide in all CM centers. Children from different age groups compete for excellence in chanting pre-selected verses of the *Bhagavad-gītā*. Hearing them chant is truly an incredible experience!

Parents: All very fascinating, but how do children benefit from BV?

Sevikā: BV enhances the overall development of the personality at all levels — physical, emotional, intellectual, and spiritual. Our Gurudev wants Indians to understand the beauty of their culture and be proud of their heritage.

Children exposed to this knowledge live more fulfilling lives. They willingly take responsibility, think independently, and do not succumb to peer pressure. Being rooted in the values of acceptance and sharing, they work for the greater benefit of humanity. Most importantly, they develop love for God and forge a lasting relationship with Him.

Parent: (*expressing joy and gratitude*) Thank you! Thank you! This is certainly the place for our children.

• The curtain falls •

Gurudev witnessed this expression of ten years of BV in Chembur. His face was aglow with joy as his eyes scanned the future horizons, foreseeing its effect on the coming generations.

In the decades since, Gurudev's vision became the enduring goal of eager devotees. As the outer world changed radically the process of evolution also touched the BV classes, but the core remained intact. Gurudev, whose love for children is an open secret, told them: "Always remember the Great Lord of Love, the flute player on the Jamuna Banks. BV is meant for this."

...A gentle hand on Shanti's shoulder brought her back all the way from 1976 to 2012. Shraddha reminded her of the time. As she rose to leave, Shanti bowed at the altar offering thanks to the Guru's infinite love and compassion!....

From Teenage Sevak to Sevak Trainer

On the occasion of the tenth anniversary celebrations of BV in Chembur, Shyamala Acharya and Shobhana Nair trained the children. They made sure that the children were in time for the program, and were by their side backstage to ensure discipline. The entire responsibility was Shyamala's.

The night before the performance, Nirmala Aunty just dropped by and said:

"Shyamala, I have an idea. Instead of the MC introducing the concept of BV, we will present it as a BV class. Tomorrow on stage, you will be a sevikā taking a class."

With half an hour's training, Shyamala was ready to enact the role she played every Sunday. At the end of the program Gurudev said, "Nirmala has given rise to another Nirmala Aunty!"

Shyamala giggled at being called Aunty. Too young to understand his vision, she wondered what he meant. Many years later reminiscing with her mentor, Nirmala Aunty, the words hit home. Says Shyamala, "Gurudev knew what I did not. Finally, I understood his vision for me!"

Bala Perspectives

Side by side on the altar in the BV class were pictures of Gurudev and Lord Kṛṣṇa. At the end of a session after the ārati to Gurudev and Kṛṣṇa, a child pointed to Gurudev's picture, and asked, "Aunty, is that Kṛṣṇa's grandfather?"

IV

The Vision Translated

TO HELP CHILDREN LEARN VALUES WITH FUN,
TO DELIGHT LIKE THE MOON AND SHINE LIKE THE SUN.
| SWAMI TEJOMAYANANDA |

This is the Bala Vihar (BV) vision statement. Coined by Pujya Guruji Swami Tejomayananda, this catchy phrase spells out the purpose of BV and clarifies its goal.

Guruji elucidates: "To delight like the moon and shine like the sun means that while shining in themselves, children must delight other people. Well-mannered children do the right thing at the right time. The result is a win-win situation, and everyone is happy."

Pujya Gurudev had emphasized this very idea in a befitting motto, for the children of the ChinmayaVidyalayas, in just two words:

• KEEP SMILING •

Also enshrined in this diktat is the objective of BV. Says Guruji, "When we smile, we make others happy. When we frown, nobody is happy. To be happy and make others happy, the formula is — Keep Smiling!"

..."That is all it takes to be happy and spread the sunshine of love," thought Shraddha. "The formula is so simple, yet we find it difficult to open the doors to our own happiness. One smiling face is enough to brighten even the darkest room."

Shraddha had heard of Gurudev's legendary love and his life transforming winning smile. Over the years, she had innumerable occasions to closely watch Shanti. Her youthful, critical eyes missed not a detail — weighing, judging, rejecting, admiring. Shanti's demeanor and her responses to situations often left Shraddha wondering what was the philosophy that Shanti lived by? Then, through years of interaction, admiration dawned in her for the thought processes and the core values by which Shanti lived. And almost through a natural process of osmosis, she was drawn to the vision and teaching of Vedānta**....**

Gurudev's unconditional love for children was a quality that influenced me tremendously. This love motivates me to spend the entire weekend teaching in five BV locations; It gives me the silent energy to deliver my very best and come to BV week after week, year after year.

— Ashok Grandhee, CM Ann Arbor

... Shraddha's interest deepened after Gopal entered the picture. Like every mother, she wanted only the best for her child. The story of Prahlāda had strongly influenced her. Without a doubt she wanted her child to be exposed, even before birth, to the beauty and depth of Vedāntic teaching. So, during the days of her pregnancy she exposed herself to the scriptures, by attending talks at the Mission center**....**

Gurudev cared deeply about the smiles on the faces of his BV children. He must have written thousands of letters to children asking them to keep smiling, encouraging them to achieve greater heights. He loved the little ones, and took care never to disappoint them. He came down to their level and played with them even through his letters!

How Gurudev Loved Them!

Swami Mitrananda, then Raju, witnessed an incident in Chennai, which makes us realize how dear children were to Gurudev. He recounts:

> Gurudev was conducting a jñāna yajña. One day at the end of his talks the children of BV Chennai were scheduled to give a cultural performance. Gurudev was well aware that once his talk finished, the audience would walk out. He also knew how hard the children had worked, and he did not want their efforts to go waste. So he did something unprecedented. He stopped the yajña!
>
> His discourse began at the appointed time of 6:30 P.M., but at 7:00 P.M., he announced, "I stop here and I will continue at 7:30 again." Majestically he rose from his seat, and he proceeded down the steps to join the audience. Nobody moved. The children came on stage and enthralled the audience for half an hour. At 7:30 he resumed his talks!

Once in Kolkata, an incident occurred that made Gurudev write to Smt. Sarla Birla. A play by the children had been canceled, and Gurudev stepped in to bring cheer to the children's hearts.

Sarla Birla

Calcutta

Hari Om! Hari Om! Hari Om! Salutations!

My BV children were extremely disappointed this time because of a thoughtless last minute decision by the Brahmachari. He suddenly decided that their programme must be dropped.

Now I am asking Sree Narayan Swamy to continue rehearsals and put up the show on Nov 21 when I am coming to Calcutta on my way to Bokaro.

Children everywhere, for their part, apprised Gurudev of all their significant milestones — laurels won and landmarks achieved. To these children, his letters continue to be more precious than all the prizes they ever won.

Gurudev's letters reveal how he kept his vision and hope alive in every child:

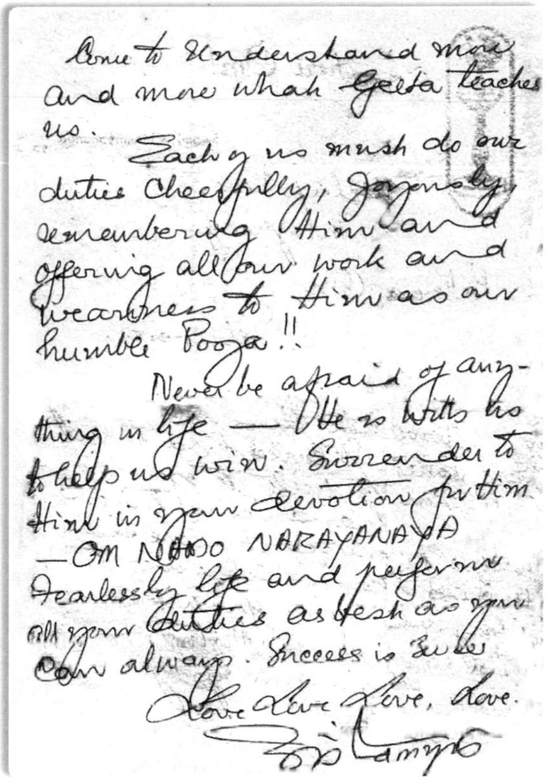
Come to Understand more and more what Geeta teaches us.
Each of us must do our duties cheerfully, joyously, remembering Him and offering all our work and weariness to Him as our humble Pooja!!
Never be afraid of anything in life — He is with us to help us win. Surrender to Him in your devotion to Him — OM NAMO NARAYANAYA
Fearlessly live and perform all your duties as fresh as you can always. Success is sure
Love Love Love, Love.

...Raising Gopal in an atmosphere enveloped in love, Shraddha began taking active interest in BV. With the one-year-old Gopal seated on her lap, she observed the BV sessions that his grandmother conducted.

As Gopal grew, she began to volunteer her time and help in conducting BV classes. Her interest and enthusiasm grew and having acquired the wherewithal to run a class, she graduated to become a BV sevikā....

When I moved to Toledo, Ohio, I was a 'casual teacher'. This meant that I would prepare every week, but just enough to teach the lesson for the day. I didn't do as much individual spiritual study. All that changed the day Guruji addressed BV teachers in Ann Arbor. He explained that being a BV sevak is a great privilege and a way to grow spiritually.

— Seema Jani, CM Atlanta

...Her devotion to Pujya Gurudev automatically connected Shraddha to Guruji who walking in the footsteps of his Guru, encouraged more and more sevaks to offer their time to the movement. She found in Guruji's message the simplicity innate to his nature and was drawn by his immense love for people, and more so, for children....

After Gurudev's Mahāsamādhī, Guruji took on the task of building bridges between parents, teachers, and children through BV. The growing BVs needed to be reminded about the pivotal points that would translate Gurudev's vision into reality.

The Right Atmosphere

Guruji gave explicit instructions on the prime importance of creating the right atmosphere for the balanced growth of the child:

Though specific to BV, this objective is in keeping with the overall vision of the Mission. At all times we should remember that teaching is not forced. It is important to maintain an atmosphere that is conducive to learning. This can only happen when we create an atmosphere of fun and caring. Then, and only then, do children want to learn.

In *Kaivalya Upaniṣad*, Aśvalāyana approaches his father Brahmāji with a request, "Please teach me Brahmavidya" (adhīhi bhagavān brahmavidyāṁ variṣṭhāṁ, 1.1). The Guru tells him to learn through śraddhā (faith), bhakti (devotion), and dhyāna (contemplation). Brahmāji advises Ashvalayana to create an atmosphere where this can manifest itself (śraddhābhaktidhyānayogātavaihi, 1.2).

Atmosphere makes a great difference and every place has its own ambience. Hospitals, airports, temples, and ashrams — all have different environments. People, without question, are drawn to the spiritual vibrations of the latter two. In the same way, children are and should be drawn toward learning with love. The environment should be inviting, friendly, and conducive to learning. When there is a blend of enlightenment with entertainment, learning takes place naturally. ***In a loving atmosphere, learning happens. The teaching is imbibed without any conscious effort or struggle.***

The Right Role Models

Gurudev wanted the BV children to be trained by their parents and elders so they could grow to be respected for their convictions and become assets to society. To achieve this goal, role models are required to inspire people. Guruji opined:

svagṛhe pūjyate mūrkhaḥ svagrāme pūjyate prabhuḥ|
svadeśe pūjyate rājā vidvān sarvatra pūjyate||

An uncultured person is given importance only in his own house. A rich, influential person is respected in his village. A king is worshiped in his own kingdom. However, a wise man is worshiped everywhere.

It is a pleasure to interact with disciplined, well-mannered children. They are indeed a blessing to the family in which they are nurtured; a blessing to society and also to the world at large. But cultured children do not just happen. *They have to be nurtured and trained by the parents and elders in society.*

...Shraddha had some pertinent questions: If discipline is important, how should it be enforced? What to do and what not to do? She had no easy answers. A sad reflection of the twenty-first century was the increased number of children needing behavioral therapy. In fact not just children, but parents, too, were taking recourse to counseling sessions.

Like millions over the centuries, she pondered over and debated with herself the age-old question: how to raise children?....

Guruji, through his years of interactions with people of different temperaments and his exposure to diverse circumstances, offers simple wisdom. Instantly, he touches the core of the issue:

The elders of today are perplexed by the different theories on child rearing that are currently doing the rounds. Some propagate the theory that children should be allowed to do whatever they like. Others say that children should be disciplined. If adults are confused, can you imagine the state of the children?

Discipline in children can be inculcated with patience and understanding. They need the guidance of their parents and teachers. Those elders who shirk this responsibility are not fulfilling their duties.

The ultimate objective of BV is to raise disciplined children and inculcate values and culture in them. We tend to invest in outward things, instead of focusing on inner development. Gurudev said: *"Don't just invest ON the child, also invest IN the child!"*

Gurudev realized the importance of the years before formal schooling begins in the life of children. He emphasized the need for proper care in tending them at this stage, to be sure of a well-rounded personality.

IN THE EARLY STAGES OF CHILDHOOD, EVERYONE IS POTENTIAL MATERIAL, WHICH CAN BE MOLDED, WITH A LITTLE PRESSURE OF DISCIPLINE, INTO SPECTACULAR BEAUTY AND COVETABLE PERFECTION

| SWAMI CHINMAYANANDA |

...Shraddha remembered how Guruji emphasized that the vision of BV is successfully translated when children get the knowledge they need, when they need it, customized to their developmental needs. Children require role models who demonstrate unconditional understanding and live by their principles....

RIGHT ANSWERS — RIGHT TIME

At a young age, it is difficult to give children the reason and rationale of all that is being taught to them. Also, too much logic and reasoning is not required for a child. There is enough time for explanations. These can be given to them in stages as they grow.

bālakeṣu ca saṁskāro vicāro yuvakeṣa ca

(Good impressions in childhood; inquiry during youth)

Besides, some people erroneously think that all the child's questions must be answered. Though children do ask questions, they do not have the ability to understand all the answers. Keeping this in mind, replies to their queries should be uncomplicated and easily understood. They should be given only as much information as is necessary and sufficient for their understanding.

In *Śrīmad Bhāgavatam*, Rājā Nimi asks the Navayogis some questions and requests them to answer only if he is fit to receive the replies. Answers should be in keeping with the age, maturity and understanding of the children. We should exercise wisdom and discretion in answering their questions.

Take, for instance, the time when a very young child asked his physicist father: "Papa, how does it rain?"

Being a scientist, the father launched forth, "With the heat of the sun, water evaporates...."

The poor child was in a daze.

> Fortunately the child's grandmother happened to be present. She rose to the occasion and saved the day. She put her grandson on her lap, used actions and mimed sound effects, and related the story of the Rain God, Indra and his elephant, Airavatha. The child was delighted.

This is how Gurudev fielded a question shot by a ten-year old, sitting at his feet on a visit to Delhi. His logic, using examples the children could relate to, unfailingly appealed to them and the message went home instantly.

When Will I See God?

"Swamiji, no one has 'seen' God. How can I believe that if I live a spiritual life I will for sure experience God, or 'see' Him?"

Gurudev looked at him mischievously and asked, "Can you see a beard or a moustache on your face?"

"No, Swamiji" answered the boy.

"Yet, are you not sure and do you not believe that in time you will grow up to see it appear on your face?"

"Yes, Swamiji."

"Similarly, the Lord is hidden in you and will manifest to you at the time of your spiritual maturity. Remember to keep calling Him!

Just as in a small seed you cannot see the trunk, the branches, the leaves, the flower and the fruit, but you 'believe' that they are all there in a potential form. If the seed is planted in good soil, with a certain amount of sunshine and water, all the seed's hidden possibilities can be seen to manifest in front of you.

So also you have the potential to make God manifest in your experience."

— Prarthna Saran, CM Delhi

Not only should the answers be child-appropriate, but also the entire approach should be grounded in strong values. Guruji is emphatic about providing children with the right beginning based on the scriptures.

Saṁskāra pradhāna

BV is saṁskāra pradhāna, meaning its main focus is and should be the creation of good impressions. The aim is to make sure children shine in their personal life and simultaneously bring joy to others. Simple things give us happiness. Parents are pleased if their children chant even a few ślokās. Children do not have to know the meaning.

At a young age, the emphasis is on creating good saṁskāras. The number of questions also grows as the children grow older. As they cross into the teenage years, they want to know even more. The meanings of the ślokās should then be told, but kept simple and easy. There is no need to give them the complete in-depth Vedāntic explanations.

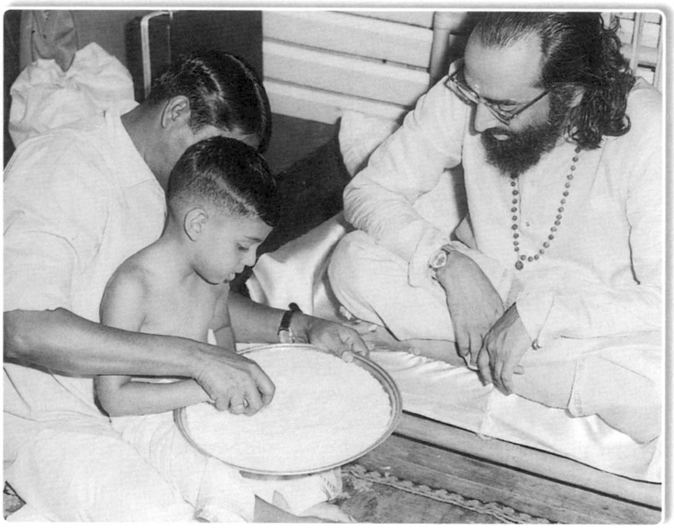

The greatest service a BV sevak can render is to simply create love for God in the hearts of children. If this is achieved, then everything else will follow. In other words, all will be taken care of. Guru-bhakti and Iśvara-bhakti are the pillars on which we can build a strong personality. If this is achieved, then the task is well done. God will do the rest!

Earlier, I used to think that 'God' and 'My Life' were two separate entities that didn't intersect. 'God' was related to the temple, BV, pujas, etc. Now I realize that God permeates everything and helps me through everything.

Posted on my desk is a śloka from the *Bhagavad-gītā*, "To those men who worship Me alone, thinking of no other, to those ever self controlled, I secure for them that which is not already possessed by them, and preserve for them what they already possess." (9:22)

— Mythili Iyer, CM Princeton

BV taught me to value and respect my family as embodiments of God. Deference to elders and value for family inputs in decision-making is an integral part of my identity. The open discussions have ingrained a deep appreciation for the wisdom that our elders can pass on. We must only be ready to receive.

— Aditya Pandyaram, CM Princeton

The vision of Gurudev in developing this program is truly humbling. Each Sunday, the families of BV choose the discipline of coming together in a powerful format — half an hour of prayer followed by one hour of classes for both the parents and their children. And, as one BV teacher (himself a BV graduate, now in college) wrote to his class of high-schoolers, encouraging them to make the time to be in class each week: "If you can live your lives by what you learn in this one hour, you will be the better for it." Like everything else in life, the choice is ours whether we go to BV or not, and once we go, whether we choose to live our lives by what we learn or not!

— Sivagami Natesan, CM Austin

The key to the success of a vision is the course of action supporting it. It is important that Gurudev's vision should be understood and kept alive at all times.

Under the canopy of the Chinmaya tree, a wide variety of projects flourish. To run these activities, a multitude of workers bring their diverse thoughts, interests, and core strengths to the fold. Probably the largest number of sevaks in Chinmaya Mission, volunteer for the BV activities. For those serving as sevaks or wanting to join the movement, Guruji has clarified the vision and purpose of BV:

The general objective of the Mission is Self-realization and service. This remains the same for all activities across the board. But for each of the specific activities or projects in the Mission, the objectives are different.

The purpose of BV, in particular, is the inner transformation of both the sevaks and the children. The goal of the scriptures being subtle, it cannot easily be explained to children. Hence other methods are required to get the message across to them.

It is logical that before we embark on a journey, we should know the destination. So there should be clarity about the goal and the methodology to reach it. The sevak should be clear about the purpose of all the different activities — chanting ślokās, telling stories or jokes, and playing games. If this is clear the child will automatically gather the gist.

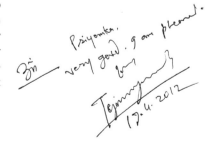

For his part, Guruji, showers children with his love to encourage their growth and development. In Auckland, New Zealand seventeen-year old Priyanka Nair, spoke at a function attended by members of the Mission and presided over by Pujya Guruji. Pleased by her understanding of the value of her BV training, he expressed his appreciation of her journey through BV. Priyanka said:

I have gained immensely from this amazing experience and learnt a wide range of things that can be applied in all aspects of life. As a young girl growing up in New Zealand it would have been easy to forget my roots and get lost in a western culture.

By attending BV from an early age we learn about our culture and the reasons behind the rituals and traditions of Hinduism; we not only learn about Indian festivals but about their significance; we not only say prayers but understand their deeper meaning; we do not just light a lamp but realize that we drive away fear and ignorance in the pursuit of Knowledge and the higher goal. This way we grow to become Kiwis proud of our Indian heritage.

A personal thing I developed from BV is faith in God, not just blind faith but knowing that there is someone there guiding us. It is an immense source of strength in the face of difficulties or trouble. It provides clarity. The values that I learnt in BV are my core values and beliefs today. When one has strong and stable moral values it becomes easy to do what is right and become the person you want to be. I am truly indebted to my teachers, Jyoti aunty and Br. Adarsh for all that they have taught me. They have helped me grow from an annoying six year old to a not so annoying seventeen year old.

Hari Om!

ॐ Priyanka, very good. I am pleased. Love Tejomayananda 17.4.2012

▲ EXCERPTS FROM PRIYANKA'S SPEECH

Mandaar Sukhtankar had the privilege of being blessed by Gurudev throughout his growing years. He sat in his lap, played with his beard, and learnt — Om namaḥ śivāya. Fed from Gurudev's thāli, he was piggybacked by him and instructed at his Upanayanam, "Eleven Gayātris every day!" Today, thirty years later, Mandaar continues his Gayātris and remembers with deep gratitude, Gurudev's presence in his life. He reminisces:

"The final year of school is always one of trepidation, fear and anxiety. I toyed with the idea of becoming an air force pilot, an army doctor, a wildlife enthusiast, a photographer, rock guitarist or a struggling writer. I had my fair share of deep thinking to do.

Towards the end of the term, I had a few options open and Hotel Management was certainly not on my list. But, I was selected to attend one of the most prestigious hotel management institutes in the country. That evening we were to meet Gurudev at a bhikṣā in New Friends Colony. Now, all of eighteen, the one raging query was whether to take up hotel management or not.

We sat there silently as people gathered around Gurudev. Finally, I gathered courage and told him 'Swamiji I have been selected for the hotel management course'. He looked at me through his glasses, smiled and said two words that have remained my motto to date, 'GO AHEAD'. The affirmation in his tone and voice drowned out everything else and that was it - as he helped me make a decision in a snap. My best and last BV lesson was by Gurudev and it was just two words: 'GO AHEAD'."

Indeed, Mandaar did just that! He is now the Executive Chef of The Park in Hyderabad. He also finds place in Celebrated Chefs of India (2013).

Misty-eyed, his mother Bharati says, "Mandaar is Swamiji's child."

Bala Perspectives

O my loving God, Hari Om. You have made a beautiful earth, if you want to come and see it, you are most welcome! — a BV child

Sunil Sachdev's whole family was embraced by Gurudev through the mother, Vimla. Deeply influenced, she conducted BV in her home for years and trained her six progeny along with other children. She protected them with the high walls of lofty ideals. At dinner, the talk revolved around great stories about the wisdom and tradition of India.

Sunil grew up in an Indian Army home and so has a special affinity for the Armed Forces. He began life as an advertising account assistant and then, following his dreams, set up his own advertising company.

During the Kargil conflict, Sunil sat glued to his television watching the drama unfold. Stories of heroism from the front lines flowed in and, like millions of Indians, he was moved by the soldier's plight. He declares, "I was overtaken with the desire to do something, to make a contribution to the nation and not be a mere observer of this terrible tragedy."

Sunil believed that while everyone respected and loved the Army, most took the soldiers for granted and failed to appreciate the magnitude of their sacrifice. He approached his partner, "Let's create and run a communication campaign to collect funds for the families of our men in uniform....Let's collect Rs 200 crores!" It was an audacious figure but the intensity of feelings was such that, "anything lesser would have been less!"

In the flow of inspiration simple, beautiful, and powerful lines were crafted for the appeal. They met senior army generals, cleared the idea with the Defence Ministry and wrote to newspapers and magazines requesting them to run this campaign free of cost.

Working around the clock, Sunil and his company scripted and put together a TV campaign, found willing sponsors and the campaign went on air. The effect was electrifying. So moving was the advertisement that even now it moistens the eyes of viewers! The impossible happened, money poured in and the Indian Army actually ended up collecting Rs 400 crores!

Not accepting credit Sunil says, "The atmosphere in India was emotionally charged. We only provided a mechanism for people to channelize their emotions and do their bit for the brave soldiers."

Sunil's design company, Designess, was privileged to design the interiors for Chinmaya Jeevan Darshan in Chinmaya Vibhooti.

Part 2

The Why

Part 2

The Why

V Divine Assurance

A transformational influence — Gurudev's promise to his children

VI Filling the Void

The special role of Bala Vihar — Linking generations and learning differently

VII Are They Yours?

Perspectives on parenting — Transforming fundamental mindsets

VIII The Ultimate Inspiration

The revered Ideal — Qualities of Gurudev to emulate

V

Divine Assurance

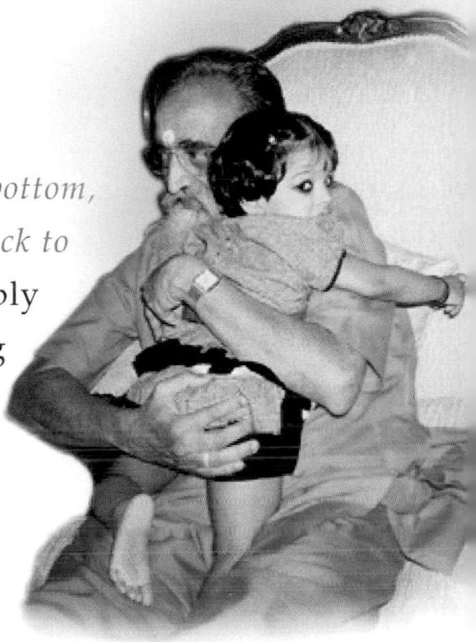

"A Bala Vihar (BV) child might go astray and sink to the bottom, but will never remain there and perish. He will bounce back to the surface and move on!" said Pujya Gurudev in reply to a question by Smt. Sunanda Shastri, a pioneering sevikā in the early years of BV.

Her question to Gurudev was: "Is it really worth teaching in BV, since the children meet only once a week and then return to their own environment?"

Sunanda's second question, "Will it make any difference in their lives?" was rather timidly put after Gurudev's powerful reply to her first query.

"Yes, it will!" Gurudev replied forcefully.

Sunanda Shastri was the first to begin a BV class in Mangalore in the early 1960s and was devoted to running it. Yet, she was not fully convinced that the children were benefitted. Her mind wondered and speculated; the thought lingered like a shadow — would BV exert an enduring and powerful influence on a child?

Gurudev's rejoinder at that juncture, both forthright and powerful, put Sunanda's doubts to rest. She had the deepest respect and love for Pujya Gurudev and wanted more than anything to follow his vision.

She was dedicated to BV, loved the children, and enjoyed being with them. Gurudev had told her to make this her sādhanā. There were no further questions, and so it was!

Many years passed. The story of BV Mangalore became intertwined with her life. When Sunanda looked back over the pages of time, she saw a stream of naughty and expressive faces, and twinkling or dreamy eyes that had come and gone through the doors of BV.

Then one day, many years after Gurudev's authoritative statement that BV leaves a lasting impact, validation came to her through an unbelievable experience.

On that unforgettable day, Sunanda had just finished her morning chores, when the doorbell rang. On the doorstep stood a young man she did not recognize. Her eyes held an inquiring look and her lips formed the obvious questions asked of a stranger at the door. But before any of her words found expression, the young man prostrated at her feet, his body in full length across the floor. That Sunanda was flabbergasted would be an understatement. She had no idea what to make of his action.

The man stood up and introduced himself. He gave his name and reminded her of the time she had taught him in BV.

"I have come," he said, "to express my heartfelt gratitude to you for giving me back my life. You really have no idea what you have done for me. You brought me out from the very depths of despair. I have no adequate words with which to thank you."

With unshed tears and in a voice choked with emotion, he poured out the story of his life. He confessed that in his teenage years he had gone astray. He had taken to drinking, smoking, and drug abuse. Things became so bad that his mother moved away and his wife divorced him. He was left alone!

Then, one day, a miracle happened. Under the influence of alcohol, when he was lying semi-conscious near a roadside creek, a voice whispered in his ears: "My child, what are you doing with your life? Is this what I taught you in BV?"

Cutting through the mist of his drunken stupor, a sudden recognition dawned on him. He realized that it was the voice of Sunanda Shastri, his BV teacher.

The love and concern in that whisper transformed him. The very next morning, he woke up with the firm determination to change his life. He did a complete volte-face; just about everything changed for him. His life took on a new meaning. Through counseling he went on to revamp not just his own life, but the lives of many more like him who precariously stood on the brink of a hopeless existence.

As Sunanda heard the young man recount his story, her eyes overflowed with tears. She remembered Gurudev's words, and in that instant, she knew that she had truly made a difference in a child's life. Her eyes closed in gratitude and prayer to her Guru. Her mind could only repeat, "Thank you, Gurudev. Thank you, Gurudev!"

The fulfilling, prized account of the young man's victory over life was her reward for the thirty-five years of being a BV sevikā. She would carry her medal close to her heart and marvel at the ways of Gurudev. While he did not need to, but through that incident, Gurudev had given her conclusive proof of the worth of her work. Though her wait was long, it was well worth it.

Sunanda understood, beyond the shadow of doubt, that Gurudev's blessings are the protective cloak that envelop his children — that BV can and does transform lives!

... Shanti had heard this story, while she was a young parent and finding her niche in the Mission. To say that it left a lasting impression would, indeed, be putting it mildly! Gurudev's power-packed words, carrying in them a firm promise, were proof enough of the greatness of the movement he had created.

With the passing decades, Shanti could not remember when she turned from a BV sevikā to a BV facilitator. She was also unaware how her faith had touched Shraddha, who took naturally to BV activities. Quite simply, BV had brought the two women together, walking the same path.

One evening during a brainstorming session for a BV teachers' workshop, Shanti related the story of Sunanda Shastri's experience to Shraddha adding, "See these goose bumps. Whenever I relate this story, it shakes me to the core. Now with the hindsight of experience, are we not witness to the glory of BV and the transformation it continues to wield in the mindsets of children across the world?"

There was silence in the room. The only sounds were the wild chirping of the sparrows and the even more strident call of the parrots settling down for the night on the trees outside. Shraddha digested the import of what she had just heard and in a thoughtful mode remarked, "Quite amazing Ma!"

"So what do you think?" asked Shanti. "Should we share this story at the seminar for parents to highlight the need for training children with care?"

Shraddha nodded, thoughtfully, "BV children may have different journeys, but they definitely evolve in the right direction!"**....**

Bala Perspectives

Children in one *Rāmāyana* class were asked to bring a present for Lord Rāma. They were asked to bring something they did not like about themselves, so that He could make it better and return it to them. One six-year-old put a chit in the 'gift box' that said, "I bite my nails". Thereafter, he never did so again. Such is the faith and beauty of innocence!

VI

Filling the Void

To understand why and how Bala Vihar (BV) took on the role of transforming childhood, we must pause to take stock of the changing times that left an indelible mark on family structure and interactions.

When India witnessed dramatic post-partition changes, families were dislocated and the bonding between family members changed. Fresh work cultures emerged and the Industrialisation ushered in a new ethos. These upheavals brought to the surface the latent good and evil tendencies. The most vulnerable were the very young and the elderly.

Gurudev was saddened by the condition of the country and its effect on children growing in these profoundly altered circumstances. He knew that proper values had to be imparted to the children in order for them to stay grounded and face the challenges of life with confidence. Only knowledge of traditions of their land could help a new, free generation stand tall in the world as proud inheritors of their ancient and glorious cultural heritage.

The need to connect the young with the old became more important as the demographics of families underwent drastic transformation in the latter half of the twentieth century with the emergence of a global culture and the fast-paced revolution in communication technology.

The necessity for this training was more keenly felt by parents of Indian origin, who had relocated to the West, more specially the U.S.

The 'hands-on dādī-nānī (paternal and maternal grandmother) syndrome' had become a concept of the past. For the vast majority, in India and elsewhere, grandparents turned into distant relatives who visited during short vacations. So the bond between the two generations weakened, with both missing out on the beneficial interaction.

To Gurudev, BV was about providing the right starting point in this changing familial and cultural scenario:

- We must give the children a glimpse of our history and expose them to our cultural tradition. When we have no respect for the past, then we have no self-respect. We must have pride in our culture, which is one of loving and serving.

To give young minds the right orientation of character, parents have to spend time and energy — thus, the need for an institution like BV to initiate the young ones into the subjective art of discovering and cultivating inner beauty, so that the growing generation may lead a purposeful life of moral beauty and inner poise. It will enable them to guide and lead the world into a more meaningful program of peaceful coexistence and all-giving goodwill, in an easy mood of joyous sharing.

...By the last decade of the twentieth century, Shanti's children had flown the nest. Free from the demands of motherhood, she now had plenty of time on her hands. So after taking an early retirement from her job at the university, she decided to work for the cause of children, by influencing the mindsets of their parents. Shanti had heard Gurudev emphasize that:

RIGHTLY HANDLED WE CAN MAKE A DIVINE
SAINT OUT OF EVEN A CROOKED,
UNDERDEVELOPED CHILD.
| SWAMI CHINMAYANANDA |

The key was right handling. Inspired by her Guru's conviction, Shanti believed that children would stand to gain the most if the approach of their teachers and parents underwent some modification. Since teaching came naturally to her, she decided to conduct workshops and seminars aimed at clarifying the concepts of child-rearing. With her background in child psychology and her teaching experience in BV, she was well qualified to organize such events.

To prepare herself for carrying the BV message to parents and educators, Shanti attended a workshop on the Chinmaya Vision Programme (CVP). The topmost question in Shanti's mind as she went to the workshop was: What relevance does this program for schools have to the BV movement?....

Gurudev wanted each of the Chinmaya Vidyalayas to be "A School With A Difference" (SWAD), producing leaders, who had the vision to steer the country confidently into the unknown future. By the end of 2012, there were over eighty-one schools being run under the banner of the Chinmaya Mission.

To run these schools in keeping with Gurudev's vision was the challenge that confronted the CCMT Education Cell. Swamini Vimalananda, the head of the governing body for schools, infused Gurudev's teachings comprehensively into the Chinmaya Vision Programme (CVP):

SWAMINI VIMALANANDA SURROUNDED BY HAPPY FACES ▲

CHINMAYA VISION PROGRAMME (CVP)

Pujya Gurudev opined, "Training the mind is the essence of education." Today's academic education is merely a lot of 'information-gathering' on many subjects. But in reality, education has the larger purpose of 'transformation' of the individual. A judicious combination of academics (information) and cultural and value education (transformation) serve as an ideal approach to education. CVP aims to give the best of modern education in the exalted, sacred spirit of the gurukula tradition.

Gurudev said, "Through such an education followed faithfully, we can more effectively complete the education of our growing generations. The secular education will make them proficient to meet the challenges in their professions, and the values of life inculcated in BV will mold them to be better persons in society."

His 'vision of education' aims to elevate children's 'vision of life' to help them evolve into outstanding men and women of character and achievement.

...At the end of the sessions, Shanti discovered that the CVP was equally relevant to BV, because it provided a practical translation of Gurudev's vision for children.

Her years of exposure to the scriptures and the experience of BV gave Shanti greater clarity about the path ahead. She realized that the process of sharing this knowledge blessed not just the recipient but the giver as well — in the language of Shakespeare, 'Blessing him that gives and him that receives.' The hands that apply the henna (a plant which is ground to a paste and then used to make decorative patterns on the hands and feet) also end up being colored by that same henna!

Shanti's seminar for the parents of prospective BV children provided an excellent opportunity to connect with them. She saw the expressions on the multitude of faces — some concerned, some curious, some deadpan, and some even a little hostile. She recognized in them thoughts that were similar to her own in the early days of doubting and questioning.

At her seminars, without too much of a preamble, she often addressed questions commonly asked by most parents:

Is it necessary to go to BV?

Are schools not enough to take care of the all-round development of the child?

Her answer to the first question was – Yes.

And to the second – The answer is a resounding "NO!"

Her seminars brought to light an important fact: the kind of education that BV offers is not available in most schools. Today's competitive world places an inordinate emphasis on academics, and grades are of paramount importance. BV, a place where learning happens with love in caring surroundings, is an oasis for this ambition-driven generation.

While preparing for such seminars, Shanti asked Swamini Vimalananda: "So what is the difference between going to school and attending a BV class?"

Swamini Vimalananda highlighted how BV holds a special place in a child's upbringing as compared to a regular school....

School is somewhere that the child has to go, whereas BV classes are optional. Parents make a special effort to enroll their children and make sure they attend, because they value the BV classes. They know that, due to a variety of reasons, they are unable to give their children the values that BV slowly but surely imparts to them.

I Don't Want To Miss BV!

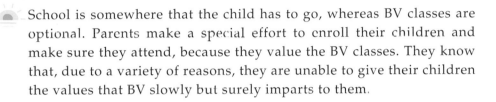

Memories of being surrounded by BV children are enough to bring joy and sparkle to my eyes....

Reticent and shy, four-year-old Krishna would sit without uttering a word, refusing to participate. And yet during a performance, she sang every word of every single bhajan with full-throated ease! Once, Sanya and Manya's mother called to say, "The girls are not ready to miss BV. I am unable to visit my mother over the weekends." A parent called from Goa, "My daughter is crying because she missed BV this week." And how can I forget Vani — a replica of the goddess herself — who comes week after week with total, unmatched dedication!

The freshness and joy with which kids enter the class, the earnestness with which they chant the ślokas or the Pledge, the love and devotion with which they sing the bhajans — says a lot about the concept of BV. What brings and binds children to BV, which has no glamorous presence, no glitter, or fancy technological distractions? For sure, there is a certain gap, a lacuna which it fills!

Back in the 1950s, Gurudev understood the crying need of families in independent India. He divined the breakup of joint families and foresaw busy and exhausted working couples. Besides numerous other things, BV definitely fulfils and enhances the role of nurturing, story-telling, and reassuring grandparents.

These children have given and taught me more than anything I can teach them. These bundles of energy spread light, love, and purity. Thank you Pujya Gurudev for your vision and farsightedness! Thank you Guruji for giving us the motivation, energy and vigor to continue the process of sevā and bring Gurudev's solemn and sacred vision to life!

— Sharda Chawla, CM Delhi

...Such reactions from BV children are not uncommon. Shanti knew how enthusiastic children are about attending; many a time even forcing a change of plans on their parents. Swamini Vimalananda went on to emphasise the need for values....

Swamini Vimalananda: The inculcation of saṁskāras, or values, in children is a slow investment, the results of which are seen after a long lapse of time and is somewhat akin to a sapling growing into a full-grown tree. BV has been around long enough for the second generation (children of BV alumni) to enter the fold. Giving saṁskāras to their children is an important necessity for parents who have grown in the BV tradition. Having lived lives based on values and having been enriched by the BV experience, they know its value. Passing on that knowledge and the security blanket of the BV community is a matter of utmost importance.

BV classes have many advantages over other extra-curricular activities that most children attend. It is a place of sheltered activity and could be termed as sāttvic entertainment. A commercial transaction is involved in every other activity, but the attitude of sevā in BV is difficult to replicate.

As for the children, they are not competing to be the best; they only learn how to be better — more compassionate, more caring — and more importantly, they learn how to think. Children in a BV class come from backgrounds with similar value systems. They strike chords in each other and long, enduring relationships emerge.

Inculcating values through BV is special, because the teaching is not pointed to one child — it is directed to the group. The synergy of group learning has a different connotation. The motivation levels are elevated and children learn better in the company of friends.

Further, BV is a good training ground for young mothers and fathers who volunteer their time in the program. Experience is the best teacher. With the insight of understanding, they are positioned to train their own children better.

Considering such benefits, BV should really become an integral part of the right upbringing of a child. Sending children to school is a compulsion. Extra-curricular activities, though important, are an option, but BV does not fall into either of these categories. For parents hard-pushed for time and unable to give their children this training, it should be choice-less because the development of the personality in the true sense begins here.

Being the visionary that he was, Swami Chinmayananda saw that, in the high-tech urban civilization, both sunshine and love would be hard to come by. Anticipating this need, he initiated BVs for the children to learn the art of living in love —the Hindu way. His idea was to provide an environment where the personality of the child could blossom naturally and spontaneously. Good conduct, emotional refinement, intellectual finesse, and spiritual awareness were to be developed by experienced sevaks through fun, play, stories, and bhajans.

Sometimes through tears, but more often through smiles, and sometimes through strictness, but mostly by persuasion, children are encouraged to be responsible, alert, and sensitive members of society. Swamiji believed that just as the strength of a wall depended on the quality of each brick, so, too, the health of a society depended on the individuals. His strategy for building a new society was to "catch 'em young!"

— Madhavi Vadhera, CM London

...Since Shanti lived in Delhi, she drew inspiration for her workshops from Swami Nikhilananda's years of invaluable experience....

In his days as Br. Manan Chaitanya, Swami Nikhilananda travelled all over Goa, the picturesque land of ancient temples and sun-drenched beaches, setting up BVs in many towns of the tiny state. His perspective on the importance of BV centered on the children themselves becoming ambassadors of the message:

BV is the locus from where good saṁskāras flow not only to the children but also through them to their families. The bhajans children learn stay with them and they sing them even after reaching home. When extended family members visit, the children regale them with stories, and in this way awareness spreads.

> The entire BV experience was very memorable and enjoyable. But what I enjoyed most was the singing of bhajans. The melodies remain and one cannot stop singing them. They helped me to connect with God and will travel with me far and wide wherever life may take me. — Alumnus, CM Muscat

Swami Nikhilananda: In some instances, a parent begins attending the Mission programs, and then the children follow. In other cases, friends or family members have acted as catalysts. But most times, concern for the future of the kids has been the motivation for parents to enroll them in BV.

> Living in the US, it is challenging for children to relate to the Indian customs and traditions of their parents. As youngsters, we generally obeyed our elders without questions. Children now demand reasons to follow a particular life-style. BV has progressively provided our children knowledge of Hindu beliefs and values which, we believe, they will cherish throughout their lives.
>
> — Sunita Mulayath, CM Houston

Swami Nikhilananda: When the family is introduced to the Mission through the children, the saṁskāras slowly but surely infiltrate the minds of other family members. It is said that 'When you teach a lady, you teach the whole family.' However, it is equally true that when you teach a little child, the saṁskāras permeate the whole family, which also learns and gains from the exposure. Life may provide the family with material comforts and luxuries, but without the right saṁskāras, the picture remains incomplete.

Vaishnavi's grandmother was upset because she was unable to purchase sufficient flowers for a festival. She felt her worship would be lacking. At this time Vaishnavi remembered a śloka from the *Bhagavad-gītā* frequently chanted by her sevikā, Uma Nagenddra.

Whoever offers me with devotion a leaf, a flower, a fruit, water, that I accept, offered by the pure-minded with devotion. (9.26)

She gave her grandmother solace by explaining that God would be happy even with a single flower, offered with true devotion.

— Vaishnavi Arun, CM Bengaluru

...Many times Shanti had seen how beginning with the child, BV brings the family within its ambit. The learning at BV that fascinates a child in turn stirs an adult's interest in the scriptures. This of course applies across the board — in India or abroad. Chancing upon an article in *Tapovan Prasad* (Chinmaya Mission's monthly magazine), written by young Anjali Madhok, (then in grade eight) made her realize how much of an anchor BV is for Indian children growing on foreign soil....

The Perfect Place to Be

It's the little things that can sometimes make me feel out of place here in the United States. People don't go around discriminating who I am or that I am Indian or anything, but sometimes I feel like I'm almost too different from the rest. From my name, to how I look, to how I act, there are days when I feel as though I'm that puzzle piece that just won't fit anywhere.

It's not like when I visit India I'm suddenly 'back home.' People there can tell that I'm not one of them either. Although my family looks Indian when we visit, the way we carry ourselves sets us apart from the others.

Even at my relatives' homes in India, I can always feel that something is a little off. I always feel like I'm 'The American' in India. So if I'm American in India, and Indian in America, then where exactly do I fit?

The one place on earth where I'm completely accepted is at Chinmaya Mission, Twin Cities in Chaska, Minnesota, a place where I perfectly fit.

I adore the centre simply because it's the one place I can just be. I can be myself without having to worry about what I'm saying, doing, or thinking. It is a snippet of a perfect world, where everyone is simply accepted, where words and actions can carelessly twirl through the air and bounce off our shoulders.

Of course, it's unreasonable for me to expect the whole world to be as perfect as this, which is why having one place like it is perfect enough for me!

— Anjali Madhok, CM Twin Cities

▲ SWAMI NIKHILANANDA AT A BV CAMP

Swami Nikhilananda described the wider psychological and social implications that accrue from following the BV system in today's world:

The influence of every individual flows outward in concentric circles. A bad person creates negative waves, while a good person generates positive energies. The positive effects of this program have far-reaching impact. The children gain values, as does the family, and through them society and the whole nation benefits.

If the atmosphere in the family and society were conducive to children imbibing both secular knowledge and spiritual saṁskāras, there would be no need for BV. Unfortunately, the present local and world situations are far from ideal. So, if little children are left to grow on their own, they will not imbibe positive saṁskāras.

After a particular age, children develop minds of their own; thereafter, efforts at inculcating good values in them are futile. In this beautiful environment of BV, children gain knowledge that is intrinsically important to life, in a simple and friendly way, without even realizing their gain.

...Children as they grow have questions of their own. Shanti was amused by this interesting exchange between Pujya Guruji, and a bold child....

Child Questions — Guru Responds

Having developed a mind of his own and hoping to outwit Guruji, a child once asked him, "Can you give me three good reasons why kids should go to BV classes?"

Guruji replied:

"Let us suppose that somebody gifts you a flute on your birthday. Does just possessing a flute make you a flutist?

A boy, like you, was gifted a flute by his uncle. A fortnight later, he told his uncle, 'Your gift to me is so good. Thank you!'

His uncle asked, 'So you like playing the flute?'

The boy replied, 'No, no, no! My mother gives me two dollars for not playing it during the day and my father gives me two dollars for not playing it at night. So every day I earn four dollars!'

But jokes aside, now tell me this: Suppose you go to a music teacher regularly; then he will teach you music. You practice and that will make you perfect. Right? When you're perfect, then everybody says, 'Please sing!'

Punctuality, practice, and perfection — the three P's happen if you go to BV classes regularly. Then these traits become a part of you."

Bala Perspectives

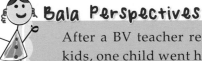

After a BV teacher recounted the Daśāvatāra stories to little kids, one child went home and asked his mom, "How come all the ten Āvatārs of Lord Viṣṇu were born in India?"

VII

Are They Yours?

TRUE KNOWLEDGE MAKES A MAN REALIZE THAT HE IS A 'SOUL WITH A BODY'; BUT NOW, IN HIS IGNORANCE, HE THINKS THAT HE IS A 'BODY WITH A SOUL.'

| SWAMI CHINMAYANANDA |

Parenthood is an intense stage of life, and in the twenty-first century, with all our advancements, we are still looking for answers to this aspect of the cyclical game of life. Our human instinct to nurture our young takes over our personalities almost unconsciously. We identify with our children deeply; our familial roles are such that we never want to let go. We get entangled in the miniscule, changing picture of our private life and fail to recognize our part in the larger scheme of things.

Guruji Swami Tejomayananda reminds us:

We are all jīvas (limited individual beings). In the *Bhagavad-gītā*, Lord Kṛṣṇa declares: "The jīvā is my part" (mamaivaṁśo jīvāloke jīvabhūtaḥ sanātanaḥ...15.7). Every jīvā is a part of the Lord and hence is directly connected to Him. The others, whom we address as mother, father, sister, brother, child, and so on, are also jīvās and, therefore, parts of the Lord as well. Everyone belongs to God. Both parent and child belong to God because they are a part of Him. While raising children, this important aspect is most often forgotten.

..."Well, everything about parenting is easier said than done," admitted one parent to Shanti as a Question and Answer (Q & A) session got underway in one of her workshops. Shraddha readied herself to listen and learn through the session that was taking philosophical flight....

Through Us, Not from Us

Q: As mother and father, we give birth to our children and raise them. How do we embrace the perspective that we don't own our children?

A: There is no doubt that the mother and father play a role in bringing the child into this world. They supply the material for the physical body. But Guruji very pertinently encourages parents to enquire along altered lines of thought:

> Do parents have the faintest idea as to how the physical body is made, what exactly happens in the mother's womb, and how it happens? For what are we taking credit? Suddenly all the notions of doership and my-ness appear to be false. Unfortunately, in the hurly-burly of our daily lives, the quiet moments of reflection are few and far between and this subtle truth is overlooked. The physical aspects of life take precedence over the spiritual essence.

Vedānta asks: Are we this physical body? The answer is an unequivocal 'NO'.

In the words of the philosopher–poet Kahlil Gibran, a similar strain of thought is summarized. In *The Prophet* he forthrightly declares:

> "Your children are not your children.
>
> They are the sons and daughters of Life's longing for itself.
>
> They come through you, but not from you.
>
> And though they are with you, yet
>
> They belong not to you."

These oft-quoted lines turn our conventional notions about the nature of the parent-child relationship on its head. Even the very first line refutes a belief dear to most parents: we have given birth to our children and hence they belong to us. Using those few deft strokes of Gibran's insight to dispel the dense fog of misconception clouding the minds of parents, Swami Nikhilananda explains:

Our children are expressions of Life coming 'through' us, not 'from' us. The bodies of the parents are merely a medium being used by Life to express Its longing for Itself. Parents are merely the soil from where children take birth. A feeling of possessiveness can even be harmful. So it is important to have the right attitude toward one's children.

...Shraddha suddenly remembered the words she had heard from her own father, "We are only caretakers. How can we claim to possess you?"....

Each to His Own

Q: Okay, if children only come 'through us,' what logic do we follow in the process of parenting?

A: This logic is what our scriptures speak about — a teaching oft repeated, but seldom absorbed. We must dare to constantly remind ourselves of this absolute standpoint: every jīvā, born in the world has a mission to complete, a destiny to follow. With some jīvās, we spend just a few moments; with some, an entire lifetime. We may be together for a while, yet inevitably part our ways. Guruji uses the apt example of a train journey to explain these comings and goings in the journey of life:

While traveling by train we do not know who our co-passengers will be. This secret is revealed only when we board the train and find out who they are. Only one karma is common to all the passengers on the train — their desire to travel on the same day, by the same train. However, their reasons for traveling and their destinations are varied and different.

Members of a family come together because of some common karma. But each one of them has come into this world for a different purpose. Each jīvā has to fulfill a certain objective. The family members spend some time together sharing good and bad times. Then, like fellow travelers, they alight at different places and go their own way. All of us have come to exhaust certain karmas and learn the lessons needed for our evolution. Once this is done, the jīvā moves on.

This is the reality of all life. So, especially while parenting, let us remove this 'I-ness' and 'my-ness' from our lives and take a more objective standpoint.

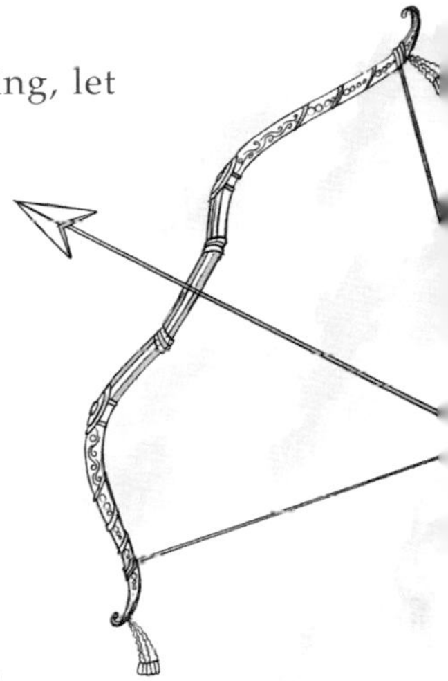

..."We do fine with friendships on a train journey, but when it comes to family, how hard it is to let go, more so where our own children are concerned!" said Shraddha to herself....

Surrender with a Bow

Q: So, how can we find that objective standpoint when it comes to guiding children?

A: To answer this question, another quote from *The Prophet* comes to mind: "You are the bows from which your children as living arrows are sent forth." Swami Nikhilananda expanded on this beautiful analogy to illustrate how that objective standpoint can be reached only with an attitude of humble surrender:

Parents are like bows and children like arrows. The one who wields the bow knows the trajectory of the arrow. An arrow does not have its own power nor does it create its own path. The Lord is the wielder of the bow; He gives the power and direction.

The more flexible, steady, and elastic the bow, the more it bends and the greater is the power that it transfers to the arrow. When it is released, it takes the correct flight path. God alone knows where the arrow has to be led. If the bow refuses to release the arrow, the arrow's power will reduce. Its flight will weaken and it will not reach its target.

Similarly, clinging attachment to our children is best avoided. Parents are bows in the hands of the Lord, and it is the parents through which children are delivered into the future. If there is no bending in humility before His will, the arrow will not go far. However, if we surrender to His will, the arrow will fly swift and far.

...Shraddha made mental notes of the messages absorbing and storing them, so as to later help enhance the joys of parenting....

Just Be Gardeners

Q: When we let go of our ownership mode in parenting, what is the most important thing that we must provide to our children?

A: We have often heard how Gurudev has likened the role of parents to that of farmers or gardeners. So, it is most important to provide a nurturing environment without the burden of doership and with the acceptance that there is more to parenting than just the parents' efforts. As Gurudev said:

Parents neither create the seed nor the soil. The potential exists in the seed; nothing needs to be added or injected into it. The farmer or gardener provides an environment suitable for the seed to grow. If the seeds have something in them, they will sprout; but if they are roasted, or if the soil is not proper, or when there is too little rain, then what can the gardener do?

Parents can only provide an environment conducive to the child's physical, intellectual, and emotional growth. But there is no guarantee that the child will grow up the way the parent desires because of a host of other reasons.

Guruji adds to Gurudev's message on the same wavelength:

Our effort is only one contributory factor. In fact, the totality of this world acts on the seed. The results of the efforts (karmaphala) do not accrue as a result of our action alone. Our duty is only to provide the right atmosphere in a given situation, and the seed with potential will grow. If, despite sincere effort, the expected results are not forthcoming, then there is no blame. Having done all that was possible, the conscience will be clear. This holds true, not just for parenting, but for every activity in life.

...Shanti often used these words to remind parents about their role as guardians. Many well-meaning parents languish in guilt when their children stray from the path of goodness. At such times it is best to remember Gurudev's simple injunction, "Do your best, and leave the rest!"....

A Duty to Fulfill

Q: What are our duties as parents? What should we do to ensure that our children grow up to be good and happy?

A: The right upbringing of a child is the sacrosanct duty of parents, given the understanding that the children do not belong to them. They cannot shirk this responsibility by pleading lack of time due to the pressures of the workplace. Guruji pithily remarks: *"Your child needs your presence, not your presents."*

The family unit plays a pivotal role in the upbringing of the child. Guruji drives home the point with his usual lively touch.

The family is the foundation of society and the nation. A family in which there is mutual love and respect, sharing and caring, joy and laughter, learning and growing, will give the right ambience for the child's growth.

Children have never been good at listening to parents, but they never fail to imitate them. Therefore, be advised, parents: mind your tongue and watch your step in front of your children. By your actions, exemplify what you want them to be.

Parents want their children to learn about their rich cultural heritage; so the children are sent to BV classes. The parents say, "You go to BV, we will watch TV!" Such double standards do not go down well with children.

Be inspiring role models for your children. Many youngsters go astray because they have no good role models or goals and find no meaningful purpose in life. They are confused about what constitutes a happy and successful life. Your role is to guide your children in setting the right immediate and long-term goals, which will enable them to achieve the ultimate goal of life — freedom from all bondage.

Shortcuts and doublespeak cannot work. If parents are smart, the children are a cut above. Being even smarter, the children are able to see through subterfuge and are deft in removing the wool being pulled over their eyes by the parents.

When my son Lokesh was a six-year-old, he loved watching the *Rāmāyana* television serial and shared a strong bond with Lord Rāma. One day, when he was being naughty, I admonished him saying that he was behaving like Rāvaṇa and not being like Lord Rāma.

Prompt came the reply, "Mama, when you become Kauśalyā, I will become Rāma!"

In that instant, my perception of motherhood changed forever. Till today, I aspire to be like Mother Kauśalyā to be worthy of a son like Rāma. – Nirmala Bharwani, CM Singapore

CHILDREN'S BEHAVIOR DEPENDS ENTIRELY UPON, AND IS EVER CONTROLLED BY, THE STANDARD OF PURITY AND CULTURE OF THEIR PARENTS.

| SWAMI CHINMAYANANDA |

LIVE THE VALUES

Q: What can we, as parents, do to encourage our children to become spiritually aware?

A: The best practical advice on this subject comes from our Gurudev, an inexhaustible treasure house of knowledge and experience. To Prarthna Saran of Delhi and some parents, eager to know how to instill spiritual values in their children, Gurudev, provided a simple solution:

- Live those values yourself. Don't preach, but practice daily. Make an everyday routine of getting the family together for the evening āratī or bhajans and leave it at that. You silently continue your sādhanā. Let the child watch you.

  You will be amazed at the teaching that is silently conveyed. The rest will follow in due course of time. You have to practice; no one becomes a millionaire by counting the king's money.

  Between the ages of three-to-five years, stories of spiritual giants of the world, recounting their experiences, their trials and inner strength in overcoming temptations, as well as the positive experience of joy that they gained, may all be passed on to your children with appropriate expressiveness.

  Let your child watch both of you praying to the Lord regularly. Make it a point for the children to pray before their meals for a short, yet serious moment.

  When your children ask questions about Nature — flowers, clouds, butterflies, or frogs, be alert to flavor your honest explanation with a hint about the play of God around us. Leave them with these small hints, do not go into details.

Even children below three years are not too young for spiritual education. Though common beliefs hold that they learn passively, by observing their parents, in a stroke, Gurudev dispels this misconception:

- Children who are below three years are not passive observers. Only after we have grown up do we learn the art of passive, dull, sleepy, and sloppy observation. Children of that age are more alert and learn much more than in later life. The rate of absorption of knowledge and experience in those early years is stupendous. Therefore, an atmosphere of religion and spiritual values around them is very important in molding and enhancing their mental life.

Q: What is the place of discipline in parenting?

A: Guruji opines:

- Obedience and living in discipline are very important in childhood. In the current day and age, no one likes to take orders; everyone wants to give them! To gain the right to give orders to others, one first has to learn how to obey. We must be vigilant about the dangers of children acting without permission, even in doing little things. When the parents are not vigilant, such inaction leads their children toward taking greater liberties, and often the situation snowballs out of control.

Parents and other adults should not take this aspect of discipline lightly for a child's development. Why? If a child does only what he likes and refuses to do what he dislikes, he is making his likes and dislikes even stronger. This is bondage from which it is difficult to escape.

A young plant has to be nurtured and protected; once it becomes a tree, it can give protection to others, too. Children lack proper discrimination and correct understanding. Thus, the guidance, instruction, and control by elders and teachers are necessary. In the beginning, we have to take care and train the children so that their minds are purified of likes and dislikes, making them capable of taking the right decisions.

... Shraddha had come to understand that Shanti's workshops gave parents food for reflection. It was important to equip them with the background that would then enable them to understand the objective of BV.

She mused, "To pass on something that we do not have, is an exercise in futility. In order to give, it is necessary to have. So, also, to transfer values to the next generation, we need to imbibe them ourselves. Who better to follow than our Pujya Gurudev himself, the ideal Master, who could inspire a person of any age, anytime!"**....**

Bala Perspectives

A young BV student told her parents who were squabbling, "Please stop being angry. Blow your anger out of the window. I want peace in the house!"

The Ultimate Inspiration

Every activity in Chinmaya Mission flourishes because of the magic of the Chinmaya name. Pujya Gurudev lived a life of the highest standards, impeccable values, and extraordinary ideals. He did not just preach, but lived by what he taught. To carry out the mission of such a visionary as Gurudev, one must keep alive the message of the Master through constant reflection on his exemplary qualities, since "what is praised, is followed."

In particular, it is important for Bala Vihar (BV) sevaks to keep the unique aspects of Gurudev's teachings close to their hearts. The most inspiring lessons of BV are born when we study his words and ways.

MAKING THE CONNECT

Though we know about Pujya Gurudev, it is always good to think about a great Mahatma and contemplate on him as the embodiment of his teachings. Listening to or reading about his life purifies the mind. Inspired by his work, we develop love for him, feel his presence, and are fulfilled. How we form this bond with him is not important. The essential point is to forge this connection with the Guru.

— Swami Tejomayananda

...Both Shanti and Shraddha attended a memorable talk by Guruji at Chinmaya Vibhooti, the Chinmaya Mission Vision Center at Kolwan, near Pune. The spotlight was on Pujya Gurudev's sterling qualities. Shanti understood that the easiest way to imbibe the qualities of the Guru is to expose, nay, immerse the mind in thoughts of his glory and carry his image in the inner eye. She had learnt that the role of the sādhaka was to be receptive to and follow the teachings of the Guru. Exposure to Gurudev's being, assured transformation, bringing in its wake the urge to become sevaks; the role models Gurudev envisaged for the young to follow.

In several informal satsaṅgs, Shanti had heard Guruji express his good fortune to have had the opportunity to live near Gurudev, observe him from close quarters and serve him. As a result Guruji learnt much and was able to draw from the depths of Gurudev's immense power. He elaborated on the qualities of Gurudev that are both venerable and timeless....

Independent Thinking & Humility

A study of Gurudev's life reflects his independent thinking pattern. From childhood, he was a disciplined, yet spirited independent thinker. When he was young, he followed the family rituals; but his mind was active on the path of inquiry. After he became a Swami, he often advised the audience during his discourses: "Do not accept something just because I am telling you." He warned against passive listening with his quip, "The longer the beard, the greater must be your suspicion!"

More than anything, he wanted people to think and contemplate independently after listening to the discourses, and then arrive at their own conclusions — to accept nothing without thinking. He wanted them to develop a questioning, inquiring spirit, without taking things at face value.

Take the case of teenagers — they have a peculiar tendency to rebel in the name of independent or original thinking. They refuse to follow their parents' advice, but curiously, these teens yield to peer pressure and implicitly follow their peers. Merely not listening to parents and grandparents is not independent thinking. Thoughtless rebellion does not reflect a questioning and independent spirit. When we have questions, we must have the readiness to inquire, understand, and accept new ideas.

Any independent spirit of adventure will find its goal only if the adventurer has enough humility, which is another important aspect of Gurudev's personality.

Hence, independent thinking must lead to a well-balanced personality; one must become strong enough to fearlessly seek the truth, but also have the humility to concede mistakes. Often people are unable to accept that they are in the wrong, even if ample proof stares them in the face. It requires courage and great strength to say, "I am wrong." Gurudev had both these qualities in equal measure; they were his greatest assets.

...Shanti was drawn to Gurudev's profile as a journalist because, unlike any average thinking person, he questioned the 'whys' and the 'why nots' of life. He acknowledged his doubts and was bold enough to inquire and find the answers. Later, when he understood the truth and found that the very fundamentals of his thinking were based on faulty presumptions, he was honest and sincere enough to accept his error. Humility made his personality approachable and human. He towered among men; yet, his head could bow down deeply to Truth, and this turned Balakrishna Menon into Swami Chinmayananda. Even as Guruji outlined that profound change, Shanti wondered at the daring honesty of Gurudev....

As a young man, Gurudev had some misconceptions about sannyāsīs. In his opinion, they were wasting their time in the mountains. So the journalist in him decided to call their bluff and off he went to the Himalayas. There he joined an āśrama, lived by the rules, and did what was expected of him. His inquiring mind absorbed the whole life style, and when he was convinced that the sannyāsīs were not wasting their time, he took the path of sannyās himself. He understood sannyās and spirituality from living in close proximity to Swami Sivananda and Swami Tapovan Maharaj. His life truly epitomized independent thinking, a questioning spirit, and acceptance of truth in its entirety.

Courage and Conviction

...Shraddha was attracted to the undaunted work ethic that permeated the life and teachings of Gurudev. She was amazed by the strong conviction with which every task was undertaken and every situation faced. No obstacle was ever allowed to remain on his path of Truth. For him there was no looking back. We can see this clearly in the Chinmaya Mission pledge where he declares the intent and prays for its fulfillment: "We know our responsibilities; give us the ability and courage to fulfill them."

On one occasion Shraddha had heard Shanti echo similar sentiments when the latter addressed a group of Junior CHYKS: "When the wavering mind stands still and a decision is taken, then the execution should be without fear. There should be no doubts and no second thoughts, but only a cheerful demeanor with complete faith in the goal and its accomplishment." Shraddha had come to recognize that questioning was the cornerstone of the Chinmaya Mission philosophy, not blind faith. This reflected in Guruji's description of the fearless beginning of Gurudev's mission....

In 1951 when Gurudev began his work, the environment was very different. India had just gained freedom from the British. Despite that independence, people's mindsets had not yet changed. In addition, Gurudev was hampered by the orthodoxy of the priestly class. The Brahmins were convinced that the message of the scriptures should be written or spoken about only in Sanskrit, and only a chosen few were eligible to study them.

Against this background, it required great courage to speak on the Upaniṣads in English, and that, too, in public! Someone even told Gurudev that his tongue either will fall off or be burned if he taught the Upaniṣads in English. But he was undaunted. He was neither demoralized nor was he afraid.

A Mahatma seems like any other person in that he eats, drinks, sleeps, and acts in the world, just like everyone else. The difference lies in the convictions that are ever vigilant and alive in the cave of his heart.

Devotion and Surrender

...As Guruji spoke about his Guru, Shanti could see that the most endearing quality of Guruji's personality was his devotion to Gurudev. Whatever Guruji accomplished had the signature of devoted surrender — "Not me. It is He!" He never missed an opportunity to salute the spiritual heights from which Gurudev operated....

To the world he appeared as a man of knowledge, action, and wisdom. But deep within was that very special quality of surrender and devotion. All Gurudev's actions were done with a spirit of complete surrender, remembering his Guru and Nārāyaṇa.

"Nārāyaṇa... Nārāyaṇa... Nārāyaṇa..." was the constant chant to which all his actions were dedicated. He was always in tune with his Guru and the Lord.

Pujya Gurudev always made his itinerary more than a year in advance. He would then offer it at the feet of the Lord and await a green signal through his direct connection with Him. Toward the end of 1992, while making his itinerary for 1994, he was often heard saying that he was not getting the go-ahead. Such was his tuning with the Lord and the Guru.

Detachment

...Shanti felt her eyes mist as she listened to Guruji's voice full of emotion. Lost in the wonder of such perfect tuning with the Guru Paramparā, Shanti's mind then focused on the degree of vairāgya (detachment) that Gurudev had imparted to Guruji. Can such devotion coexist with utter detachment? Shanti had always marveled at how that quality created Mahatmas....

Gurudev worked for the joy of working, immersed in the moment, alive to the present. There were no clinging attachments to any labor or effort, or people, or place, or past, or future.

He was often asked what would happen to this huge Mission after he had gone. With total lack of concern, he would say that he had done his work and dedicated it to the Lord. If his disciples and devotees wanted to continue the work, they would do so. His surrender being total, his detachment was also complete.

Gurudev had detachment even toward his own body. I have seen him happily sitting in a chilled air-conditioned room. The room was so cold that I could not bear it and had to come out immediately. Also, I have seen him sweating on the railway platform in Allahabad in the sweltering heat, sitting patiently, without any complaint.

...Shraddha had read in an article somewhere how Gurudev had sat meditating on a hot tarmac of an airfield, completely oblivious while others around him fretted about the heat....

Patriotism

'He viśvaci mājhe ghara,' (the whole world is my home) said Sant Jnaneshwar. Pujya Gurudev lived true to that saying, looking on the whole world as his home. His love for humanity took him to different countries and cultures, and he went happily. But Bharat had a special niche in his heart, and he was happiest when he was on Indian soil.

Pujya Gurudev loved everything about India — her culture, her history, her people. He would travel all over the world but was at home only when he returned to India! In the Jagdeeshwara temple, Mumbai, he would sit cross-legged on the ground in the traditional manner, feeling the oneness with the land and the Lord.

He had love for all beings (sarvabhūtahiterataḥ — engaged in the welfare of all living beings, *Gītā* 12.4). People often have patriotism and bhakti for their own country, but ill will for other nations. Gurudev had a very special love for his motherland, but there was also respect for other nations. His love was all encompassing (viśva prem).

...The idealistic Balakrishna Menon had fought for Indian independence before he fought for spiritual renaissance, thought Shanti. Indeed, India was part of his soul....

Value of Spirituality

...As Guruji spoke, Shraddha's mind was filled with awe, "Can the work done by Pujya Gurudev ever be quantified? Can statistics tell the story? Any numerical evaluation of the work by Gurudev can only be a poor estimate. It will fall short because numbers can only account for the overt — what is seen or perceived — but what about the millions of lives and homes that have benefited from the forty-three years he spent in the service of mankind?"

Almost as if he read her thoughts, Guruji presented a perspective of how Gurudev endowed the Mission....

Gurudev began his work from a small Ganesh temple in Pune. From this modest beginning, slowly the Mission grew into a force and then became a movement. Today we can list the number of jñāna yajñas he conducted and maybe even put a number to the aśramas, temples, schools, and colleges he established.

However, countless are the benefits received by the millions across the globe from the logic of spirituality that he gave to the world. People have different notions about spirituality. Some think it is meant only for those who have retired or are unable to live a productive life. To others, spirituality means sitting in a cave and escaping from life.

Gurudev removed such erroneous notions and revealed that spiritual knowledge is a great science founded on sound reasoning. Through his lectures, he explained the rationale behind spirituality, religion, and culture in a language that could be easily understood by everyone. After listening to him, people were convinced that Gurudev's teachings were indeed a great and definitive science, not bogus information or a figment of imagination.

The Unique Trademark

...Shraddha's mind was caught in a question — a long time before Gurudev began his discourses, the tradition of giving lectures on the scriptures had already existed. What, then, made Gurudev's style of teaching so distinctive?....

Gurudev took learning to another level and made it a different experience. In his lectures, everyone was seated with a book in hand. Every word was chanted, repeated, and explained. And he did not hesitate to take everyone to the very Source, to the Vedic foundation. He established this tradition of learning, which became his trademark, and it continues to be the special feature of Chinmaya Mission lectures worldwide. In further describing Gurudev, Guruji said:

Generally, people listen to talks based on ideas and thoughts expressed in the scriptures without knowing their original source. As a result, many people become attached to a particular book or person. Gurudev spoke on the original texts — the Upaniṣads and the *Bhagavad-gītā*, thereby taking our minds to the very sources of Knowledge itself.

Once at the source, there is no need to look elsewhere for this Knowledge. This takes you to the very source of happiness. It is due to his efforts that we are aware of the Upaniṣads, the *Gītā*, and other prakaraṇa granthas (books of categories, that is, the foundation of logic) of Vedānta. The names of great Masters, which would have otherwise been forgotten and lost, are today a part of our living heritage.

Also, if there was a demand for knowledge, he made sure it was fulfilled. It was Gurudev's love for the seekers that took him on travels to far-flung places around the world. This is why the Mission is represented on practically every continent.

In two words his life work can be described as '***transforming lives***.' In a short span of forty-three years, he set up so many Mission centers and touched innumerable lives. It is not possible to count the number of lives he changed and transformed by his mere presence, teachings, letters, or work. To the extent that even if a little child wrote to him, he replied, and so changed the person!

Pujya Gurudev, a great Mahatma of modern times, had a unique personal touch that sublimated the lives of many.

Vision into Action

...The practical idealism of Gurudev was what Shanti had admired from the beginning. She had carefully watched it unfold in his every initiative....

The fructification of vision lies in its translation. Gurudev's vision was that of a Master; yet, he implemented it with the compassion of a mother. Understanding the needs of all, he reached out to each one at the level at which they were:

Vision must be translated into action and there has to be a proper program that includes and reaches out to all levels of individuals.

Gurudev was not a mere visionary. He knew how to implement his vision. While some visionaries remain mere dreamers and some act without a vision, he knew how to give shape to his dreams. In him, we had a visionary who worked with the zeal of a missionary.

A newborn baby gets nourishment from the mother's milk. The child grows, but still needs to be nourished by milk. So the child is fed using a bottle. Later, the child drinks milk from a glass. We find that milk remains constant but the method of giving the milk changes.

In the same way, Pujya Gurudev created programs for all age groups at their levels: BVs, Yuva Kendras, and Study Groups are based on age, thus reflecting a steady progression. Even though at every stage nourishment is in the form of knowledge, the methodology is different at each level.

Guru-Śishya Paramparā

...Shraddha was overwhelmed when she first entered Chinmaya Vibhooti, as this symbolised the underlying strength of the Guru-Śiṣya paramparā (teacher-disciple tradition). The phenomenal growth of Chinmaya Mission is entirely due to the blessings of this tradition that Gurudev faithfully followed. When Guruji explained the vision that supported Chinmaya Vibhooti, Shraddha visualized this as the living roots of the Mission, nourishing the future....

Since Gurudev's Mahāsāmadhī in 1993, the Mission has grown in leaps and bounds, in every possible field of service. Ideas need implementation and implementation requires people with a vision and the ability to perform. Gurudev's most cherished agenda was setting up institutions to train brahmacharins in the understanding of Vedānta.

Perhaps his most important contribution to the Guru-paramparā was the way he maintained and kept it alive through the Sandeepany Sadhanalayas. He knew that individuals can work only up to a certain time and level. For work to continuously flow, there must be a tradition, which must be protected. The most important work of the Mission is the teaching of the scriptures in the Sandeepany Sadhanalayas. If all the other programs were to continue but this were to stop, the whole Mission would become stagnant and the stream of work would come to a standstill.

Life demands perennial flow. By setting up institutions to teach the scriptures in various languages, he encouraged the spread of Vedānta. His passionate commentaries on many scriptures gave rise to priceless books. As a result of this constant flow of Knowledge, Chinmaya Mission has the sustaining guidance of its many ācāryas and a vast body of excellent literature in different languages.

The unprecedented cultural renaissance that Gurudev sparked has connected the sages to even our little BV children! The children of today know about many different aspects of Indian culture. They know the significance of prayer and know why they should prostrate. That in itself is a great revival.

...The auditorium in which Guruji was speaking seemed to fill with a spiritual energy as the audience listened to the description of Gurudev's qualities and achievements. His words etched the image of Gurudev in every sevak present. As Guruji paused to summarize, Shanti reveled in all that she had heard: "Every talk, every letter, every memo carried his signature. Gurudev's message came from the core of his heart, and it found its target deep in the psyche of the listener, to remain there for all time. His teaching was the Truth, it brooked no denial."

The compassionate voice of Guruji once again flowed through the Sudharma Auditorium as he listed the key mantras to remember from Gurudev's repertoire....

The cornerstone of Gurudev's philosophy was: *"You Change."* Since we cannot perfect this world, we have to perfect ourselves. In short, he preached: *"World perfection through individual perfection."*

The winning attitude that Gurudev advocated was: "KEEP SMILING." Life throws up challenging situations; through them all, we can and must smile. If on some occasion he was being served by a solemn-faced volunteer, Gurudev would say, "Smile!" Once he even autographed a serious photograph of himself saying: *"There is no harm if you smile a bit!"*

His advice in a world of action, based on the *Gītā* was 'Active resistance to evil.' Spiritual life was about active goodness, not passive submission.

Gurudev's firm belief in the innate strength of human beings echoed in his resonant voice, "We can. We must!" Repeatedly, he asserted that only mankind has the capacity to achieve the impossible — to Realize!

..."Each of these mantras is worthy of reflection," mused Shraddha, "but practice is not an easy task." Grappling with an obstinate mind, she knew that the power of satsaṅga alone could cut through the vicious tyranny of thoughts that occupied the mind from sunrise to sunset. All she could do for now was diligently take the first step in sādhanā (spiritual practice) — śravaṇa (listening).

Shanti was happy that Shraddha was here with her at this particular lecture. She knew that anyone who entered the Mission could not but be touched by the power of Gurudev's being. For some, the light was ignited in an instant, while in others it lay dormant to shine forth at a later time. This magical aspect of his personality had a powerful impact on many lives. Shanti herself was still connecting the dots to understand the full picture of her own transformation. The prayer in her heart that day was simple, "Gurudev, let your Grace envelop Shraddha. Let her make the connection with you!"**....**

Bala Perspectives

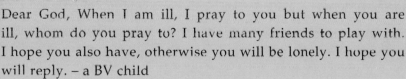

Dear God, When I am ill, I pray to you but when you are ill, whom do you pray to? I have many friends to play with. I hope you also have, otherwise you will be lonely. I hope you will reply. – a BV child

Pramodini Rao is recognized in the Chinmaya family through her mellifluous voice, which enlivens several bhajans CDs in the Mission repertoire.

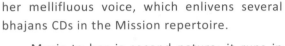

Music to her is second nature; it runs in her veins. Her music training began very early in life, under her mother, Susheela Acharya, a musician and a gifted writer of verse. The lyrics of many bhajans sung by Pramodini have flowed from her mother's pen. Says Pramodini, "Even as a child people would comment, 'She sings well'. So whenever any singing was required I would be pushed into the spotlight."

As a young girl, Pramodini was quiet and reserved, content to enjoy her own company. This changed when in class eight she became a teenage sevikā in Nirmala Chellam's cluster of BV classes in Mumbai. Here, Pramodini blossomed. She recalls:

"Being trained as a sevikā brought about a huge transformation in my personality. The confidence to address a group of people, the ability to think independently and organizational skills are all by-products of this training.

Music has always been the one great love of my life. Guruji urged me to adopt music as a profession, but I chose not to heed his advice, and went off to the workplace. After several years, when those vasanās were exhausted, I realized I was ready to work for the Mission fulltime and offered my services at the feet of Gurudev."

Guruji handpicked Pramodini to lead the Chinmaya Naada Bindu (CNB) team. And in 2009, when CNB was inaugurated to propagate India's Vedic and spiritual traditions through the performing arts, Pramodini Rao was appointed its Resident Director. She had come home.

Pramodini discloses, "We encourage artists to attend the residential Dance and Music intensives at CNB, in the serene, sylvan surroundings of Chinmaya Vibhooti and through music bring peace to the mind." With Guruji's blessings and her able leadership CNB is inching towards a place in the top echelons of the world of music.

She says, "As Director of CNB, the impressions left by Nirmala Aunty's teachings help me to be level-headed and balanced.... I am indebted to Gurudev and Chinmaya Mission for all that I am today. The leadership and organizational skills that others acquire through expensive MBA programs, came to me simply by being a part of the Mission!"

Part 3
The Know How

Part 3

The Know How

- IX Value the Action

  The Highlights — Inspiring avenues for creative and interactive learning

- X The Literary Trail

  Ideals through pages — Books, magazine and website for children

- XI Toward Uniformity

  The Bala Vihar curriculum — Prototype booklet to grade-wise books

- XII Nurturing the Flow

  Training empowers — Guruji on the role of a Bala Vihar sevak

IX

Value the Action

Through a story or a song, a verse or a game, the values that Pujya Gurudev idealized come alive for every generation of Bala Vihar (BV) children. He wanted every action in BV to leave a valuable imprint on young minds. For every child to feel the wonder of scriptural learning, he encouraged the use of different creative forms as learning tools during the weekly classes and annual camps.

Be it a regular class that lasts an hour and a half, or an extended summer camp that ranges from a week to two months, every aspect of BV is focused on building a firm foundation of values.

Gurudev was certain that, at BV, children would imbibe the timeless principles of Sanatana Dharma, build inspired friendships, and develop a lifelong bond with the scriptures — all in an atmosphere fostered by selfless sevā and unconditional love.

...Like many Chinmaya Mission centers, the center at New Delhi comes alive during every summer vacation. Children's voices fill all the rooms — because it is the BV annual summer camp. Shanti looks forward to these days with great enthusiasm. The whole project lasts a total of three to four months and releases a great deal of bonhomie. Over years, a strong synergy has fostered lasting relationships among the sevaks, and everyone awaits this event with joyful anticipation. The sevaks first come together to conceptualize, then to research, and finally to deliver the package of fun-filled learning in an action-packed three weeks....

All that is taught in BV is of great importance for the overall development of the children. They learn something from every activity. A day at the camp includes all the activities that happen in a regular BV class, along with some additional programs. An inside look at some of these activities gives the complete flavor of the BV experience.

Once Upon a Time...

... Shanti's forte was always the storytelling sessions. She loved observing the changing moods on the young faces of children seated before her as the narrative took them soaring into lands of fantasy. This took her back to her own childhood, when seated in a circle with her cousins, she had heard these very same stories from her silver-haired and oh so soft-skinned Nānī!**....**

At the last camp, Shanti had invited Deepa Kiran (a former BV child, now a professional storyteller) to conduct a session with the children. Deepa, a delightful solo-act, came with her band packed in a pull-along suitcase and, as in days of yore, she spoke, sang, and danced through the narration.

Said Deepa, "The 'once upon a time' beginning often helps illustrate a point far better than facts. The beauty and power of storytelling lies in the strength of 'realization through revelation.' Through the stories the teller 'reveals,' and the listener 'unravels' truths for himself. The listener is taken on a journey during which he can gather new insights. The narrative becomes a medium through which a child learns to distinguish between acceptable and non-acceptable behavior. A skilled storyteller can kindle curiosity so that a child questions the actions of the characters in the story."**....**

The Bard Par Excellence

Gurudev, a masterful storyteller who could spellbind any generation, urged parents to spend time telling and reading stories to their children:

"Storytelling is an art that should be cultivated by all conscientious parents; it is an unavoidable must.

If you spend half an hour each day with the children and read something interesting out loud to them, their vocabulary will improve, and they will learn to talk in coherent and meaningful sentences — no more will any baby talk issue forth from them. Also this practice teaches them the art of listening, which will stand them in good stead when they grow up, not only in their early education, but also in their later life in the outer world of strife and strain."

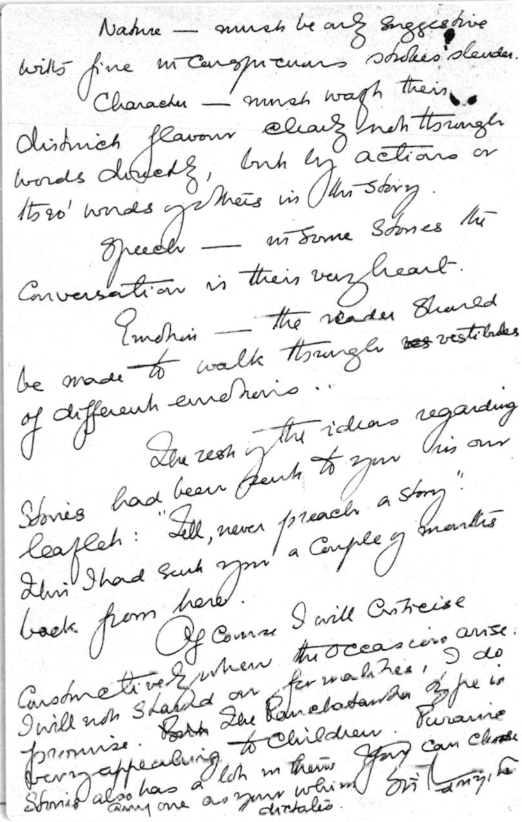
Nature — must be only suggestive with fine inconspicuous strokes' slender.
Character — must [illegible] their distinct flavour clearly not through words directly, but by actions or through words of others in the story.
Speech — in some stories the conversation is their very heart.
Emotion — the reader should be made to walk through vestibules of different emotions..
The rest of the ideas regarding stories had been sent to you in our leaflet: "Tell, never preach a story". This I had sent you a couple of months back from here.
Of course I will criticise constructively when the occasions arise. I do not stand on formalities; I will not stand on [illegible] promise. Both the Panchatantra type is being appealing to children. Puranic stories also has a lot in them. You can choose any one as your whim dictates.

Values Come Riding

...During the planning of the camp, the sevaks met with Swami Nikhilananda to clarify the concepts and goals. While explaining the need for stories to introduce values, Swami Nikhilananda said, "Children may not understand the concept of truthfulness through a talk, but when they are introduced to the value through the story of a truthful person, they comprehend it easily."

Swami Nikhilananda alluded to a passage from Gurudev's writing where he states that values are best imparted through storytelling....

Values are so subtle that even an elderly person will not be able to conceive of the idea unless it is concretized in an individual acting on those values in a given set of specific conditions.

Thus, when you relate Harishchandra's story to the children, they understand the compelling situations: Harishchandra's own son had died. The mother brought the body for cremation to the very burial ground where Harishchandra, her husband, stood guard.

He said, "Sorry, ten paise is the tax; you need to pay it."

She said, "I haven't got even one paisa."

"Then get out of here. My master has placed me here to collect the tax. Or, you can wait here, and when the master comes in the morning, you can discuss it with him. If the master says he has no objection, the matter could be settled." (Harishchandra, who gave up his kingdom in a test of his truthfulness, would not bend the rules, not even when he saw his only son dead in the arms of his pleading, penniless wife.)

So the truthfulness, the honesty of words, you gather from the story alone. You may forget the story, but the idea goes in. This is the method used in BV. In today's modern education, the children are not provided with any ideals. Data is given but no ideal to pursue. Ideals must be given. The story is not for history, it is for imparting an ideal. Give it to them in a story and they will always check whether their action was morally good or not, beautiful or not. These children will grow up, and in their togetherness, they will constitute the society.

First we have to conceive of, understand, and appreciate these values ourselves. Thereafter, mere possession is not sufficient. Each individual should learn to live up to them. In order to impart these values to our growing children, there is no way other than concretizing them through the heroic stories of people who have lived these values. Hence, the need for stories.

VALUES COME RIDING ON THE BACK OF A HERO!

| SWAMI CHINMAYANANDA |

The story of Shravan Kumar's dedication to his blind parents moved me deeply and made me want to live like him — I vowed to be the best child to my parents. I am happy when their friends tell my parents they are blessed to have a son like me. — Srijit Nair, CM Bengaluru

My inspiration for storytelling Sunday after Sunday is:

The shine in the children's eyes when they 'get it'; I look for the point in the story when they stop moving and their minds are completely absorbed. It is thrilling to have a child's complete attention, but you have to be careful with such impressionable minds.

The most touching moment was when I was telling a story on how association with a sage can make you a better person. At the end of the story, I waited in silence for a moment to let the message sink in. Then the class was dismissed. A boy came up to me and said, "Look, Aunty, my hair is still standing up." — Nanda Subbarao, CM Princeton

During BV I narrated a very well-loved tale about a little boy who was told by his mother to call out for Gopal Bhaiyā (Śrī Kṛṣṇa) when he felt scared. Among the students was a young boy suffering from cancer. After hearing this story, his mother said he would call out to Kṛṣṇa all the time.

And two weeks later he passed away, saying, "Kṛṣṇa Bhaiyā."

— Bina Sutarwala, CM Ottawa

The BV story telling sessions were my favorite activity and the stories unlocked a new gateway in my imagination. The description of the heavens, the gandharvas, apsarās and devas were splendid, though somewhat overwhelming and introduced me to a fascinating world.

— Mohit Wadhwani, CM London

Dramatize and Reinforce

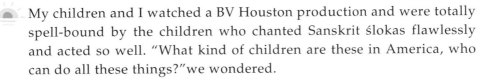

A favorite aspect of BV is to showcase a story on stage. Stories linger in memory, and when they come alive in a play, the impressions are more impactful. From humorous skits to elaborate stage productions, BVs around the world have taken the cue from Gurudev's dramatic flair.

My children and I watched a BV Houston production and were totally spell-bound by the children who chanted Sanskrit ślokas flawlessly and acted so well. "What kind of children are these in America, who can do all these things?"we wondered.

The kids said, "We are coming for BV!" and from the next week onward, we became a part of CM Houston. Chinmaya Mission is where my daughter made her friends, where she found her bearings. This is where she fitted into the American society.

— Punam Malhotra, CM Houston

Releasing Wonders of Creativity

For Gurudev, values could be evoked through varied artistic mediums. He encouraged sevaks to experiment with different art forms to coax the joys of creativity from young hearts. He said:

> Never can children's education be complete unless we impart to them a true appreciation of the eternal values of life and also help them to open up their sense of beauty and rhythm, their aesthetics and ethics. That is the reason why we not only try to mold them with our stories of heroism and excellence in character, but also to give them a free choice to discover and develop their inner secret talents in music, dance, painting, and so on. It has been found very rewarding in all our centers.

Given the chance to express their individuality, children give their creative best. The wonder in their hearts expresses as visual art. The arts and crafts sessions allow their imagination to flower, self-esteem increases and children feel pride in their creations.

...Shanti was an old hand at BV and could lend a hand in any department that required her expertise. Her little grandson Gopal, one of the youngest participants at the camp, was registered in the junior-most section. To him the Chinmaya center was not a place that held any secrets, because he had roamed its halls and corridors for as long as he could remember.

Now the little tornado came running towards his Dādī, weaving his way through the groups of children sprawled on the floor, absorbed in a world of their own making — with colors, papers, shapes, paints, crayons, and much more.

Shanti settled down cross-legged beside Gopal to help him create his masterpiece. To each his own they say, and so it was with these children. Every one of them viewed their artistic creations with pride. The hall full of children, though quiet, was palpably joyous.

In response to a query from some parents, Anand Sharma, the camp Ācārya said, "The art and crafts sessions ensure active involvement; the children are completely absorbed in doing something themselves. Making a mask of Śrī K⍰⍰⍰a is an opportunity to pour out their creativity. In the process of trying to visualize Him, a connection is established. This leads to further involvement, and they aim to make Him as beautiful as possible."....

Hands Hold the Key to Learning

The fun of using one's hands brings with it great learning. Children can experience even a tough concept like, 'God is everywhere, in all of creation' — when out of clay, they make several objects and then blend back those objects into a single, huge ball of clay! Acārya Darshana Nanavaty, sums up the logic behind this playful activity:

> When one sense is involved, there is some impact. When more senses are involved, children remember better. Giving them projects that involve all the senses will create deeper grooves in their minds, and they will remember the concepts.

...Shanti found that Junior CHYKs were a great resource when it came to arts and crafts activities. They were helpful and eager volunteers and loved planning activities for the younger children....

> Most of the summer was spent coming up with ideas and preparing material for BV projects. The experience was transformative, as in the process I discovered my own interests and passions. It became an avenue to serve the Mission, doing what I had an aptitude for and also enjoyed. — Pooja Merai, CM Chicago

Fun Time – Let's Play!

Ask any child, "What do you like best?"

Ten times out of ten, the answer will be, "Play"!

Gurudev was an expert child psychologist, and knew that teaching would best take place through the medium of games and activities. It infuses them with team spirit, discipline and patience.

They understand the art of 'playing without anything'. In time they connect to the Vedāntic truth, that material things are not the true source of happiness.You don't need things to be happy.

...Shanti saw the children milling around Anand, wanting his attention. The shrill voices could be heard calling, "Anand Bhaiyā! Anand Bhaiyā!" Joking or serious, loving or stern, Anand had them wrapped around his little finger. After the completion of the Vedānta course from Sandeepany Sadhanalaya, Anand Sharma has been with the Delhi Center, involved with children in BV and in the Chinmaya Vidyalaya, Delhi.

Anand told Shanti, "Children draw their own parallels. They understand that just as a game cannot be played alone, so also, in life we need help from others to successfully accomplish goals. They recognize that being a good human being living a life of discipline will help them evolve. They learn: Try again. Do not give up!"....

Joining the Festivals

Song... dance... drama... delectable food... mouth-watering delicacies... pujas... special clothes... visiting friends and relatives — are the ingredients of any celebration. Hinduism is utsav pradhāna (with an emphasis on celebrating festivals)! This is the not-to-be-missed fun part of Indian culture. So at BV, all festivals are celebrated zestfully; care is taken to explain the importance of each festival, and parental participation encouraged.

At many Chinmaya Mission centers, during Janmāṣṭamī celebrations, clones of Kṛṣṇa and Rādhā can be seen running around — the boys tugging at their dhotī, the girls hanging on to their dupattās! From center to center, the approach may vary, but celebrating is a common denominator in the BV ethos.

Having celebrated many such festivals with children Swami Nikhilananda spoke of his experiences:

> Stories of the life and pranks of Kṛṣṇa make the festival come alive for them. In an atmosphere of celebration and excitement, children learn about the adventures of Kṛṣṇa and Rādhā. They also unconsciously imbibe the glory of bhakti and true love.

...Shanti heard how in one US center, children celebrated Śivarātrī by building their own massive Śivali⍰ga. For Rāma Navamī, they took individual idols of Lord Rāma and offered Him play clothes and made-up ornaments — all in line with the sixteen steps of a traditional puja. Every year the style of celebration changes. This novelty makes children and adults look forward to festival times. Not only do children understand the significance of religious festivals but they also learn about their symbolism. Indian culture comes alive for them....

In Tune and In Step

Values always take on a special noteworthiness when they come through bhajans. Favorite bhajans set up a direct connect with the Lord. Several BV choirs have produced musical talent that has gone onto the world stage.

Values also have their own rhythm in the world of dance. Indian classical dance themes are all based on the scriptures and so instantly capture the hearts of children.

I started to sing bhajans at the age of five — they were fun, and the catchy tunes and beautiful meanings always stuck in my head for replay as I grew. Now, it serves as an escape from daily life and schoolwork. Singing in front of Guruji and Gurudev's pratima are experiences to be cherished forever. Bhajan singing is a part of my life. It has made me who I am and will continue to play a vital part in it.

— Sumedha Rao, CM Houston

...Shanti was awed by the abundance of fine art capabilities exhibited by BV children worldwide. She loved singing bhajans with children and found even their dance performances totally charming. According to her even the toddler who danced slightly out of step to the music seemed to add beauty to the program....

Attuning to Divinity

Every BV camp and class integrates prayers from the scriptures in varying degrees — melodious chanting of selected ślokas (verses) from the *Bhagavad-gītā*, mantras, and stotras.

...In every camp, the parents expressed a common doubt, "Will the children be able to master such difficult Sanskrit ślokas?" Shanti had learned to allay their fears with smiling eyes that said, "Wait and watch. They may yet surprise you!"

When parents enquired, "What are the benefits of chanting? How does it affect the mind?" Shanti explained, "Everything we say affects the mind. The chanting of ślokas and mantras involves the repetition of Bhagavān's name, and results in calming the mind. Even without knowing the meaning, we experience peace and serenity, which then spreads to the surroundings. As children grow, a desire to know the meaning arises — which is the first step in their spiritual quest."

Her confidence stemmed from years of experience and Gurudev's assertion....

- Our effort is mainly to encourage the children to chant the verses musically (throwing in stories and historical anecdotes here and there) so that when they grow up, there will spring forth in them a desire to understand the meaning and value of these verses.

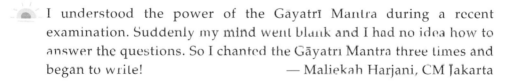

Powerful results accrue from the practice of this ancient tradition. Chanting helps attune the minds of children. They learn about the great ṛṣis who have given us these prayers and mantras with such beautiful and profound meanings.

Even more powerful than chanting individually is chanting in a group. The power of the multiplier effect ensures that the vibrations generated are purer and more powerful.

The sound of hundreds of voices chanting the āratī and the Mission Pledge are among my most memorable memories of BV.

— Mythili Iyer, CM Princeton

I understood the power of the Gāyatrī Mantra during a recent examination. Suddenly my mind went blank and I had no idea how to answer the questions. So I chanted the Gāyatrī Mantra three times and began to write! — Maliekah Harjani, CM Jakarta

Chanting Calms the Mind

Nicknamed 'the Vedic sisters' by Pujya Gurudev, Brni. Shruti, one of the sisters says:

Sometimes if I wake up and am unable to go back to sleep, I begin to chant some mantras. While chanting, the meaning of the mantras comes to mind, pushing it into introspection or reflection. When faced with potentially explosive situations, instead of dwelling on or releasing unnecessary emotions, I take to mental chanting. This helps to remain in the present and also prevents any over-reactions.

I was teaching the first-grade class about Lord Śiva. We had just started to learn the Mahā Mṛtyuñjaya mantra. We taught that the mantra was life-giving and that when chanted with love for Lord Śiva it had the power to save one from death and extend life.

One child raised his hand and softly asked, "If I chant this mantra, will my Grandma wake up from her coma?"

"Of course," I said, "Lord Śiva is all-powerful. When we call out to Him sincerely, He comes running to save us."

We chanted the mantra eleven times in class and the child continued chanting at home. Within a week, his grandmother came out of her coma; in a year, she started walking.

This powerful incident moved me tremendously — the simple faith of the child and the power of the Lord's name.

— Charu Ganesan, CM San Jose

Gītā in Growing Voices

Gurudev envisioned the chanting competitions as an introduction to a life-long friendship with the *Gītā*. The children were embarking on a progressive path of 'Chant-Study-Know-Live the *Gītā*.'

The *Gītā* was Gurudev's life breath. He wanted the Lord's Song to echo among people of all ages and across all continents. He launched the 'Chant *Gītā,* Land Washington' competition in 1991. It was planned to coincide with Gurudev's 500th *Gītā* Jñāna Yajña. The event resounded with success, captivating over 10,000 children and youth in India. Jyothi N. Iyyer from Nagpur and R. Sudha from Delhi were the winners. Their reward was a month-long trip to the U.S. visiting various CM centres.

Ācārya Sharada Kumar, CM Ann Arbor, recalls how *Gītā* chanting grew into prominence in the United States:

▲ GURUDEV WITH JYOTHI AND SUDHA

Gurudev asked us to coordinate a Chant *Gītā*, Land Ganga competition in the BVs of the U.S.A. Vidya Kumar of Ann Arbor and Gauri Patankar of Houston, respectively were winners in the senior and junior categories. While handing them their trophies Gurudev congratulated the two girls and praised the way the competition had brought his vision alive.

The promised all-India trip to the winners was beautifully coordinated. On their last stop, in Uttarkasi, the children heard the sad news of Gurudev's Mahāsamādhī. It looked like Gurudev had timed every detail of that unforgettable 'Chant *Gītā*, Land Ganga' trip, to the last minute.

Guruji in a succinct Sanskrit śloka conveys the great importance of *Gītā* chanting:

गीतापाठेऽर्थजिज्ञासा ततोज्ञानंभविष्यति।
कृतार्थताहिज्ञानेन तस्माद्गीतांपठेन्नरः ॥

From the recitation of the *Bhagavad-gītā* arises the desire to know its meaning. Thence arises the Knowledge (of the Self). From this Knowledge arises fulfillment. Hence an individual must recite the *Bhagavad-gītā*.

In India annual *Gītā* Chanting Competitions are held in every state, spanning villages, towns and cities. BV sevaks work with devotion to involve children from schools in their areas. Teachers from the Chinmaya Vidyalayas are also committed to annually increase its scope. The magnitude of the activity being so enormous, it is well nigh impossible to assess its outreach in numbers!

In many U.S. centers the annual competition is conducted around Gurudev's birthday on May 8. Participation in it is their way of acknowledging his grace and saying, "Gurudev, this is our gift to you!"

Uma Kamath, a seven-year-old in BV Houston, has been participating in *Gītā* chanting for the past five years! Even as a two-year-old, she would chant a few verses of the *Gītā* to an astounded audience. Innocently she says, "God wants me to do it, and when I work hard, He always helps me."

To spread the benefits of chanting, CM Houston began the Slokathon program. Envisioned by Darshana Nanavaty, the main aim of this program is to give children the confidence to chant in Sanskrit. More than 250 verses from the scriptures, divided into fifteen sections, are taught throughout the year by a team of dedicated teachers and continues to have far-reaching impact.

Look What I Know; See What I Can Do…!

Parents and children enthusiastically await the cultural performances at the the end-of-the-school-year or end-of-camp celebrations. On stage, the children are in another world, eyes twinkling and enjoyment writ large on their innocent faces. Their parents are astounded to see their budding talent and feel grateful for the nurturing by the sevaks.

Swami Nikhilananda summarizes the effects of such shows:

> Often, we notice that shy children become fearless after coming to BV. In this friendly and loving atmosphere, they drop their inhibitions and begin to speak freely and interact easily. Nobody is judged; they are not given any ranks or certificates. All children are treated equally and in the warmth of this acceptance, they shed their fears and step into a life of assurance and self-confidence.

... The sevaks worked tirelessly to make sure that everything was in place before the curtains went up for the finale — a grand ending to the camp. Shanti watched the preparation with a sense of déjà vu. "Amazing," she thought, "each year the excitement levels are the same — the same for the children, and the same for the sevaks. It is almost like waiting to see the face of a newborn!"**....**

> The success of any annual day program depends on minute detailed planning. The quantum of organization behind this event is truly immense and can only be accomplished by the spirit of true cooperation. I saw how much time and effort was required of everyone in the community to ensure the smooth execution of the event.
>
> As a child, while preparing for a BV annual event, the import of the first line of the Mission pledge presented itself. "We stand as a

family bound to each other with love and respect." I truly felt a part of one big family and for life learnt the important lesson of teamwork!

— N. M. Sundar, CM Mumbai

And What a Finale!

In 2003, Chennai celebrated fifty years of the Center's existence on Marina Beach with the Indian Ocean as witness. And what a celebration it was! Months of planning and toiling led to this grand event, to be indelibly etched in the minds of all those privileged to be a part of it. An eyewitness account:

> It was a grand vision — the vast blue expanse of the sea and the sky and thousands of children gathered on the sandy shore. There were separate enclosures for each school, clearly identifiable by their uniforms. The children looked like huge bunches of flowers in different colors, nodding and swaying joyously in the breeze. Far away, framed against the sky was the raised platform of the famous and historical Seerani Arangam, beautifully decorated. This was the last program to be held there, as it was demolished a couple of days later.
>
> Seated there on the dais was Pujya Guruji, in flaming orange, the leading light of the movement. The rich booming voice of the famed and legendary singer of Carnatic music, Śrī Balamuralikrishna, rose above the waves, and the voices of the children subsided.
>
> Slowly, after the inaugural speeches, the children chanted in unison more than 35,000 young voices singing the eternal song of the Lord, the twelfth chapter of the *Bhagavad-gītā*. The intonation flowed flawlessly, up and down, wave upon wave, verse-by-verse, teaching the rhythm to the waves that vied to reach the children and hug them in glee. It was glorious to be alive then and to witness the grand vision of Gurudev unfolding in the vast arena!
>
> — Parvathy Raman, Editor, Tapovan Prasad

Bala Perspectives

Said one child with conviction: "When we die, our body dies, but God is inside us. He does not die. He goes to another body and that person is born. So, we should not cry when someone dies. God never dies!"

X

The Literary Trail

Before paper was available and when printing was still unknown, knowledge passed by word of mouth from the teacher to the taught. In some cases, carvings on stone and metal tablets preserved the legacy of ageless wisdom. Ancient handwritten manuscripts captured the secrets of the world, but with the advent of the printing press, the process of sharing words and thoughts became much easier. Today giant strides in technology have changed forever the world of books and publishing.

Children's books today have much to offer in terms of design, content, and presentation. Children's literature by Chinmaya Publications has grown exponentially and from humble beginnings has risen to a place of eminence.

Gurudev sowed the seeds of literature that catered solely to the needs of his beloved children. He wanted to keep alive the glow of inquiry in their eyes and to see the light of idealism grow in their hearts. The objective was to translate the children's admiration for idols, like Śrī Hanumān and Śrī Rāmacandra, into their ideals for life. Children's literature has served as important resource tool for teachers in the Chinmaya Vidyalayas and for Bala Vihar

(BV) sevaks. The available content caters to the needs of children from three to fifteen years and, in design, vies with the best.

...Up until her introduction to the Mission, Shanti was blissfully unaware of the wealth of literature available in the Hindu scriptures. Her exposure to the Mission changed her understanding and so opened the doors to a whole new world. One day while cataloging books in the Mission bookstore, her eyes fell on the familiar covers of the *Bala Ramayana* and *Bala Bhagavatam*. These served to remind her of the time when she met the author of these books — Bharati Sukhatankar! Bharati conducted the classes that Shanti's children attended. The two women struck a friendship and during conversation one day, out came the story of the very first children's book written under Gurudev's directive — published by CCMT Publications Division — *Bala Ramayana*. Bharati's engaging account was still fresh in Shanti's mind....

The First Release — Bala Ramayana

I was a goggle-eyed teenager when I heard Swami Chinmayananda at the *Gītā* jñāna yajña in 1968 at New Delhi. I walked home in a daze that first day, wondering where the Swami had been all these years of my life. Over the next few days, something wonderful happened to me and I was never the same again. This had to be destiny.

After the Delhi yajña, Gurudev went into 'retreat' for the first time at Uttarkashi. My very first letter to him was a six page missive filled with questions such as: How could I serve, when, and where? Almost immediately, he wrote back saying, "Write a *Bala Ramayana* for children." I was totally unprepared for this task and thought, "I am a Science student. What do I know about creative writing?"

But I had implicit faith in Gurudev's wisdom. He had commanded, and obey, I must.

So with every pore of my being bursting with inspiration, I sat with the two versions of *Rāmāyaṇa* by Sage Valmiki and Saint Tulsidas — reading, absorbing, interpreting, and writing. And that is how *Bala Ramayana* poured out in handwritten pages, twenty-to-twenty-five pages at a time. I would send them to Gurudev. And he, in turn, would read them and send them back to me, always with a lot of encouragement and guidance.

GURUDEV WITH BHARATI ▲

Nothing less than excellence was acceptable to Gurudev, and Bharati was determined not to let him down. Bharati reminisced about the way the book took over her life:

> Somewhere along the way, I had ceased to exist. I do not know when my mother would feed me or gently put me to bed. *Bala Ramayana* was completed in two months, by July 1968. Swamiji released the book during the November yajña at Shivaji Park, Mumbai, that same year.

During the yajña by Gurudev in Belgaum in 1979, Ahilya Naik, Bharati's mother, promised him that she would start a BV class. She kept her word and continued as a BV sevikā for twenty-five years, till she became too old and frail to carry on. At any given time, she had around forty children in a class. Often on the streets or in the market, youngsters would walk up to her and ask, "Do you remember me? I used to come to your BV."

Before I could start wondering "What next?" came a letter saying, "Read *Bhāgavata*. We will take it up next, after August, say in the middle of September. Okay?"

FIRST COVER OF BALA BHAGAVATAM ▲

BALA BHAGAVATAM IS BORN

Never having heard about the *Bhāgavata*, Bharati had no clue as to what Gurudev wanted. So with the wisdom of a teenager, she thought:

> "*Bhāgavata*? Surely he meant *Mahābhārata*? Where had this *Bhāgavata* come from...? Soon a 'cartload' of books came from Calcutta; it was a twelve-volume hard cover set, bound in red cloth, with a print like tiny ants marching across the pages. Flicking through the pages I thought, "What has Swamiji got me into? How am I going to interpret this for children?"

Gurudev wrote: "When you learn to forget that you are doing the work, when you retire, He starts His work Divine.

Be in tune with children and talk to them while at the typewriter. Let hundreds of innocent chubby faces be uplifted to you all around. See in your mind their anxiety, fear, love, compassion, tears, smiles, and Thy Own Self..."

Gurudev's words had a rousing effect. I took up the challenge to write "healthy, robust, talking, speaking, lively stories, dashing in action, suggestive for the innocent minds of the children."

Slowly but surely, the *Bhāgavata* took over my life. At one place, in the story of Gajendra Mokṣa, the elephant cries out to Lord Nārāyaṇa in distress, "I am a lowly creature, please come and save me."

Gurudev rejected this prayer outright. "Remember," he said, "We are molding young minds. When we call them amṛtasyaputraḥ, Children of Immortal Bliss, we cannot offer them negative ideas. Use positive ideas only, so that they discover the depths of their own strengths and grow in stature and spirit."

Along the way, I drew some sketches in accordance with the guidelines that Gurudev supplied. "The sketches must speak to the children. Forget about adults. Dhruva must still be a baby, doing tapas on one leg. Narada must not have a kamandalū — he must have a tāmburā across his left shoulder; in the right hand, either a mālā or a chiplā (small wooden clapboards) to keep time in singing. He must wear a mālā."

The work was tedious and at times difficult. To condense and write a child-friendly version of Vyāsa's masterpiece was a Herculean task. What sustained me were, undoubtedly, Swamiji's letters — almost one per day.

The Tata Press in Jamshedpur printed *Bala Bhagavatam* and, as Gurudev had wanted, it was released during the yajña in Mumbai in October 1969. His words still ring in my ears, "Long after you and I are gone, people will still read these books."

... The story left a lasting impression on Shanti. She was most touched when Bharati expressed her deep sense of humility and gratitude for the privilege of the bylines on *Bala Ramayana* and *Bala Bhagavatam* – 'Chinmaya and Bharati'**....**

...That was just the beginning of the long row of titles that would flow out from the CCMT Publications slated exclusively for children. Shanti had learned much about the history of Chinmaya Mission's literature for children through interesting encounters, at the Powai ashram, with people active in the publication field.

Shanti recalled meeting Uncle Mani, From him, she learned about the journey of *My Prayers* – the book, which has anchored BV for years!....

My Prayers I, II, and III

BV did not just begin - it took off! Classes grew in number, mushrooming in various cities; new sevaks joined and there was a need for printed support to achieve standardization. Uncle Mani of Mumbai stepped in to compile *My Prayers I*, followed by *My Prayers II* and *III*.

My Prayers was published along with audio support around 1969 for children of non-resident Indians, so that both the sevaks and children could achieve perfection in chanting.

Indira and Leela (later Swamini Pavitrananda) from CM Bengaluru were responsible for setting the melodies to many of the songs and mantras, which have been universally and enthusiastically accepted. To this day the very same prayers and melodies are followed in BVs and Mission centers world over.

My Prayers Gets a Facelift

Then, in 2006, a team began work as to give a facelift to *My Prayers* — Brni. Nishita took responsibility for the designing and Brni. Aparna for the funding. Pramodini Rao and the members of the Chinmaya Swaranjali, Mumbai, set to music and sang all the ślokas and bhajans featured in the book. The three books were consolidated into a bright and cheerful new edition, which came with an audio CD.

...Shanti admired the colorful visuals that cheerfully leapt out of the pages of the new book and enjoyed the soulful music of the audio CD....

Tell Me a Story and the Tarangini Series

...Bharati and Shanti had come a long way in their relationship. So, after her work at the Mission center that day, the two friends met in Bharati's home.

Having much in common they could spend hours discussing fables passed down the ages, sung by bards or narrated by grandmothers and mothers to the young clustered around them. They shared experiences on how children readily lap up the love of the narrator and the moral of the story.

Conversation turned to the mother in Pujya Gurudev, who understood the value of these mythological tales; and how along with Swamini Saradapriyananda and Bharati, Gurudev began to author short stories with a moral, to be put together as a collection. These tales became the *Tell Me a Story* series, published in 1968....

Ten years later, the Tarangini series, authored by Brni. Sarada (later Swamini Saradapriyananda) and Pujya Gurudev was published. As a graded series, primarily for students of the Chinmaya Vidyalayas, these were edited by Bharati. In her opinion, "These may have been a response to the Moral Science books, which were in use by most secular schools at that time. Gurudev felt that we should have our own value-based books." The series is now being redesigned; the stories brought alive with illustrations, vibrant and colourful are a visual delight.

Chinmaya Bala Katha

...Shanti shared with Bharati the details of her meeting with Brni. Nishita, who initiated the Chinmaya Bala Katha, a range of picture books directed towards a younger age group, from four to eight years. Shanti had asked, "Brni. Nishita, where do you get inspiration to write these children's books?"....

In reply, Brni. Nishita took a trip down memory lane...

She had grown in Australia, was in Mumbai for the duration of the Vedānta course, and was thereafter posted in Hong Kong. The culture in this world-class, buzzing metro was unlike anything she had ever experienced. For the first time, she had the opportunity to meet the parents of BV children, who belonged to a different genre. In private conversations, they would point out that some stories from Hindu mythology were violent and hence, not fit for child consumption.

They would remark, "How can I tell my child that Gaṇeśa's father cut off his head? He will start having nightmares!"

Another remarked, "Kṛṣṇa was always engaged in mischievous pranks — what kind of a role model is He?"

The tragedy was that these mothers themselves were not intimately acquainted with their own culture and had no clue that these tales were symbolic and had to be told with the care that Gurudev always advised.

The turning point was a conversation with a particularly belligerent mother, critical of Hindu culture and the Purāṇas. That night, sleep eluded Brni. Nishita as she tossed, turned, and pondered over the situation.

A new train of thought emerged, "If these stories are not handed down to the coming generations, they will dwindle and eventually die out. In India they may stay alive but certainly in the West, they would be lost for all time."

She thought, "Gurudev showed us brahmacārins and swamins how to teach the *Gītā* and other scriptures. In the same way, through these books, parents could learn how to tell stories to their children.

Working with inspiration and assisted by a CHYK volunteer, the draft of her first book, *Ganesha Goes to a Party*, saw the light of day. Brni. Nishita said, "It was an amateurish effort, but nevertheless I mailed it to Guruji, telling him about my dreams." Guruji gave his nod and the first book was released.

The response was heartening; mothers were reading it out loud to their children, and these little ones were going around their homes with book in hand, chanting — Gaṇeśa goes to a party… Gaṇeśa goes to a party!

Brni. Nishita next turned to acquainting children with stories from the life of the mischievous Kṛṣṇa.

To ensure that they could compete with the glossy publications available in the bookshops, she dedicated much time and effort on the artwork. Her bold steps paid rich dividends. Adorned with fetching visuals and printed on glossy art paper, the books enticed children and parents alike. Following the trail blazed by these books, other Mission books also took on a more vibrant appearance.

Balvihar Magazine

Children were constantly in Gurudev's thoughts, and he did not stop with only books for children. He wanted BV groups in Asia, Australia, America, Europe, and Africa to share a common bond and platform. And so they were knit together through the pages of the monthly *Balvihar* magazine, the Chinmaya Mission's magazine for children, published by CCMT Mumbai.

In his message for the inaugural issue of the *Balvihar* magazine, Pujya Gurudev wrote, "We shall, through this journal, build bridges of love and understanding between children everywhere, and we shall learn to create a greater world out of what our parents have given us now."

The official international children's magazine was released in November 1969 with Aruna Sheth as its first editor. Professionally run it got a healthy response from the Chinmaya family.

In 1995, the magazine faced administrative difficulties. And one evening, in Guruji's kuṭiyā, it became the topic of a heated discussion, in which Bharati Sukhtankar was a participant. There were suggestions that perhaps the *Balvihar* magazine should stop publication.

This appeared to sadden Guruji as he said, "Everybody comes to me with problems. But nobody wants to work toward solving them. Gurudev started *Balvihar*. I will never let it close down."

After a pause, he turned to Bharati and asked, "Are you ready to work for it?"

Her response was an immediate 'Yes'.

In January 1996, Brni. Vividisha Chaitanya (now Swamini Aaradhanananda) was appointed as the Chief Editor and Bharati Sukhatankar became the Editorial Advisor of the magazine. Since then, uniting their love for children and talent for writing, they have worked with dedication towards its growth and success, reinventing it for the modern world.

...Bharati shared with Shanti the story of how the old *Balvihar* magazine burst into a new world of bright color. This is what happened....

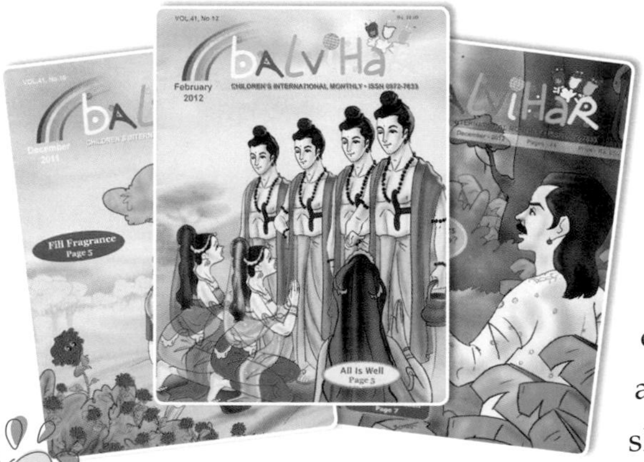

Balvihar's New Appearance

One fine day, Providence stopped by to visit. Sonal Soni, the owner of Soni Scan Graphics (a printing company), walked into the CCMT office with a copy of *Balvihar* and demanded, "What are you people doing? This magazine should be in color!"

Sonal then made a fantastic proposal offering to print an all-color issue for a nominal increase in the printing charge. And so, with the January issue of 2005, *Balvihar* went into full-color production; it shifted gears and became a truly international children's magazine.

From the Editor of Balvihar

Swamini Aaradhanananda joyfully admits, "BV kids have worked wonders on me and changed me for the better. Assuming charge as chief editor of *Balvihar* meant entering the kids' world. I had to get under their skin, think like them, and see things through their eyes — in short, be like them. I had to learn to be simple, fun-loving, and carefree!"

From Bharati's desk

Writing for a children's magazine is exciting. I realized that being a child has nothing to do with chronological age. Freshness of approach, a sense of wonder, a sense of fun — that's what childhood is all about. That is also when I grasped the beauty of the compliment that Gurudev once paid me when he said, "You! You will never grow up!"

...As Shanti sat engrossed in the story, the telephone rang and Bharati answered. Bharati listened to the voice at the other end of the line and let out a yell of joy. Her eyes were dancing with excitement as she exclaimed, "*Balvihar* has won an award! We have been declared 1st runner up for the best in-house magazine amongst NGOs an ICE (In-house Communication Excellence) Award instituted by the Shailaja Nair Foundation.

Indeed it was a congratulatory moment— for the team steering the magazine, for its writers, and for BV!

While celebrating this achievement Shanti paused to take a look at an unusual find. Rummaging through the Chinmaya Archives Shanti came upon a letter from Gurudev to the enterprising children of BV Ernakulam who were publishing a hand-written magazine! Gurudev wrote....

10.5.63

Dear Children,

To read and learn the Great Books of the Rishis, to approach a teacher and try to understand their deep meanings, and reflect and keep them all as your own knowledge to guide you in your life is the full duty of every Hindu child of the eternal Rishis.

After acquiring anything in life we have the most sacred duty to share what we have with others. Knowledge also is to be shared. To explain to others our own ideals through words spoken and written is called "Pravachanam": to study the text ourselves is called "Swadhyayam".

By publishing this hand-written magazine I find the Bala Vihar children are trying to do both swadhyaya and pravachan. Glory to you all.... May you all shine like Sankara, Ramanuja, Madhwa, and the great saints of all religions....The best preaching is in your own perfect action. That is a magazine ever published. Be careful in your words, thoughts and deeds. Be good. Do Good.

Thy Own Self,

Website for Children

...Leaning on the wall in a corner of Guruji's room in Powai, Shanti was present when Arti Shah unveiled her plan of a website for children. Her mind raced, "And so BV steps into the fast-paced world of the twenty-first century — an exclusive platform for children."....

Arti Shah dreamed of a website for children that would provide them the perfect platform to share their ideas, dreams, poetic and artistic talents. The sevikā Arti had helped to organize several BV camps in the Powai ashram. She witnessed first-hand the explosion of creativity that BV unlocks among the sevaks and children. She thought, "What if this fount of creativity and imagination could be shared between people the world over? BV sevaks anywhere in the world could dip into this common-idea pool and make their classes more innovative." It was then that she became Arti Shah, the website designer.

Conceptualized in 2003, *www.chinmayakids.org* was designed to offer mental, spiritual, and emotional avenues of growth to children. It was a trendsetter in its day. Chinmaya Kids aims to subtly, but firmly, ingrain in the child the importance of mindful living. It strives to remove misconceptions regarding religion, regardless of nation, cast, or creed, while emphasizing Universal Oneness. A click of the mouse can create more sevaks, create more classes, and reach out to more homes, schools, and even workplaces.

BV children the world over could, in the future, connect electronically. From the days of the traditional gurukula teaching and learning, the transfer of knowledge had moved to yet another level of interaction.

> The Chinmaya children's books are interesting because of their simple language, colorful pictures and apt explanations. They are a great help in answering the innumerable questions which children come up with!
>
> Once I narrated a story featuring Sage Nārada posted on the Chinmaya Kids website, which left such a lasting impression on the BV class that they began to remember the Lord and pray not only in times of distress but also when they were happy and all was well.
>
> — Kalpana Shankar, CM Gurgaon

Bala Perspectives

Dear God, If we live after we die then why do we have to die?

— a BV child

XI

Toward Uniformity

Apart from the books that feed the thirsty minds of the children, Chinmaya Bala Vihar (BV) has a structured and well-thought-out printed curriculum. This landmark was reached after years of research and innovative thinking. Faith in the scriptures, the words of the Guru, and a love for the goal were the raw materials with which the early stalwarts set course.

...Flipping through an old file of BV papers, Shanti came upon some early thoughts of sevaks, garnered from their experiences, on how to run BV. Keen to learn how the first BV curriculums were put together she wondered, "It would be good to know who first thought about documenting the procedures to be followed in a typical BV class."

Almost as if in answer to that, she chanced upon a treasure in her archives.

Chinmaya Bala Vihars - How to Organize and *Run* was a tiny booklet launched in Calcutta on November 1, 1967, perhaps the first documentation on the modalities of organizing and running a BV. On this occasion, Pujya Gurudev had written:....

We have been working at this for the last seven years, and that it is now catching the imagination of the people is a very rewarding encouragement for the Mission. Requests are pouring in from all directions asking us for the 'know-how' of starting such independent children groups. Śrī Hariharan of the Calcutta Bala Vihar has done beautiful work codifying the various activities of the Chinmaya Bala Vihar, modeled after and evolved through the suggestions and thoughts that I had given at various centers from time to time. This tiny handbook of instruction, I hope, will be useful for the workers to, at least, intuitively feel what the direction is in which we are planning this march to the future.

More details we refuse to give as they would stereotype the entire activities of all the branches and would tarnish the natural beauty of this sacred work. Each worker should know only the direction of the entire program, so that in the day-to-day approach there would be fresh creativity gushing from each one. Uniformity in such programs has always been the danger of importing the ugliness of militancy to the organization. Once the militancy comes, it will no longer be an evolutionary progress of the children, but it might flounder to become mere brainwashing.

Many years later, Ācārya Darshana Nanavaty of CM Houston elaborated on this initial effort to guide sevaks in their quest to become BV teachers. She wrote a set of ten books entitled *BV Teachers' Handbooks.*

...Shanti had heard of her substantial contribution in writing the BV curriculum and greatly admired her dedication. Here also in the story behind the writing of these books, Gurudev played a pivotal role....

The First BV Teachers' Manual

Darshanaben had often heard Gurudev reiterate that the torch of learning should be lit in the earliest years of childhood, to shine strong and steady throughout life. BV was to be a garden of values for children and its curriculum should touch their hearts and evoke the highest ideals in their minds.

As the number of BVs increased worldwide, Gurudev recognized the need for a graded curriculum in order to give a common base to the content. And so one fine afternoon, he took Darshanaben by surprise. He said to her, "Prepare the books for BV and show them to me when you meet me in Piercy (the CMW Headquarters at Krishnalaya in Piercy, California)!"

The Master had commanded and his voice brooked no denial. Darshanaben did not know what to do or how to do it, but she did not have the courage to say anything to Pujya Gurudev.

She later admitted, "I remained silent, and on returning to Houston I resigned from my job as this daunting deadline loomed just six months away."

What kept the goal in sight and approachable were Pujya Gurudev's words heard at a satsaṅga. These kept dancing in her mind, allowing her no rest. He had said, "Give your children to me for their first twenty-five years and we will have world peace."

She thought, "In America, children learn so much through the popular educational show for children, Sesame Street. So why not create BV books with age-appropriate games and activities along with scriptural messages? The children can then learn our scriptures, while having fun in the classrooms."

These two thoughts were the signposts that her mind retained while conceptualizing the plan. The work began, and needless to say, help came from all directions. She sat for endless hours, capturing on paper the lessons that emerged from intense, daylong brainstorming sessions. Sevaks involved with the project recall the incredible effort of those days:

> We would bring piles of children's books from the local library and pore over them for ideas on illustration and presentation. At one point, the library staff thought that some of us lived there! Darshanaben visited local churches, and met organizers of weekly Sunday Schools and yearly Vacation Bible Schools. She even enlisted to study their lesson packages, while some Montessori-trained teachers in her team reinforced the creative structure of the booklets. — Madhavi Vaidya, CM Houston

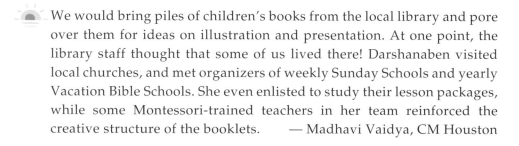

In six months the draft Pujya Gurudev desired was ready. When it was presented to him, he glanced at the folder and handed it to Rudite Emir to edit. Shortly thereafter, the contents of the folder translated into ten small booklets — a consolidated manual for BV teachers.

Darshanaben's labor of love received Gurudev's blessing at Piercy during the summer of 1991. He encouraged teachers worldwide to use the manual and invited Darshanaben to train BV teachers in India. With inimitable candor Gurudev told her, "Land in Mumbai. I'll tell you what to do. We, in India, like foreign material. So, if you come from abroad and talk about Hinduism, our people will like it!"

... The seminars that Darshanaben conducted in those early days laid the groundwork for further efforts on the curriculum. Going forward in history, Shanti found that Guruji, who also has the uncanny knack of producing the right idea at the right time, later reinforced Gurudev's insightful instructions**....**

From Booklets to Books

On a visit to Houston in 2004, Guruji instructed Darshanaben, "You will formulate the BV curriculum so that it can be used worldwide by all centers in our Mission." Blissfully unaware of the enormous responsibility being entrusted to her, she respectfully nodded her head.

It was time to turn the concepts outlined in the booklets into full-scale lessons across a well-defined, graded curriculum. Thus began an interesting journey, which manifested as the *BV Teachers' Handbook*!

Darshanaben envisioned the BV curriculum as centered around the Chinmaya Pradeep — the emblem of a well-lit lamp of Consciousness fueled by the oil of right living and decorated with swan-like discrimination. She firmly believed that even abstract concepts can be communicated to children in a way that they can understand.

Darshanaben paid attention to even the smallest of details in producing these books for every grade, beginning with kindergarten.

Holding them all together in a garland is the eternal thread of the scriptures, reflected in every page and lesson.

A Puppet in His Hands

Under the guidance of Darshanaben, a group of BV teachers began work on the project. Within a year she was reasonably satisfied with the outcome. At this stage, Krish Ravishankar was co-opted to provide editorial support. With his induction realization dawned that the job was far from complete. He suggested that the messages be organized into lessons and made user-friendly.

Darshanaben recalled, "While organizing the material into lessons, I recognized I was a puppet whose fingers were moving on the laptop. I found myself opening different texts written by Pujya Gurudev and Guruji, picking out excerpts and inserting them into appropriate slots!"

After much hard work, the content for the lessons was ready, but the books had to come alive and speak to the children. Punam Malhotra took on the challenge.

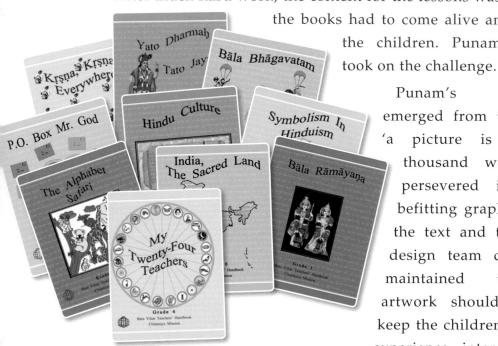

▲ BAL VIHAR TEACHERS' HANDBOOKS 2007 - 2013

Punam's inspiration emerged from the saying, 'a picture is worth a thousand words'. She persevered in finding befitting graphics to suit the text and theme. The design team consistently maintained that the artwork should serve to keep the children's learning experience interesting and valuable.

Presently the books from kindergarten to ninth grade are complete. Three more books wait in the pipeline before this mammoth project successfully concludes.

...Shanti and Shraddha were both present at the BV sevaks conference when Guruji released the first six books. He applauded the sincerity, hard work, and dedication of the team, reserving the maximum kudos for its leader. The ovation from the audience was sincere and long — a tribute to all those involved in this production....

Darshanaben said, "We are truly grateful for and appreciative of Guruji's profound trust in us. He never once asked what the curriculum consisted of, nor did he look at a draft manuscript. It appears that he knew all along that Pujya Gurudev and his vison would shape the curriculum."

Guruji, in his foreword to the new books, wrote:

> Our children are our joy. No amount of efforts put in or time given to them can be considered enough. Our efforts, however, ought to be in the right direction, and the time given must be quality time. There was a long-felt need for a systematic syllabus to conduct the classes efficiently and professionally.
>
> I heartily congratulate Darshanaben and her team for their stupendous efforts in producing the fantastic graded series of BV books. I exhort all our BV teachers in all our Mission Centers to take full benefit of these books.

...Shanti and Shraddha met Darshanaben to get some interesting perspectives into her journey. Darshanaben credited her team for their creativity and perseverance and revealed that Gurudev had all along been their guiding light....

Said Darshanaben, "Flipping through a Mananam publication titled *Education: Toward Inner Transformation*, my eyes alighted on an article by Pujya Gurudev on 'Our Children,' which resonates with the thought development of the curriculum. It occurred to me that Gurudev, in his infinite wisdom, had, as early as 1985, laid out the blueprint. In an instant, I felt humbled and blessed, because here I saw how the fundamental precept on education, envisioned and outlined by Pujya Gurudev, had come to bear and shape the curriculum. It is his vision, his making, and HE DID IT. We thank him for using us. We have just been puppets in his hands!"

The BV curriculum is about igniting inspiration in the mind of the child; not about just cramming it with loads of information about Sanātana Dharma. With inner inspiration, right actions are effortless.

— Raghuveer Akula, CM Houston

The focus in the BV curriculum is on questioning and discussion so the teachings are more likely to have a lifetime of practical implications for the student. — Shobha Mahadev, CM Los Angeles

A Flashback...

Many years earlier, Gurudev had handed over some BV material to Darshanaben, with instructions to plan a syllabus on similar lines. This was the draft framework conceptualized by Nirmala Chellam, (the legendary sevikā from Mumbai) when the BV movement was in its infancy. Gurudev was pleased with the outline Nirmala had supplied. Connecting the dots, he passed it on to the person who many years later would design the BV curriculum — Darshanaben Nanavaty!

...Darshanaben acknowledged the contribution of the author of the original draft in an informal chat with Shanti. The syllabus came back to India in a vastly improved form, embellished with words, illustrations, and challenging activities for the growing mind. It was the ageless nectar of the scriptures, translated for young modern minds packaged in a colorful and appealing format!

But what did the end users, the BV sevaks, have to say about the curriculum? Shraddha collected some of their thoughts during a Skype session....

Instead of trying to simplify the scriptural teachings too much, Gurudev had high expectations for his children. He knew that they were capable of thinking on a higher level and understanding abstract concepts. The children have justified the faith he had in them; this is demonstrated through the questions they ask and the quality of the discussions in the class. — Seema Jani, CM Atlanta

The new BV curriculum is remarkably interesting and informative. The methods outlined by Ācārya Darshanaben at a recent BV workshop are truly innovative and fun-oriented. Had I been ten years younger, I could have taught BV children with more energy, for more years to come, adopting this unique method!

— Ganga Ramachandran, CM Kochi

Giving More Than What We Take

On Halloween, in America, merry bands of children go from house to house, colorfully dressed as characters of their choice. They chant, "Trick or Treat" and are given candy by each neighbor they visit. On one such occasion, a BV household ran out of candy. A group of young merrymakers were walking up the driveway and would soon ring the doorbell to demand their share of the treats. They could not be disappointed. What was to be done?

The youngest member of the family came to their rescue: "I will give them all the candy I collected. Do we not pledge to give more than what we take?"

She had not only assimilated the teachings and but was able to apply them at the appropriate moment.

The profound wisdom of Vedānta is beautifully conveyed and absorbed even by the kindergarteners. Teachings that adults struggle so hard to assimilate and apply in the interactions are effortlessly imbibed and applied by even the tiny tots in BV.

The teachings are simple but extraordinary. Children are introduced to values in a fun way through *Alphabet Safari* and the *Vedanta Alphabet*. Complex questions like: Where is God? What does

He do? If He is everywhere, why can we not see Him? — are logically answered. Through the medium of storytelling they learn to love the Lord as Hanumān, Rāma and Kṛṣṇa and strive to emulate their qualities.

Each week a specific value such as caring, sharing, forgiveness is taught and discussed. In the following class the children share with their friends whether and to what extent they practiced that value. The children learn from each other. Śravaṇam and mananam start in childhood itself. This is a unique and remarkable feature of the Curriculum.

What each child takes away from BV will, of course, vary; but, without a doubt, the seeds of transformation that have been sown will certainly sprout when the situation is conducive. A BV child will definitely be a positive contributor to society!

— Shashi Dwarkanath, CM Boston

...Looking through the newly released books, Shraddha remarked, "Ma, a textbook comes alive only in the hands of an able teacher. These books are a tribute to Gurudev's vision and the competent teachers of BV who will now carry it forward!"....

Bala Perspectives

One child told his teacher – "God is everywhere. So, we are in God."

XII

Nurturing the Flow

BALA VIHAR IS MY TEMPLE
CHILDREN ARE GOD
TEACHING IS MY WORSHIP
AND THE VISION OF GOD IS MY REWARD
| SWAMI TEJOMAYANANDA |

To begin a program is often fairly simple, but to sustain it requires a vision backed by systematic training. Gurudev's grand vision for Bala Vihar (BV) requires dedicated sevaks to guide children to an appreciation of universal values and scriptural knowledge in order to raise the leaders of tomorrow.

BV Sevak Training Camp

In many centers in the West, BV programs are the fulcrum around which the other activities of the Chinmaya Mission are structured. For many years, their programs have been running on the strength of these centers. Thousands of dedicated sevaks give of their time to this program which nurtures children. Being perhaps the most important grassroots activity of the Mission, there was a need for BV volunteers to understand Gurudev's vision and the necessity of keeping it alive in its pristine form.

In May 2009, Guruji conducted an international camp to focus on training of BV sevaks worldwide. His aim was to help them understand the import of the BV activity in the context of future generations.

...Chinmaya Vibhooti, in Kolwan, turned into a hub of activity. Sevaks from the Mission's foreign centers in Asia, Africa, America, Europe and Australia, drawn by the cause, had traveled great distances to be part of this path breaking experience. Eager anticipation produced an aura of excitement. Cars and buses carrying committed BV workers from across the world converged there for a unique event — the first BV Sevaks Training Camp. Among them were Shanti and Shraddha eagerly looking forward to the rich global exchanges and the introspective moments that would follow.

Surrounded by softly rolling hills and host to magnificent sunrises and sunsets, Chinmaya Vibhooti is the Chinmaya Mission Vision Centre. This hallowed spot, picturesque and intrinsically soothing, instantly calms the mind. Conceived of and built for undertaking projects of this magnitude, Chinmaya Vibhooti provides ideal conditions for deep learning to take place....

Guruji inaugurated the camp with an introduction to the life, work, and teachings of Pujya Gurudev and the journey of Chinmaya Mission. Then, more specifically, he spoke of the relevance and importance of BV in the overall context of the Mission.

Guruji highlighted the need to bring together sevaks from an expanding network of BVs so that improvements could be made in the

system through a mutual exchange of experiences and ideas. He pointed out that though values are eternal, society constantly changes. It was important to innovate and keep abreast with the times.

He wasted no time in clearly spelling out the sevaks' role and the attitude required to successfully implement it. The sevak must understand the need to serve, the children being served, and most importantly, the benefit of true service:

Sevā is often understood as a particular act of service. In Chinmaya Mission, Pujya Gurudev's birthday is observed as Sevā Day. While planning the day, our thoughts immediately go to an orphanage or a place for the homeless. We think of the distribution of food and clothing, or educational material to the needy. Our minds go toward acts that will alleviate the state of the materially underprivileged.

Spirit of Sevā

...Unbidden, a question arose in Shanti's mind: But can sevā be confined to just a few acts, or is it in fact an energy that has much deeper implications? What is the genesis of sevā? As Guruji continued his address, Shanti's silent questions were answered. Her fingers raced across her notebook as she noted Guruji's explanation on the attitude behind sevā:....

Mahatma Gandhi made a pertinent point when he said, "There is not a single moment in man's life when he cannot serve." Attitude is the most important aspect of sevā. The spirit is of greater significance than the act. Charitable acts done in a routine or mechanical manner, without the spirit of service, cannot be termed true sevā.

Sevā need not be anything big. Words of consolation in times of distress or advice in moments of confusion are also sevā. Even a sincere prayer said with a pure heart, for the well-being of all, is sevā. It could even be just a smile. It is not a particular act, but the spirit that pervades all our actions.

People misunderstand the connotation of sevā. They erroneously believe that the jñāna yajñas conducted by Chinmaya Mission are not a service to mankind. Our minds are conditioned to think of sevā only as an act of giving material goods. According to our scriptures, the gift of knowledge (vidyādāna) is the highest of all sevā.

In simple words, sevā is the fulfillment of any need of another person. It could be the desire for food, clothing, or knowledge. The *Bhagavad-gītā* considers the imparting of knowledge as a great service or yajña.

BV is the best form of 'Bālakṛṣna' sevā. It has helped me expand my love for all children and treat them equally. Its practice perfectly blends karma yoga and bhakti yoga and is my spiritual sādhanā.

— Chandrika Pradeep, CM Bengaluru

Service is Worship

...Shraddha marveled at the clarity and simplicity in Guruji's elaboration of the word sevā. It completely transformed her understanding of service. It expanded to take on a whole new meaning....

Guruji identified sevā as the greatest expression of godliness in humanity:

Some social workers, though atheists, serve society on humanitarian grounds. They are mānavtāvādi (humane). That is good. But in a spiritual organization, the spirit and attitude are different. The two are lifted to still greater heights.

Ramana Maharishi expressed this sentiment beautifully:

jagadiśadhīyuktasevanamaṣṭamūrtibhṛddevapūjanam

Serve the world with the attitude that the Lord pervades it all. In serving the world, I am serving the Lord. This is my worship. (*Upadeśa Sāra, 5*)

This is a much higher attitude than mere humanism or service to a cause. Serving the world as the Lord Himself is worship. "Work is worship."

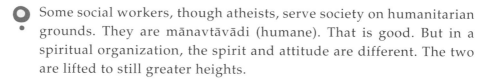

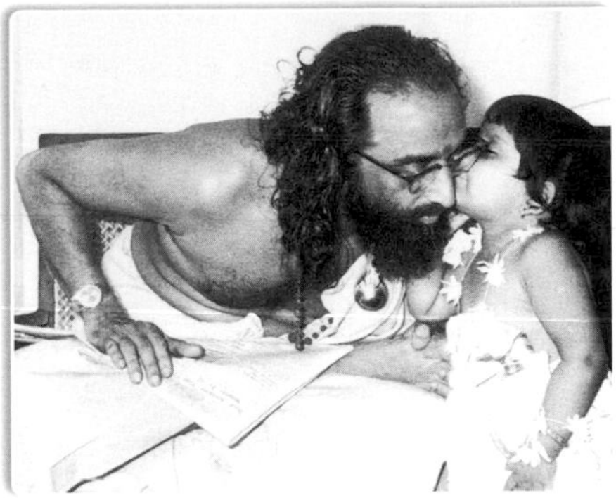

In an act of service, the benefactor thinks of the beneficiary as being needy and a few notches lower. If the spirit of service is lacking, we may entertain thoughts like, "I would always like to serve. I never want to be served." The corollary to this is that the other person should be in need of service.

However, we have to learn to be recipients as well as benefactors. Pujya Gurudev said we should, "Give more than what we take." He did not imply that we should not take at all for we must also learn to be receivers. He advised us to take the minimum and give out the maximum.

When we say, "Service is worship," are we obliging God? An element of obligation creeps in when we serve other beings, but as worship of God, there is no question of obliging anyone. When the opportunity to serve is taken as worship, it is indeed a great blessing. Then we act with an attitude of gratitude.

My relationship with God has changed from worshipping him in the temple to worshipping Him through everything I do. I worship Him through my service to the children of BV; through my service to the customers I serve at work, through service to family and friends.

The endeavor is to treat everything around me with equal vision and feel this life is a dialogue between God and me; a journey to divinize every relationship. — Ashok Grandhee, CM Ann Arbor

And what happens when service is born out of pure love? Guruji uncovered the hidden benefits of selfless sevā:

Selfless service is both a means of purifying the mind and also a great unseen blessing. Sevā fulfills the need of both the giver and the receiver. Those served benefit because their needs are fulfilled, whereas those serving gain by the purification of their minds.

Sevā offered to God increases our love for Him. So sevaks gain on all fronts because through such sevā an attitude of devotion, gratitude, and love develops and permeates all actions. It is not just confined to teaching children.

Social service done without this attitude sometimes leads to frustration. Resentful feelings often surface, "I did so much for society, but what did I get? Society is so ungrateful." The basis of this attitude in work is material self-interest. Material benefits mean not only wealth, but also include accolades, which the mind seeks. As opposed to this, spiritual sevaks only want to know, "How did the world gain?" Such an attitude leaves no room for frustration.

...Shanti knew that the biggest trapping of social service was unstated expectation. The human mind turns even service into an avenue for recognition. Guruji was hitting the nail on the head. Shanti realized that BV could bloom only where there were no weeds of desire for personal gain....

THE ATTITUDE OF THE SEVĀK MAKES THE DIFFERENCE
BETWEEN MEDIOCRITY AND EXCELLENCE

| SWAMI TEJOMAYANANDA |

Guruji reiterated:

Enter the BV class with an understanding of the spirit of service and with the proper attitude. Then, for sure, great heights can be scaled and success thus assured. It is not possible to choose the children who come to the class, like parents cannot choose the children who are born to them! They have to serve the jivā that comes into their lives.

Look at the children who come to the class as 'God sent' and not 'parent sent.' Consider it a great opportunity to serve them and to worship God. Then make teaching an act of worship, with children as the altar, and do the best you can.

Nirmala Chellam told her teenage sevaks: If you don't enjoy BV how can you expect the children to enjoy and come back the next time. The children act as your mirrors. They will not excuse your mistakes — they will point them out to you. If they like you, they will listen to what you say and do as you do. But if they don't like you, nothing you say or do will matter to them.

Understanding Children's Needs

For the children to gain the most, the sevaks need to be attuned to the minds of the children they are blessed to serve.

As a BV sevak, Swami Chidrupananda (Ācārya, CM Noida) won the hearts of the children he served. His secret: Merge your mind totally with the minds of the children. Talk like them, laugh like them. Children love silly talk. If the sevak can be like them, the day is won. To win over their hearts, the sevak has to view the world through their eyes and speak in their language. Once they are convinced of your love, they are yours for ever.

Gurudev urged the sevak to enter the dreamlike world of a child's mind, to connect with the creativity therein. Guruji similarly advocated:

It is important to understand the intrinsic nature of children and appreciate that they are neither the same and equal, nor are they clean slates to be molded in any fashion.

They are the same because they are all children; they are equal because they have their own potential and unique talents. The commonalities they share are their potential and divinity. But they are not the same – each child possesses different potential, abilities, and talents. As the sevaks' rapport and understanding with them increases, the distinctiveness of each child's individual nature is revealed.

Children are not clean slates because they are jivās who come with their own karmas, vāsanās, and saṁskāras. They are individual entities and do not fall into a single category. We must understand and deal with these differences without praising or condemning them. Moreover, differences are not a measure of superiority or inferiority.

Each child is unique and no one common principle works. One venerable gentleman said, "Before marriage, I had six theories about raising children. Now I have six children and no theories!" Some children are calm and contemplative, others are hyperactive and outgoing; some are leaders, some are followers, and yet others are counselors. Thus, all children will not respond in the same way — their latent qualities manifest as the differences we perceive.

Observation shows us the different levels of absorption and concentration. If the inactive child becomes proactive, or the active one become contemplative, treat it as an achievement.

Tips for Sevaks

The key factor contributing to the success of the class is the regularity of the sevak. Come rain or sunshine, if the sevak is present, the children are sure to remain. — Nirmala Chellam, CM Mumbai

A teacher must know how to keep the attention of the class. If the class is bored, promptly divert the children's attention. Tell a story about a great person, share an anecdote, or crack a joke. Within a couple of minutes, the class is refreshed and you have the children's attention!

— Shyamala Acharya, CM Mumbai.

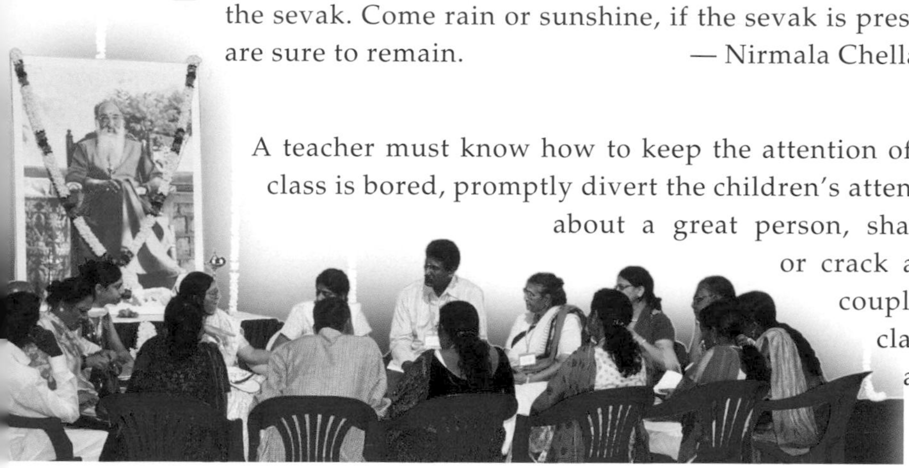

▲ SEVAKS IN ANIMATED DISCUSSION

Once a BV child – now a BV sevak

Bringing a different perspective to the table, Br. Atharvana says:

Having risen from the ranks of BV children to the status of a BV sevak gives me better insight — experiences of sitting on both sides, helps me communicate better with children.

I understood what perhaps, I was unable to as a child and it helped me devise methods of conveying concepts in easy to understand modules. I learnt much as a student but more as a teacher. Learning they say brings humility and as a sevak I had so many children to learn from! I was fortunate because I was given this opportunity to teach and so the learning continued.

...The Vibhooti camp was a complete, rewarding experience. During the camp, sevaks were like children — laughing, playing, singing, and exchanging stories. The camp refreshed their spirits and strengthened their motivation.

Homeward bound Shanti carried back one particularly poignant tale of the grace of Lord Rāma at a BV camp, which was related to her at Vibhooti....

Rāma Kṛpā (Divine Grace)

The setting: Krishnalaya Ashram, Piercy, USA — just a day before the Fourteenth Chinmaya Youth Camp. Its Theme: Lord Rāma.

Ācārya Uma Jeyarasasingham was occupied with last minute details. Suddenly, there was the sound of a halting car. Piercy is on a remote stretch of the freeway. We wondered, who had come to the ashram?

A man and his family driving by, noticed the buildings and walked in. His name was Ram and his seven-year-old twin boys were Luv and Kush! He was from the Fiji Islands and used to hold *Rāmāyana* satsaṅgs there regularly.

He was extremely keen that his boys attend the Camp. Uma Aunty politely informed him, "The camp is already full, and your children are too young to attend." Disappointed, he left reluctantly, telling her that if she needed help to call him in Santa Rosa (a drive of two and a half hours from Krishnalaya). Uma Aunty thanked him and forgot all about the incident.

The next day, we arrived at Krishnalaya by bus. After some time, we noticed that a 'mold' of Lord Rāma - a vital part of the camp activities was missing. We searched frantically and finally gave up. As a last resort, we called the bus company (in Santa Rosa). Yes, the mold was there! But how would it get to us? Uma aunty remembered Ram from the previous day.

So Ram was contacted and the next day, Lord Rāma 'in mold form' arrived. Ram and his family were invited to stay for a few days. Luv and Kush finally ended up attending the camp!

A string of 'coincidences' or indeed the Līlā (divine play) of the Lord?

— Aruna Nataraj, CM San Jose

Bala Perspectives

Dear God, I know that Gandhiji said turn the other cheek but what if your brother socks you in the stomach? – a BV child

Bhaskar Raman has been blessed and loved by Gurudev right from early childhood. On one occasion, Gurudev sat silently in front of a group of devotees with his eyes locked on the one-year-old Bhaskar who was peering innocently back at him. Finally, as if from a great distance, he softly said, "He is looking into Brahman...."

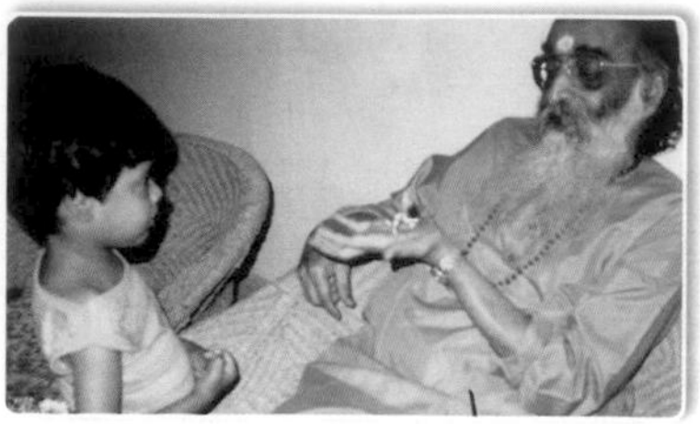

Growing in the serene environs of Sidhbari Ashram, Bhaskar was exposed to the values of BV every single day. He and his family experienced Gurudev's unconditional love time and time again.

Gurudev, whose strict insistence on discipline often scared even the most intrepid generals, never intimidated children. Once, Bhaskar woke up early only to find nobody around. He cried for a while, but receiving no response, climbed out of the window in search of mommy.

Meanwhile, in the lecture hall, Gurudev was conducting his morning meditation class. The students sat on the floor in perfect silence, their backs straight, eyes closed. Gurudev's rich, sonorous voice spoke in soft, deep tones, "Observe the breathing. Thoughts will come and go. Do not dwell on them. Remain a witness....As the mind grows silent, watch the silence...."

His voice grew hushed as everyone in the room slowly moved into inner silence and peace. At this moment, the big doors to the hall burst open and in walked a little child, wailing at the top of his voice.

Says Bhaskar, "Immediately people were shaken from their meditation, but I didn't care. All I wanted was my mother. She, terrified that Gurudev's wrath would be directed at her, scooped me into her arms and ran out as fast as she could."

Gurudev opened his eyes gently. He smiled. "Call out to the Lord the way that child cries for the mother. He has to respond and envelop you in His divine love. That is the attitude you must have in your spiritual pursuit! Come what may, that boy wanted his mother, he did not care for what anyone else thought of him, he did not care that he was interrupting the class and people would get angry, he did not fear anything! All he knew was that he wanted his mother and nothing more. That same fearlessness, the same ruthless, single-pointed desire for truth is the only way for you to get results."

Part 4

The When and Where

Part 4

The When and Where

- **XIII Spreading Wings**
  The movement in India — In the main Metropolitan cities
- **XIV Pillars of Support**
  The grand elders of Bala Vihar — Stories of their continuing inspiration
- **XV Embracing the World**
  The movement spreads — From India Eastward and to the West
- **XVI The Reigning Stronghold**
  Established in the U.S.A. — Common trends via select stories of centers

XIII

Spreading Wings

The source, always special, has a different fragrance, and is uniquely significant. As Gomukh (the source) is to the Ganga, so is Chennai to the Chinmaya Mission. The journey of the organization began in this cultural capital of South India in 1953. It was first registered there and came to be known as Chinmaya Mission. In fact, the metropolis of Chennai has many firsts to its name, in connection with Chinmaya Mission. The first study group began there, and also the first editions of *Usha, Tyagi,* and *Tapovan Prasad* magazines were created there.

Chennai was possibly the place where Gurudev first introduced the concept of Bala Vihar (BV) and also the venue of the very first formal BV class, but....

Under Gurudev's directions, Janaki Seth from Delhi arranged the first exclusive, out-of-town expedition, for children of all ages. The highlights of this historic trip were that Gurudev accompanied them and the youngest participant was just three years old!

• So began the Bala Vihar movement with the •
saṅkalpa (resolve) of the Master!

..."Now we are into the second decade of the twenty-first century and there is little documentation on this worldwide movement. Very soon, the generation responsible for planting the first flags would have passed on, carrying with them their memories and experiences," thought Shanti, filled with an urge to document, for the sake of posterity, the spectacular spread of BV.

Shraddha became a willing partner in this ambitious venture. Enthused, they decided on a plan of action. Shanti would be the traveling partner and Shraddha would take charge of documenting the observations. Shanti would initiate the process by contacting some centers in India....

The best way to start was at the beginning. So Shanti went off to Chennai, where she began unearthing the beginnings of BV....

In 1956, Gurudev undertook a journey with the children of Chennai to the Guruvayur temple, where the main idol is Bālakṛṣṇa (Lord Kṛṣṇa in the form of a child).

◀ GURUDEV LEADING AS ALWAYS

It is quite likely that on this trip, Gurudev narrated one of his characteristic stories. Or he may have had a conversation similar to this, held on another occasion:

"Why do we go to temples?" Gurudev asked the children.

"To see baby Kṛṣṇa," replied one child.

"To pray," said another.

"Because my mother wants me to go," said a third.

"Yes... that is why we go, but we also go for one other reason," he said. "It's a playground for your mind!"

Some children looked confused. "Swamiji...," one girl began, smiling, "how can the temple be a playground?" Swamiji was too old to understand, she thought to herself.

"Don't you go to the playground every day?" he asked the children.

"YES!"

"And what do you do there?"

"We play!" shouted the children in chorus, "On the jungle-gym."

"Ah! Your body gets to exercise in the playground so you can become strong, doesn't it?" said Gurudev. "If you go to the playground, but never play; if you only sit, then will your body get its exercise?"

"NO!"

"So also we come to the temple to exercise our mind. If you want your mind to be good and razor-sharp, you have to go to the temple and tune your mind to the Lord."

The children understood.

Gurudev took it to the next level. "God is everywhere, but when you come here to this temple, Bālakṛṣṇa is there, right in front of you. See! Here you can contact Kṛṣṇa directly!"

From the classes that slowly took form in Chennai, the offshoots traveled not only to the other metros — Bombay (Mumbai), Calcutta (Kolkata), Bangalore (Bengaluru), and Delhi — but also to the numerous cities, towns, and villages that Gurudev visited all across India!

Typically, the BVs followed a certain pattern. Through the sixties and seventies, the inspiration came directly from Pujya Gurudev. He drew people to him as a magnet attracts iron fillings. When Gurudev sat majestically in the place of honor, his gaze would also travel to the children playing among themselves. Gurudev knew their potential:

> The present-day children are smarter, with a high I.Q., with more sense and power of judgment, to know and analyze things and beings around them. We must strive to evolve a method to meet

satisfactorily the urgent needs of the children in their homes and in their community.

The sapling sowed by Gurudev has now matured into a mighty banyan tree… extending fresh roots as it spreads. From India's shores, the seeds of tender transformation were carried both eastward and westward, where they took root in other parts of the world.

In the U.S., the movement has touched great heights and has its strongest presence. At some venues, from 1,200 to 2,000 children attend BV every week and the numbers are still growing.

BV, from humble beginnings, is today an undertaking of unimaginable magnitude. It is impossible to trace its history in every city, town, and village. A sampling of the histories of some of the established centers is representative of the pattern followed in the others. One can confidently state that there are no parallels to such a movement!

Bala Vihar in Some Indian Metros

Chennai (Madras)

At an informal satsaṅga with Pujya Gurudev, the conversation turned to children. Finding himself in the midst of a band of devotees wishing to serve, he directed, "Train my children to chant the *Gītā* during the yajña in Mylapore, Chennai, in May 1956. They will chant for me!"

…Shanti had heard about this path-breaking event. It was the first time that BV children showcased their talent at a public function. Knowing Gurudev's penchant for perfection and flawless chanting, no pains were spared in their training**….**

During that particular visit, Gurudev spoke extensively about the need to set up children's activities in his discussions with devoted followers. Radha Sadashivam and Radhalakshmi Chary accepted the challenge and took the lead in initiating the program in Chennai.

... Shanti had reached the source. She realized, "This, in a manner of speaking, marked the creation of BV not just in Chennai, but in the world! The message of Bhakta Prahlāda was being handed down for the children of the twentieth century and later."**....**

All India Chinmaya BV Mahotsava

In September 1959, Chennai bagged another first by hosting the first All India Chinmaya BV Mahotsava (an occasion where all the BV children of a city or a state come together for an event or a camp). Inaugurated by the then Union Home Minister, G. L. Nanda, this grand event spread greater awareness and gave a further fillip to the movement in the city.

SWAMI MITRANANDA ▲

Among the sevaks of the 1960s was Mr. Chandrabanu. He was responsible for molding the mind of young Raju, who came to the fold at the tender age of three and grew up to become Swami Mitrananda, the current Ācārya of CM Chennai.

... Shanti learned how all the BVs in the Chennai center functioned under a centralized scheme. Under Swami Mitrananda's guidance, a system of learning evolved in which, every year, a new theme is taken up for study. Divine Vehicles, Divine Mountains and Rivers of India are some of the interesting themes that the BV students have studied so far. Each year culminates in a grand finale based on the annual theme.

Swami Mitrananda explained, "The finale is designed as a mega theatrical performance, to keep alive these powerful messages in the minds of the children. So virtually the whole year, the sevaks and their wards are immersed in one thought-flow."

The last one on 'Rivers of India' was presented as an outdoor sound and light show — an unimaginably artistic presentation witnessed by a mega audience of nearly two thousand people!**....**

The search for new concepts ended in COOL, or Creating Optimistic Outlook. Initiated in 2004, this is an eight-day, non-residential camp for children between the ages of eight to thirteen years. It fosters value-based learning in a lively, supportive, and participative environment. Run entirely by members of the Chinmaya Yuva Kendra (CHYK), the program over the years has reached four thousand children and their families.

BV camps in rural areas of Tamil Nadu are another initiative of CM Chennai. Conducted with the help of the youth wing of the Mission, several camps have been held in and around Salem, Tamaraipakkam, Tirunelveli and Tuttukudi, with help from the local Mission members. A completely novel experience these camps add another dimension to many young lives in the villages.

... Shanti could see that the BVs of Chennai were vibrant and still growing, thanks to the innovations and interest of all the sevaks and students**....**

Mumbai (Bombay)

From Chennai, the action branched out to Mumbai sometime in 1964.

... Following the Metro trail, Shanti journeyed to Mumbai. Here she discovered that Śrī Ananth Narayan, also known as Uncle Mani, was the first commander of the BV forces. A sprightly 88-year-old in 2012, Uncle Mani is an institution unto himself.

Shanti spent a lively hour with him, reminiscing over the 'good old times.' At the end of that session, Shanti wondered, "What enthusiasm! What inspiration! Even now he is able to animatedly involve the listener with his tales of years past."**....**

GURUDEV WITH UNCLE MANI ▲

Inspired by Gurudev, Uncle Mani became a sevak, and the first children's classes began at his home in the RBI quarters, Mumbai. Six months later, at the venue of the yajña by Gurudev in 1965, he noticed a stall giving information about BVs in other cities, and asked Ram Batra, a Trustee of CCMT, "Why should these not be officially run under the Mission banner and called BV?"

Gurudev gave his approval to Ram Batra and directed that the children chant a week later in the yajñaśālā. Uncle Mani was a bit flustered, but on the appointed day the sixty children trained under his wing chanted — when they finished, Gurudev announced that this was the launch of the first BV in Mumbai!

Growth happened when with Uncle Mani's help, Nirmala Chellam, took her first steps toward setting up classes at Chembur.

...Shanti was narrating this story to Shraddha, and in her excitement, forgot to introduce these important characters. Shraddha interrupted, "Wait a minute, Ma. Who are Uncle Mani and Nirmala Chellam? Tell me more about them."

Shanti stopped her narrative and laughed, "Sorry. Sorry. There is so much to share; I forgot that you do not know them. Their journeys are worth recording. I will tell you more once we complete the history of BVs in the metros."....

Nirmala Chellam did not seek to be a sevikā; she was commanded by her Guru to assume the mantle. Once cast in the role, she refined it to perfection, innovating and adapting, along the way to the changing needs of her students.

Affectionately known as Nirmala Aunty, she developed a unique system in Mumbai, whereby senior children between the ages of twelve and fourteen, became sevaks for their juniors. Through 'Leader's Retreat', a training program, she groomed them to become teachers. The ripples from this system were extensive. At one time, in Chembur (a Mumbai suburb) alone, over twenty BV classes with a combined strength of 500 were run simultaneously under her guidance and leadership.

The classes in Chembur created a high benchmark for others to follow and the rest, as they say, is history!

Taking the message further afield, BV sevaks run dedicated BVs for schools in Mumbai, benefitting large numbers in the process.

Chinmaya Nursery School

The Chinmaya Nursery School founded by Pushpa Jaisinghani with the blessings of Pujya Gurudev, is worthy of note. Based on the teachings and vision of BV, this school has expanded to two locations under the leadership of two very competent BV sevaks, who began life as BV children — Padma Jaisinghani and Suprabha Rao.

▲ GURUDEV AT THE CHINMAYA NURSERY SCHOOL

Says Padma, "Pujya Gurudev had the highest respect for all religions but he used to say, 'All mothers are worthy of respect but my mother is my mother'." So though the children learn about other cultures and religions, they follow Hindu traditions. Padma makes no compromises and tells parents who question her, "Missionary schools are run on the lines of Christianity so why should the Chinmaya schools be afraid to proclaim their Hindu leanings!"

Aditya Birla World Academy

'Life Skill Program' is the nomenclature under which BV functions in the Aditya Birla World Academy. Smt. Neeraj Birla, spouse of Śrī Kumar Mangalam Birla, invited Vishakha Nanavaty, to hold regular classes in their IB International School to bring home the message of Gurudev to children of the school.

The classes are compulsory for all children whatever their faith. The wonder is the extremely positive feedback from even parents of different religions.

One Muslim child from Class Six wrote, "I used to think God is in heaven, but now realize that He is everywhere, even in my heart."

The Mumbai of the twenty-first century is a city of distances and traffic snarls. Hence neighborhood BVs have sprung up in various parts of the city to keep spreading the message. On special occasions and camps the children from all the BVs meet at the Powai ashram, and the place resounds with sounds of their merriment and laughter.

Kolkata (Calcutta)

At about the same time that Uncle Mani began the Mumbai chapter, BV established a presence in the capital of West Bengal.

...On her arrival at CM Kolkata, Shanti was greeted warmly by the BV sevaks. Responding to her quest, Gayatri Krishnamurthy had put together the early history. She told Shanti, "Thank you, for giving us the opportunity to ponder over the past. But for this exercise, we would have never known how much work was done in BV Kolkata to bring it to its present stature. It amazes us to know how many people have worked with such dedication for thousands to imbibe the Chinmaya ethos."....

The BV presence in Kolkata has been very strong since February 1965, when Śrī A. Hariharan assumed responsibility. Under the dynamic leadership of the early sevaks, classes were conducted across the city in twenty-four locations, reaching more than six hundred children.

▲ GURUDEV BEING WELCOMED

Subsequently, under the guidance of Śrī T. V. Narayanswamy and Śrī R. S. Nathan (later Swami Nityananda), BV activities increased manifold. Śrī Swamy recalls, "Over a period of twelve years, we built the movement brick by brick. The result was that we had more than fifty centers with over fifteen hundred children — conducting classes in English, Hindi, Tamil, Gujarati, and Bangla."

The organizational strength of the Kolkata chapter was evident from its early days. Responsibilities were systematically divided and shouldered to ensure the smooth functioning of classes. Since youth activities had not begun, a class for teenagers, targeting the age group of fourteen to twenty years, took care of their needs. Kolkata under guidance from Śrī Swamy helped publish the very first teaching aid for BV sevaks — *How to Organize and Run Balavihar Classes.* For a while, the center also published a monthly magazine for children called Chinmaya Bala Vani — a forerunner of the *Balvihar* magazine.

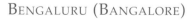

The children of BV Kolkata grew up with a mantra:

Tune in your mind with a healthy habit,

Make BV your weekly habit.

For many it became a habit of a lifetime — a habit that changed their lives forever!

Bengaluru (Bangalore)

...The wonderful thing about visiting Chinmaya Mission centers is the feeling of belonging that envelops the visitor. The "Hari Om!" greeting, said with folded hands, is a magic password that opens doors of friendship and ensures a warm reception – even with total strangers.

Bengaluru being another important center, Shanti chose to combine her visit there with devotional stopovers at Tirupati and other famous shrines of the South. She also decided to visit the Coimbatore ashram to meet with Nirmala Chellam of Chembur.

There again, she found that substantial work had been done to encapsulate the history and highlights of the activities at the center. Shanti was invited to the home of a devotee who shared the story of BV's birth in Bengaluru....

GURUDEV WITH YOUNG ▲ SWAMI BRAHMANANDA

The setting was Dr. Sirur's house at Malleshwaram during the Bengaluru yajña in 1958-59. Pujya Gurudev instructed Smt. Usha Bai and Smt. Kumudavati to begin a BV, "You both have small children, teach them with other children in the neighborhood. Your children will learn and others will also benefit. The seeds of spirituality must be sown at a very young age. Every child should know about the *Bhagavad-gītā*."

Others followed the pattern set by this center. And soon, Shankarpuram, Jayanagar, Basavanagudi, and the Cantonment area became locations of active BV classes. Children participated in all events in the Mission and looked forward to the Alaya Yatras (temple visits). These were their special treats.

...During her visit, the sevaks organized a wonderful day-long excursion, to famous nearby temples, alongwith the BV children. Feeling the blowing wind in the open truck, and hearing the children singing bhajans, Shanti wondered, "Can the joys of children glued to their television sets compare in any way with the joyful abandon of these young ones? How rare it has become to raise children this way!"....

"Jñānenavatu Kaivalyam," a skit based on an incident in the *Śiva Purāṇa*, was the highlight of the fifty-year

SWAMI BRAHMANANDA WITH ▶ CHILDREN OF BV BENGALURU

celebrations of Chinmaya Mission, Bengaluru (2007). In this poignant story, Lord Śiva takes avatār as an ascetic to convey the sublime Truth of the Upaniṣads to sages entrapped in the snares of karmakāṇḍa (rituals). Swami Brahmananda together with a band of dedicated sevaks guided this mammoth organizational feat. It was a resounding success and nearly one hundred children from all BVs in Bengaluru took part in this music and dance performance.

Since its inception, the Bengaluru center has hosted annual competitions for *Bhagavad-gītā* chanting, bhajans, public speaking and BV Meets —where children present cultural shows. The focus is now on holding two to three week-long summer camps in various parts of the city.

BALAMAHOTSAVA AND CAMPS

The first All Karnataka Balamahotsava was held in Mysore in 1962, in the presence of Pujya Gurudev. His charismatic personality guided the event and encouraged the children. In a carnival-like atmosphere, competitions were held for *Gītā* chanting, storytelling, and public speaking.

As a part of the preparations for Pujya Gurudev's birth centenary celebrations, Swami Brahmananda conceived the idea of one state-level event every year. The first in the series, Balagokula 2011–Akhila Karnataka Balamahotsava, was held in Shivamogga. Over fifteen hundred children from centers all across the state participated in the event.

In Bengaluru the aim is to have a BV within comfortable reach of each locality. The center has set a goal of one hundred BVs by Gurudev's birth centenary year and is working towards it.

...With the inputs from Bengaluru, Shanti headed home to Delhi. In the debriefing sessions Shraddha registered: every BV center, big or small, strongly held the Chinmaya ideal and pursued it with its own local flavor.

Shanti still had to piece together the history of the spread of BVs in Delhi and take a quick look at some of the current activities in the Indian capital and the surrounding areas of Noida, Gurgaon, and Faridabad....

DELHI

There may have been some children's activities in the early years in Delhi, but there were no records available to substantiate them. The turning point came in the late 1960s when Bharati Sukhatankar came to Delhi. Gurudev encouraged the storyteller in her with a steady stream of letters to open the doors of her home to the children of Delhi.

...This information was brought alive in Shanti's visit to Bharati's home. As the two friends browsed through the memorabilia — precious letters from Gurudev, all neatly documented — thoughts of the past surfaced to enliven the present....

In the 1980s, Sita Juneja (now Swamini Gurupriyananda) was attracted to the cause and began classes from her home. Later, in 1994 Mission activities saw an upsurge with the arrival of Br. Manan (now Swami Nikhilananda) in Delhi. CM Delhi got its own center at 89 Lodhi Road in 1997. Since then, there has been a steady expansion in BV activities and classes are also regularly held at the Chinmaya Vidyalaya.

...The three-week annual summer camp is a much-awaited event in the BV Delhi calendar, generating excitement among parents and children alike. Both Shanti and Shraddha are integral to these camps and help wholeheartedly to make them successful....

SWAMI NIKHILANANDA ▶
AND BR. NAVNEET LEAD THE WAY

In the Chinmaya tradition, camp activities revolve around a selected theme. A dedicated band of workers silently provide the nuts and bolts of the camps, ensuring its successful execution. The grand finale sees large numbers of parents and grandparents applauding the efforts of the children and sevaks, convinced that the quality bar at these camps is being continuously raised every year.

...Shraddha offered to help Shanti with information from the Noida center. One event caught Shraddha's fancy, and she immediately registered Gopal for a colorful morning of creativity. Both mother and son reached the venue in Noida and watched an exciting spectacle unfold before them....

Brilliant sunshine, bright colors, and children's voices all blended together in the excitement of 'Rang Bharo' — an annual series of drawing and painting contests for children. In 2011 nearly 2,300 students from twenty-two schools registered for the contest.

Talks and workshops for student and teacher development held in schools, over the last few years by Swami Chidrupananda, and his band of devoted youth are the reason for this unprecedented success. Good will has its own way of spilling over!

...Gopal was — literally, a portrait of joy after painting to his heart's content! His shirt, face, and fingers had happy splashes of paint, and he proudly showed his painting to Shanti on his return home!....

CORD (Chinmaya Organization of Rural Development)

Gurudev loved the smiling, happy children from the villages around Sidhbari, Himachal Pradesh. His love was the inspiration for Dr. Kshama Metre (National Director, CORD) to include BV as an integral part of CORD in 1992–93.

...Sidhbari held a special place in Shanti's heart because it was at Gurudev's Samadhi, in the shade of the Dhauladhar range of mountains, that she pledged her unquestioning loyalty to Gurudev's mission. He, in turn, from the deepest quietude, promised to carry all her burdens!

Shanti never needed an excuse to return to this hallowed spot. During one of her visits, she took time to be with the children of the hills. She saw for herself the miracles that BV had worked in the villages through CORD....

Special Schools

Kshama Metre recounts an interesting anecdote about a bālavādī (preschool) in Jool, a tribal village. The adults queried, "Why do these little children need to study when we did not go to primary school till we were six-to-eight-years old?"

It was a while before the parents started appreciating these 'special schools' where their kids learned simple prayers and manners. The children in turn taught and delighted their parents with their newfound learning! The journey from resentment and incredulousness to clamoring for more such programs followed a gradual upward path.

...Seated on the cārapāī (rustic bed) at one of the centers, enjoying lunch with her hosts, Shanti realized that the sevaks had a great role to play in the lives of their wards. Paying tribute to the backbone of the program, Kshama said....

The BV sevaks have to constantly shepherd wayward children back to school. In addition, children are mobilized to work on issues such as health, nutrition, sanitation, disability, old age, water supply, and alcohol abuse awareness. As they work enthusiastically to accomplish assigned tasks, they are rewarded with enhanced self-confidence and

> fledgling leadership skills. This training also decreases gender barriers and related problems.
>
> The BV groups are run by the active participation of the village women and elders. These simple rural ladies are tutored in stories, games, bhajans, and stotrams, and are thereby empowered to run the classes. Over the years these teams of enabled sevaks have proved to be the backbone of this program.

Today CORD runs 175 BVs in as many villages, and its outreach benefits 3,700 children in its centers in Odisha, Tamil Nadu, and Himachal Pradesh.

...The simple, serene setting of Sidhbari had a way of overwhelming Shanti, more so after the visit to the BVs in the village where the values of service and knowledge are strengthened in the hearts and minds of its children....

Innovative Initiatives

Sunday School, Chennai

Every Sunday morning, since 2010, Chinmaya Vidyalaya at Taylors Road, Chennai, bristles with activity. It is back to school for grandparents and parents, who along with children eagerly await the classes on the art of living life joyously. This is the Chinmaya Sunday Family School (CSFS), a novel project conceived by Guruji, and guided by Swami Mitrananda.

The Sunday School, as it is popularly called, acts as a forum for the spiritual rejuvenation of the family as a whole. Both Chennai and Ahmedabad have taken the lead and begun running classes on these lines. In Chennai the success rate was so high, that classes are now being held at all three Chinmaya Vidyalayas.

The two-hour school, held for three Sundays in a month starts and ends with common sessions for all the participants. For the rest of the time, the children, youth, parents and grandparents pursue activities appropriate for their age groups and mindsets.

Ahmedabad Innovates

Br. Atharvana accepted the challenge to introduce the concept of conducting classes on the pattern of a Sunday school in Ahmedabad. He comments:

> Based on the American pattern, classes for parents are held parallel to the children's classes. This has contributed to the success of the experiment. According to Guruji after joining the Mission people go through three stages: participation, involvement and complete commitment. Following Guruji's advice in stage one, people were just allowed to participate without making any demands. After a year or so, they automatically came forward and became involved. Stage three is yet to arrive but this too will surely follow.

CM Ahmedabad has also adopted the Graduation Ceremony advocated by Gurudev. Children who have crossed the age limit for their group and have 75% attendance, are deemed fit for graduation. During the ceremony children are individually called on stage and spoken about by the sevikā. They are given a tulasimala as a token of initiation and handed over to the sevak of the next group.

...Back in Delhi, Shanti and Shraddha, shared notes; their fledgling efforts had yielded an immensely rich insight. Then, Shraddha reminded Shanti: "Ma, now tell me more about those pioneering sevaks whom you met during your travels."....

Bala Perspectives

At COOL Camps children are 'punished' if they sleep or yawn in class. Once a young sevak was caught napping. The children demanded that a punishment be meted out to him. The sevak was asked to sing a song for the children. One cheeky little boy quipped, "But Swamiji, that is a punishment for us!"

strident cry was, 'Train the trainer.' In response, Uncle Mani took up this task with great earnestness and zeal.

Organizers like Uncle Mani are an invaluable asset in any organization. In 1991, he was posted to Chicago to take charge of the ashram. His assignment was crisp and single-pointed: to promote grassroots activities. Not one to let time slip by, he had a Study Group operating within three days of his arrival followed shortly by BV! Enrollments increased at a phenomenal pace, and in just three years, 800 children had signed up for the program.

He encouraged teachers to follow a simple philosophy, "You do not require any special qualifications for the job. All you need is love. You have your own children. Now just add a few more to your own."

Gurudev greatly approved and valued his work and called upon Uncle Mani to conduct sevak training programs within India as well as abroad. Even today, when duty calls, he cheerfully rises to the occasion!

...Uncle Mani's simplicity and its outer expression as service fascinated Shanti. For Divinity to manifest, all we have to do is, open up our hearts. Love without expectation inspires the one on whom it is showered, to follow in the footsteps of the giver. That is how Nirmala Chellam trod the path illumined by Uncle Mani....

▲ NIRMALA CHELLAM

...Shanti had heard from Nirmala Chellam's former students of her stellar role in building BV Chembur. Gurudev fondly addressed Nirmala's group as 'the giants of Chembur.' One call and they gathered together to recount and revel in the joyous moments of the past. Having heard so much, Shanti just had to travel to the Coimbatore ashram to meet that grand old lady who evoked such generous praise from her students.

A frail picture of kindness, Nirmala Aunty, who was ninety years old at the time of Shanti's visit, needed persuasion to reopen old chapters. However, touched by Shanti's interest, she soon warmed to her subject....

Beacon of Learning – Nirmala Chellam

The first lady of BV, Mumbai, Nirmala Chellam is remembered for her extraordinary dedication to BV. Her amazing voyage began when she became a part of Uncle Mani's Study Group — a sincere seeker, she drew her core strength from the scriptures.

Her saga with children began while traveling with Pujya Gurudev in a car in Chittoor, Andhra Pradesh. In his loving authoritative, and yet nonchalant style, he simply said to her, "You teach BV!" The power behind that sentence instantly changed her world. She protested, "Gurudev, I have no training for the job. I am single and have no experience with children. There are so many more competent people!"

But Gurudev had spoken. He heard her out in silence, and then again, all he said was, "You teach BV!"

As she mulled over several options, she finally concluded, "Gurudev wanted me to begin a BV class, so I will do just that!" It was in 1966, on a sunny morning in the sleepy suburb of Chembur, that Nirmala Chellam was about to commence her first class:

> I was sitting with all the children and their parents arrayed before me. I felt alone, sitting in front of Pujya Gurudev's portrait. Then I said to him, "You have put me here, now you take the BV." Following this, I closed my eyes, chanted Om, and started the class.

This was just the beginning....Over the years, Nirmala found that the attendance of children over eleven years of age began to diminish. Bored with chanting and bhajans, they began to drop out. She came up with a novel solution – the BV class for this age group was converted into a Study Group, with *Rāmāyaṇa* as the text.

...Nirmala told Shanti, "Gurudev then instructed me to train the senior children to take classes for the younger children."....

Soon teenage sevaks with some adults were running BVs for all age groups of children across Chembur. Nirmala Chellam's motivational power was so great that younger students eagerly anticipated the day when they, too, would conduct a class. She made it a point to oversee each and every one of the more than twenty classes, and regularly provided feedback and suggestions for improvement.

Susheela Acharya's Role

Singing was not Nirmala Chellam's strength, so she persuaded Susheela Acharya to help train sevaks to lead the bhajans in BV...sequentially a weekly bhajan group formed in the Acharya home. From teaching bhajans, Susheela Amma started composing bhajans. Soon the Chembur BV Bhajan group began receiving invites to sing at functions and festivals all over Mumbai. Susheela Acharya and her troupe for many years led the bhajans at Mission events in Mumbai. Chinmaya Mission devotees round the world are familiar with her bhajans through thc CDs: *Archita*, *Ranjeeta* and others.

▲ SUSHEELA ACHARYA AND NIRMALA CHELLAM

Susheela Amma recalls, "The first time the group performed for Pujya Gurudev at Paramdham in Chembur, the founder of ISKCON, Srila Prabhupada Swamiji, was also staying there. It was a memorable occasion. The atmosphere was charged with devotion. The high point of the evening was when Pujya Gurudev and Srila Prabhupada Swamiji began to dance in ecstasy!"

Her students' fondness, admiration and devotion for her are an acknowledgment of the transformation she wrought in their lives. Her life is a testimony to the dedication that Gurudev inspired in his followers. A woman with no children of her own became a mother par excellence to hundreds of children in the community.

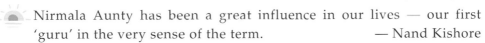

NIRMALA CHELLAM AND SUNDAR ▲

She saw herself only as a sevikā and insisted that each of us turn to the source of her own inspiration — Pujya Gurudev. While Gurudev caught my imagination and fired up my zeal for sevā, Nirmala Aunty brought alive the ideal of a true sevak. — N. M. Sundar

Nirmala Aunty has been a great influence in our lives — our first 'guru' in the very sense of the term. — Nand Kishore

Nirmala Aunty allowed each one to bloom according to their nature. She neither dictated nor preached, but emphasized practice. She handled us in such a manner that we understood what was expected and acted accordingly. — Ram Raju

Inspired in the Park

Ashok Patel, a particularly bright child had the makings of an achiever, but the atmosphere at home was not conducive to study. Nirmala counseled him, "Son, do not be disheartened. You can sit in the park and study. Your mind will be quiet and you can concentrate on your work."

Ashok took her advice and started to study regularly in the neighborhood park. His dedication paid rich dividends. He went on to study abroad, and is now the Purchase Manager of a large multinational firm in Mumbai — an eventful journey for a boy who studied under the open skies in the park!

Nirmala Chellam served the Mission for fourteen years as a BV sevikā. Although the classes in Chembur were not the first to begin in the Chinmaya Mission, they contributed significantly toward the firm foundation of the BV movement!

Going the Extra Mile — Śrī T. V. N. Swamy

The Kolkata success story, though scripted at a later date, was by no means less spectacular and can be traced to the commitment and love of Śrī T.V. Narayan Swamy.

Also an octogenarian, Narayan Swamy now resides in Chennai. From the recesses of his razor sharp memory flowed the past. He happily shared details of his extraordinary story, revealing his great love for Gurudev and the children of BV.

▲ GURUDEV, ŚRĪ N. SWAMY AND SEVAKS OF CM KOLKATA

He is best introduced through the accolades showered on him by Pujya Gurudev: "Calcutta has become the best Bala Vihar center after Śrī N. has taken charge of it. India owes a lot to him and his family."

On another occasion, Gurudev said: "What I am doing for the Mission, he is doing for the children!" High praise indeed from someone with such exacting standards as Gurudev!

Love for children was a bond shared by both. And so whenever they met, Gurudev's very first question to Śrī Swamy was, "How are my children?"

...Śrī Swamy recalled, "I wanted to do something creative for present-day children, so they could grow to live up to our ancient culture, traditions, and values. I joined the movement, learnt the rudiments of BV and started classes in Ranchi."....

Writing came easily to Śrī Swamy. His creative urges propelled him to write short English dramas based on religion and spirituality, which the children staged during yajñas. Gurudev witnessed a few of these at the Bala Mahotsavam in Jamshedpur, and there the author made the first personal contact with his Guru.

...“The ways of the Lord and the Guru are mysterious,” thought Shanti. Gurudev had a knack of bringing out the best in his disciples....

Śrī Swamy remembered how Gurudev encouraged him: “Gurudev applauded profusely and advised me to write more and more dramas. Struck by his magnetic personality, it was like meeting one, who was very specially and spiritually known, guiding me from past lives. My surrender at His holy feet was instant and spontaneous.”

Of all the dramas scripted by Śrī Swamy, the one Gurudev liked best was *Himavat Vibhutī*, a play on the life of Swami Tapovan Maharaj.

In 1974, Śrī Swamy was transferred to Kolkata, and the very next year, Gurudev appointed him the BV Chief Sevak at Kolkata. Toiling hard and planning thoroughly over a period of twelve years, he saw the BV strength growing from ten to more than fifty centers with over fifteen hundred children.

...Amazed by his account, Shanti was convinced, “Devotion never goes unrewarded. When the Master and the disciple are in tune, wonders happen!” But there was more to be astounded by ....

44 YEARS...STILL SERVING!

Seventy-seven year old Smt. Malati Shah is the ‘grand old lady’ of Chinmaya BV in Kolkata. A shining mentor to hundreds of BV children, she is still actively involved in Mission activities.

She must be the longest serving sevikā. A booklet on BV activities dated 1968 mentions her... which makes for an impressive forty-four years of service!

At the urging of her husband and in-laws, Malti started taking classes at Bhowanipur Gujarati Balmandir, where she teaches to date. She would leave her baby son asleep and go after-school hours to conduct the BV class. She was and is still popularly known as ‘Gita’ Aunty by the BV children!

...At the Chennai center, Shanti met Surekha Raghavendran, who provided insights about her mother, Usha Bai. A creative and dedicated sevikā, Usha's personality mirrored the staunch loyalty and commitment common to the early devotees....

BV Must Carry On – Usha Bai

Usha Bai's BV class in Bengaluru never closed, not even for her daughter Surekha's wedding. The marriage was on a Sunday, and Usha Bai taught the class on Saturday! At the same time, a Yuva Kendra camp was underway in the city, so she just added the campers to the wedding guests and supplied food for the entire camp!

Years earlier, Usha Bai had gone to listen to Gurudev and was irresistibly drawn to him. The Mission and its activities became a vital part of her life. She toiled with love, purely for the joy of working, ever ready to help promote the Mission. To create awareness about the newly-built Chinmaya Mission hospital, she even went on a pada yātrā (walking tour) from house to house distributing pamphlets.

Her daughter, Surekha remembers, "In my mother's absence, my sister and I conducted the classes. Every week our house was host to nearly seventy children. Her rule of thumb was to teach the children all that the school and their parents were not teaching them!"

▲ GURUDEV WITH USHA BAI

Usha Bai wanted the children to chant the Mahāmṛtuñjaya mantra once a day, but being unsure whether they would remember, she made them chant it seven times in the weekly class. When she died, one of her children said, "Let's chant the Mahāmṛtyuñjaya mantra...she will come back to life!"

Usha Bai would never impose anything on us; she would just expose us to the ways of the world, without being judgmental. There was no right or wrong. This trait has stayed with me till today, even after a lapse of so many years. — Meera, CM Bengaluru

Even now, her legacy continues. The classes are still conducted, with sincerity and regularity, by her older daughter — every Saturday, same place, same time.

Grateful appreciation is the hallmark of a BV child and sevak. Surekha Raghavendran spoke with humility of her mother — her teacher and mentor, "Whatever we are is because of Gurudev. Through our work, the organization may not benefit, but when we work for such an organization, we get organized!"

... As Shraddha nodded in agreement, Shanti said, "Is it not astounding how such a widespread organization has been built solely on the strength of volunteers, who wished to serve Gurudev? The niche that Chinmaya Mission has carved out for itself around the world is also due to their unswerving committment. Now let us trace the history of BV around the world."**....**

Bala Perspectives

A young BV student of *Ramayaṇa* said — "Rāma's mother Kaikeyī was not really bad. She had a bad friend who made her do bad things. If she had Rāma as her friend, she would not have done bad things."

Embracing the World

Gurudev traveled around the globe to quench the thirst of spiritual seekers, far and wide. The very epitome of compassion, he crossed oceans to meet potential seekers on their doorstep. In his quest to light the lamp of wisdom in the hearts of multitudes, Gurudev spared no thought for his own comfort. And so, in 1965, began a new phase — spreading the message of Vedānta in Southeast Asia and beyond.

... Shraddha began to follow the trail through emails and Skype calls. She was lucky to meet many sevaks from different countries in Delhi itself. It became clear that after taking firm root in India, Bala Vihar (BV) traveled overseas with Gurudev, following his imprints on the invisible sands of time, to spread the brightness of knowledge in young minds in far-off lands. BV found new dwellings in the homes of kindred minds seeking spiritual succor for their children — children growing up in foreign cultures far removed from their ancestral origins, who, but for the vision of this great ??ī, would never have known the wonders of their cultural heritage woven into the texture of Indian thought**....**

The Spread Eastward

..."Ma," said Shraddha, "let me take you on a guided tour of the nations that have welcomed BV — first, east of India, and then across to the west. As in India, Pujya Gurudev's electrifying presence was the catalyst. After his Māhāsamādhī, the spark came from Guruji and, in some places, other Swamis laid the foundations for the local BVs."....

The march eastward reached the Southeast Asian countries and beyond, all the way to Australia and New Zealand.

Pujya Gurudev visited Hong Kong, Singapore, Manila, and Jakarta in the late 1960s. As a natural follow-up, BV classes opened in each of these cities. Later, Br. Susheel (now Swami Swaroopananda) nurtured BVs in the region and guided early sevaks to build a strong movement. Currently, Brni. Nishita is shaping the destiny of BV in these countries. Evidence of her love for children is the Chinmaya Bala Katha series of books she has authored.

BRNI. NISHITA WITH BV CHILDREN AND SEVAKS ▲

BVs in the cities of this region have many memories to share. Below is a snapshot of their history.

Hong Kong

The residence of Śrī K. P. Daswani and his wife Vindu was the venue of the first BV class in this island city known for its financial muscle power. With time the number of children attending BV grew, dwindled and then settled around three hundred.

Using imagination the center produced a day of unadulterated joy — the Kṛṣṇa Mela. Brni. Nishita and her sevaks created over twenty-five different games with themes around

AT THE KṚṢṆA MELA ▶

the antics of Kṛṣṇa. Life-size cutouts of the Lord adorned the venue. A resounding success, the whole day was dedicated to the children enjoying games and other activities with Kṛṣṇa…Kṛṣṇa…Kṛṣṇa.

Another burst of creativity to 'catch them young,' initiated by Brni. Nishita is Chinmaya Shishu Vihar, or 'Mommy and Me' classes for newborns to four-year-olds. The rule book for the class reads: Love them to bits. Let them do whatever they like!

…Shraddha excitedly shared with Shanti a video clip on Shishu Vihar….

It was a world of cute, adorable babies — some on their backs, kicking away; others crawling or swaggering from one object to another...

Meanwhile prayers were being chanted; some tiny tots tried to chant along haltingly, cheered on by their mothers. What better way for mother and child to bond? Mandatory for both to attend, mothers learned the specially created nursery rhymes with their children, and later became enthusiastic facilitators.

…Fortunately Shraddha met Brni. Nishita in Delhi and got a first hand update….

Brni. Nishita said, "The little ones have strong retentive power and are quick to learn. The double benefit of mothers also learning is that the rhymes and stories get strongly embedded in the minds of the children. Even three-year-old children can chant the Hanumān Cālīsā!"

…Imagining the great times with these adorable infants, Shraddha now wanted, more than anything, to begin a similar class at the Delhi center!….

Manila

…Moving to Manila, the capital city of the Philippines, Shraddha uncovered a curious fact: the Hindus were a miniscule minority in a Christian stronghold, and they were working dedicatedly to keep their culture alive….

Gurudev's reassuring presence provided much-needed support to the Indian diaspora; floundering in a setting rich in contrasting traditions, trying to find the moorings to reconnect with their ancestry.

...Shraddha learned that the sparks of inspiration from Gurudev ignited a desire in Nina Hathiramani to plant the BV flag in this terrain. She worked against huge odds to bring children,who were finding it difficult to withstand the onslaught of the Christian influence, into the fold.

Her hard work and persistence paid off. Her motivation was Gurudev. At their very first meeting he said to her, "She can do it!" Says Nina, "I couldn't let the Master down; if he thinks I can do it, I WILL do it. It is His mission, I just have to do my best and the rest is up to Him." Nina worked with inspiration to inculcate discipline in these children, put together lesson plans, innovative games and puzzles to sharpen their intellects and keep their interest alive....

The sevikās, drawn mostly from the Sindhi community, pitted against Christian missionary zeal, faced dire straits. Then, convinced of the purity of Gurudev's message, they rose to the occasion to become focused and structured. Their singular dedication made the children understand and appreciate the beauty of their own religion. The conversion rate to Christianity began to decline.

One thought became firmly implanted in the minds of these children:

• "I AM SPECIAL. I AM GURUDEV'S CHILD!" •

If numbers are the only criteria of success, then the Manila center, with only 150 children, may seem to have underperformed, but the challenge there was far greater. To have made those children feel proud of their own Hindu heritage is a laudable feat in itself.

Roma Sujnani, currently in charge of the program and passionate about her work, proudly declared: "BV is my life's calling!"

SINGAPORE

...In the island state of Singapore, Shraddha found a chequered history. Initial success was followed by extinction, but the embers remained smoldering and were once again resurrected with the passage of time....

▲ GURUDEV ENJOYING SINGAPORE

In 1968, founding members Dr. T. P. Paran and his wife initiated a modest beginning for BV in Singapore. The numbers grew and, by 1975, eight classes catered to the needs of almost 250 children. Subsequently, due to a variety of reasons, the classes dwindled and then completely stopped.

...Nirmala Bharwani and her family hosted Gurudev during his visit in 1987, and reopened the doors for BV. On a Skype call with Shraddha, Nirmala was quick to acknowledge her earlier inadequate knowledge of Hinduism and how she made amends, "I immediately wanted to rectify this with my children so they would grow up knowing their roots and the expansive glories of Hindu Dharma!"....

On Gurudev's subsequent visit Nirmala communicated her desire to conduct BV classes for children. He closed his eyes and told her to start with the attitude of serving Kṛṣṇa in the form of little children. He counseled, "Don't think you are teaching them and doing them a favor, but be grateful to them for giving you a chance to serve the Lord in their form."

The tradition of service to BV continues as the second generation of daughters and daughters-in-law, keep the institution alive. The Guru's blessing passes on!

...While chatting with Brni. Nishita, Shraddha was amazed to hear about the fledgling presence of BV in Malaysia as well....

In the 1980s, after Pujya Gurudev made two trips to Kuala Lumpur and Penang, Swami Swaroopananda assisted in setting up the BV infrastructure, but the momentum could not be maintained. Since 2005, Brni. Nishita has been visiting regularly, and the outcome is three BV classes. The center has shown steady increase in its followers and, will be soon a registered Chinmaya Mission center.

... After her Internet research about Indonesia, Shraddha understood that the country's past history was entrenched in Hinduism, even though it has the largest Muslim population in the world today. Its ancient temples and present-day sculptures carry the fragrance of a vibrant and spiritually evolved culture**....**

JAKARTA

Harish and Lakshmi Lasmana are, and have been, the mainstay of the Mission in Jakarta, playing a pivotal role in all its activities. Lakshmi said, "In the late 1980s, during one of Gurudev's visits to Singapore, he pointed to our kids who were playing in the room and said, "These children are your future. You are responsible for them."

Lakshmi understood. And with the blessings of Indonesia's ancient Hindu inheritance and Lakshmi's active support, BV was introduced to the local Hindu community.

The threat of conversion is also a stark reality in Jakarta. The BV children realize this and are grateful for what they learn about Hinduism in their classes.

Many children in the Jakarta chapter belong to the expatriate community, and their numbers keep fluctuating because of parents relocating from and into the city. Surprisingly, here finding teachers was easy — the challenge was to get children to attend and to convince parents to make BV their priority!

... Shraddha also discovered that the Southeast Asian centers were well networked and had their own little fraternity. Hong Kong, Manila, Singapore, and Jakarta pool together their resources, share ideas, and get inspiration or help from each other, when required! Nina Hathiramani even set up a think-tank that worked out a syllabus and guided the other centers**....**

Australia

The BV trail moved south to nestle in Australia, a country with a teeming population of Indians.

When compared with its counterparts in other parts of the world, BV in Australia is fairly young. It took birth in 1982 at Dr. K. T. Ganapathy's residence, which was aptly named 'Gurukripa' (Guru's Grace). Fondly known as Mataji, her name is well known in CM, Australia. She spearheaded the movement in Melbourne; other sevaks replicated her efforts in Sydney.

...During Gurudev's maiden visit to Australia in 1984, he unfolded his vision for children. Christine Grimmer penned for Shraddha her account of that day. She wrote, "I was greatly moved by his farsightedness. I realized the import of what I had heard and wanted to capture it for posterity. So I rushed home and jotted down phrases from Gurudev's talk: "Catch them early and harness their energy. They are pure while they are young, so instill in them virtues and teach them their Hindu culture. Let them grow to be strong in values and to have love for the Lord."....

Gurudev made the sevaks understand the children's intrinsic need for play and fun. The teacher in Christine was captivated by this vision. And after a brief internship under Dr. Ganapathy, she was entrusted with teaching BV.

> In a letter dated 1986, Gurudev noted: "As the BV classes grow bigger and bigger we must discover new sevikās to conduct the classes. Very large numbers of children cannot be served by one individual. Children need a personal touch and counseling and must feel that each is a special child of the sevikā."

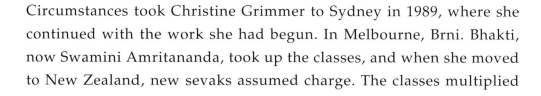

Circumstances took Christine Grimmer to Sydney in 1989, where she continued with the work she had begun. In Melbourne, Brni. Bhakti, now Swamini Amritananda, took up the classes, and when she moved to New Zealand, new sevaks assumed charge. The classes multiplied across the city, with parents and senior Yuva Kendra members being inducted as teachers. Branching out, BV established a presence in Adelaide, Canberra, and more recently in Brisbane (2005).

AFTER THE SHOW WITH BR. GOPAL ▲

...Shraddha was like a child on a treasure hunt, when every morning she opened her laptop with anticipation. Her thought was, "What will I learn today?"

Sharing her amazement with Shanti, Shraddha said, "It is interesting how BV evolves in keeping with the needs of different countries. Over the years, Melbourne specialized in BV camps, and Sydney designed weekend family camps with separate programs for adults and children. Often led by Swami Swaroopananda, these camps are based on the adage that 'the family that prays together stays together.' Sydney also hosts an annual New Year picnic and a cricket match. The inclusion of fathers in these programs has established a value for BV in both parents. There being something of interest to draw in each member, the family as a whole comes together to make these events memorable for all!"....

JYOTI WITH GURUJI AND ▲
SWAMI SWAROOPANANDA

New Zealand

The pristine beauty of New Zealand, tucked away to the southeast of Down Under, shone brighter when BV came to town. Mission activities started when Brni. Bhakti, (now Swamini Amritananda), moved to Nelson. But BV struck roots in Auckland, only after Jyoti Raj, its roving ambassador, moved there in June 1999.

...Jyoti and Shraddha became acquainted via the Skype route, and Shraddha came to know about the activities in New Zealand, including the birth of BV. Jyoti said, "Our younger son Vaidik was turning five. I thought the best gift would be to start a BV class — a gift from Pujya Gurudev."....

▲ BR. ADARSH WITH CHILDREN OF BV AUCKLAND

The first class consisted of her two sons and five neighborhood children. Raji Nair and Ratna Dubey added their support and helped stabilize the program in Auckland. They later moved to Perth, and replicated BV there as well.

Two years later, it became necessary to set up a youth class to accommodate the kids who had outgrown BV. Around the same time, Br. Adarsh was assigned to Auckland and became a great hit with the children. In 2009, Auckland acquired its own center — Chinmaya Nikunj and the work continues with enthusiasm.

The Spread Westward

The BV's trail westward includes Mauritius in the Indian Ocean and the Arab nations of Dubai and Kuwait. Farther west, it branched out to Kenya, Tanzania, South Africa, and also established a presence in the United Kingdom. But it is across the Pacific — in the U.S.A. — where the movement has its strongest bastion.

Mauritius

Mauritius and the Reunion Islands are tiny islands in the Indian Ocean. But despite their size the BV flag has been flying high. Swami Pranavananda guided and nourished the Mission presence in French-speaking Mauritius from its inception. He set up BV in the late 1970s and took care of its needs until the mid-1980s. By then, Maya Murday, a talented singer, and Sheila Ghurbinsingh, both BV alumni, were trained and competent to assume leading roles.

Over time, sustained efforts by several brahmacharins brought a steady transformation and the movement gathered more momentum. As the children matured, Junior CHYK and Youth classes were instituted. From 2005 to 2010, Br. Shripad (now Swami Ramatmananda), took a keen interest in the program. He developed interesting activities to keep the children motivated and to ensure their continued participation.

MIDDLE EAST — KUWAIT, DUBAI, BAHRAIN, MUSCAT

...Moving from islands in the Indian Ocean to affluent cities surrounded by miles of shimmering desert sands in the Middle East, BV established a strong presence in Kuwait, Bahrain, Muscat, and Dubai. Their stories being similar, Shraddha decided to showcase Kuwait as representative of the changing landscape....

In 1971, Pujya Gurudev first walked over the sands of Kuwait, a city famous for its glorious sunrises and golden sunsets. Chinmaya Mission in Kuwait was born and grew with the growth of the country.

...Som Oberoi, a staunch supporter from those early days, met Shraddha in Delhi and was happy to learn about her project. Their chat led to further communication via email. He wrote, "The facade of Kuwait changed from sand dunes to water towers, from camels to Cadillacs. Through all this, the Mission stood strong. Subtly and unobtrusively, the sevaks maintained their course and continued to spread the messages of Sanātana Dharma."....

Pujya Gurudev's presence inspired the listeners at his yajña in 1971 and a group of enthusiastic ladies set up two different classes. The seeds sown by him sprouted fast and blossomed into strong trees branching into various areas of Kuwait. By 1999 the strength of BV children was 300. Today, a devoted team of thirty-five sevaks serves more than 400 children, enrolled in fifteen BVs.

▲ GURUDEV ON A SAFARI

Nairobi

The landscape changes yet again, from the Middle East to the continent of Africa: Nairobi (Kenya), Dar Es Salaam (Tanzania), Lagos (Nigeria), and Durban (South Africa).

In February 1991, Pujya Gurudev made his third visit to the city. On the last day of the talks at a bhikṣā in Śrī Manubhai Patel's home, he made an electric announcement. He declared, "Jyoti will start a BV class and a Study Group in Nairobi." Jyoti Raj and her family had just moved to Nairobi in December 1990.

...Jyoti's eyes had a nostalgic look when she narrated her state of mind to Shraddha. She was transported to that historic day. "Gurudev took me by surprise, and speech simply deserted me. My mind screamed, 'Say no, say no! You cannot do this. You have never attended BV. What will you teach? You do not know anything!'"....

▲ GURUDEV WITH JYOTI AND HER SON

Unperturbed, Pujya Gurudev left the next day, knowing full well that his will would prevail. Assistance came, like it always does, to fulfill his wishes. Manubhai offered his old house in the middle of the city as the venue, and seven children turned up for the first session. Additional children trickled in as word slowly spread. The base was established. In early 1992, the Raj family moved to another country, passing on the reins to Ramesh and Murli Pattni and family.

After a break, Shayur Pattni renewed the BV movement in 2002 at Muljibhai Ratna's office in Westlands. Shayur further passed on the mantle. Willing hands received it and the BV flag continues to flutter in the African wind.

Dar-es-Salaam

...Shraddha now took Shanti into a narrative about the adjoining lands, from Kenya to Tanzania, BV moved to these new lands with Jyoti Raj, who was fast becoming its trusted ambassador-on-wheels!....

Early in 1993, Jyoti and her family were transferred to Dar-es-Salaam and, within a month, she had organized herself to break fresh ground. The BV flag was hoisted with her son and a few children of her husband's colleagues.

In just over a year, the class outgrew the space in their residence. Providence came to their rescue: they were offered a hall, free of cost; able assistants came forward; they planned events and worked to establish the program.

To spread awareness of BV, the group organized a grand Mātṛ Pujā in Chinmaya Mission style, which gave huge publicity to the Mission. The increased attendance over the course of four years spells out an unmitigated success story!

...Jyoti had a wealth of BV history to share in the several sessions of Skype with Shraddha. Listening to this Shanti was amazed at how, through all her travels, Jyoti's devotion to BV never wavered....

In 1996, Jyoti moved again, handing over the reins to other empowered sevaks. With the next port of call being Moscow, she even managed to run a BV there for a duration of two years!

Durban

In the mid 1980's BV made an appearance on the Durban landscape thanks to the efforts of Ishwar Beesunlal. The classes continued on a moderate scale till they received an impetus with the arrival of Br. Pithambar in 1998.

More recently with Swami Abhedananda's, guidance and the able support of dedicated sevaks, BV South Africa gained in popularity. Inspiring camps entitled 'Man to Hanuman', 'Arise, Shine and Smile' were conducted every alternate month and attended by about seventy children. Since Jan 2013, these camps have become a monthly feature. And today approximately 1900 children are associated with the Mission in some way or the other!

...Even if the teaching transforms one child it is well worth it. Shraddha found the story of the Spronk children absorbing and most fascinating....

Holland

Living in Holland, Paula and Frank Spronk could not send their children Gerard and Anton to BV; instead they exposed them to the depth and beauty of Gurudev's vision in their very home. Older now, both children attend satsaṇg with their parents and can be frequently seen at camps in India and Europe. Surrounded by Gurudev's blessings the boys are growing into unusually gifted musicians, in the western classical music tradition.

▲ THE SPRONK FAMILY WITH GURUJI IN CHINMAYA VIBHOOTI

Says Paula, an alumna of Sandeepany Sadhanalaya, Powai, "As a family we have walked the tightrope, exercising discipline to accommodate concerts and schoolwork. A spiritual dimension and the attitude of surrender has been our underlying strength. These children have attended a unique BV, not confined to a day in the week. Their whole life has been a study of spirituality, which their music exudes. As a family we share an eagerness to serve mankind in the form of music and spiritual knowledge, finally leading to the understanding of music as an ornament of silence."

Trained by their father, Gerard plays the violin, whereas Anton coaxes music out of the cello. Their strong spiritual leanings have no doubt, contributed to the flowering of such perfection so early in life. Born and reared in Holland, the children chant the Gurustotram and other Sanskrit hymns and also sing bhajans. To hear them play Tapovan Ashtakam is to experience divinity.

They have performed several times for the Chinmaya family, in the presence of Guruji. Paula and Frank pray, "May the children be His instruments through their instruments. Nothing is ours, it is all His!"

United Kingdom

...During an overseas trip to London, Shraddha had an opportunity to meet a few Mission members and gather the history of BV in the United Kingdom....

On a visit to the U.K. in 1993, Gurudev talked about the BV program at the home of Kavita Chanrai and in passing suggested that it should be started in the U.K. But no word from Gurudev was ever just a casual remark!

In 1994, the year following Gurudev's visit, a handful of CHYKs and a young mother came forward to offer their time to the program. And so it was that Gurudev's vision for BV manifested in the U.K. at St. Christina's School with three sevaks and just five children. And now BV in U.K. caters to two hundred children with thirty sevaks. Some specialties from the U.K. are:

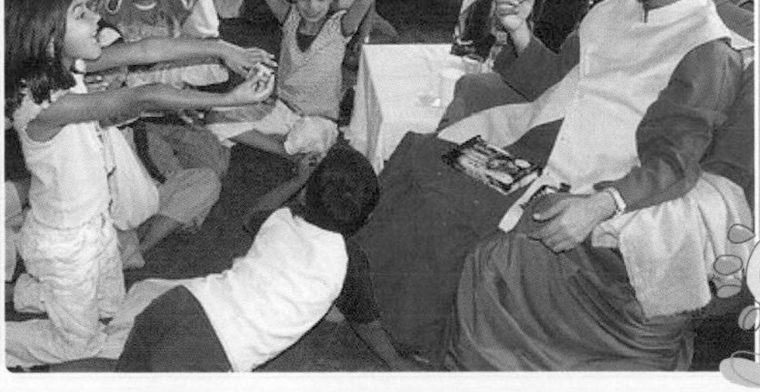

▲ SHISHU VIHAR IN PROGRESS

In response to a vocal demand from young mothers in London, the idea of Shishu Vihar flowered here as well. In 2012, this program, became an add-on to BV. Many of the young participants were past members of the Yuva Kendra, who after marriage and children found little time for sādhanā and study. They felt the need to expose their tiny ones and themselves to the positive vibrations of stotra chanting and bhajan singing.

Shishu Vihar's dual focus benefits children and mothers. When the children are otherwise engaged, the mothers can practice sitting in silence or are stimulated by discussions on books relevant to parenting. Br. Paritosh, the resident Ācārya says he looks forward to the hours that he spends in the company of like-minded children!

General Certificate of Secondary Examination (GCSE)

The U.K. chapter of BV prepares its teenage stars for the paper on Hinduism in Religious Studies — a subject in the GCSE, a national qualification exam taken by youngsters fourteen to sixteen years of age. The Chinmaya Mission intertwines the prescribed syllabus with Mission texts, such as Hinduism: *Frequently Asked Questions*, *Symbolism in Hinduism*, and *Why do We?* The highly successful program started in 2007 with just five teenagers, has become an annual feature, with thirty to forty BV children taking the exam and achieving high grades in it.

Junior CHYKs are also encouraged to participate in community projects. Recycling plastic for residents and fundraising initiatives for CORD are some of them. Children actively support the local community by visiting old-age homes and work in coordination with mainstream Harrow schools to encourage children to revere their grandparents.

SEVĀ OF THE ELDERLY ▲

Councillor Bednell, a community leader, appreciated the Mission's initiative: "In an age when young people seem to prefer blowing up digital monsters on video consoles, to taking their grandmothers for walks in the park, this attitude is very welcome; it is a perfect catalyst for youngsters to inspire dialog with their elders."

The movement crossed the Atlantic and travelled across the breadth of the United States of America, to the shores of the Pacific Ocean. In the land of immigrants, BV found its stronghold and Gurudev's embrace of his children worldwide was complete!

Bala Perspectives

An alumnus from U.K. recalls: "BV was my introduction to God. Here I was taught to 'call' God by a technique, which involves taking my right hand, and vertically aligning it with my left hand so that each type of finger touches its corresponding one. I would then shut my eyes, and force myself to recollect the picture of the deity in front of me, whilst reciting a strange poem in a foreign language of which I had no idea."

XVI

The Reigning Stronghold

As in India, yajñas by Pujya Gurudev were the genesis of Bala Vihar (BV) in the United States. His quest was not just to illumine the minds of the adults; it was to embrace the children of Indian ancestry as well. So, in the early 1970s, when he visited Ācārya Sharada Kumar's residence in New York for bhikṣā, his gaze fell on the bright-eyed little kids accompanying their parents. He expressed his concern: "I am not worried about the adults who grew up in India, because they will know where to find answers for their problems in the scriptures. But I am worried about these young ones, who will be lost in the dual culture."

Turning his piercing gaze on Sharada, who had been chanting for his lectures since 1969, he asked, "Why don't you start a BV for them?"

Momentarily taken aback, she confessed, "Gurudev, I do not know how to start one." Ready with a solution, he gave her a letter of introduction addressed to Nirmala Chellam in Chembur, Mumbai.

And said, "Go get trained!"

So, in 1974, Sharada Kumar visited Mumbai and received directions and relevant materials from Nirmala Chellam. Also guidance flowed from

Br. Krishnamoorthy, who, in 1970-71, had moved from Mumbai to New York to start groundwork for various Mission activities.

SHARADA KUMAR ▲

Sharada began the first BV in 1976 in Long Island, New York. She recalls, "Of course, people had no concept of BV then. So it was tough to convince them to bring their children to the classes!"

The cyber world had not yet stormed Planet Earth, and so interaction in the 1970s was not as swift as it is today. Using out-of-the-box marketing strategies, Sharada reached out to the Indian community. In supermarkets, whenever she and her daughter spotted any Indians, her five-year-old daughter, would run up to them and ask, "Aunty, Uncle, can you bring your children to the BV at our house, please?" Every week, Sharada made mouth-watering Indian savories to distribute as prasādam, an appetizing lure for the parents to stay. Soon word spread and people began coming on their own!

...Shraddha and Shanti noticed that the movement had a pattern: dedicated messengers carried the BV word wherever they went. So it was that the pioneer of the movement in the U.S., Ācārya Sharada Kumar kept the BV torch burning as she moved from New York to Michigan in 1984....

Ann Arbor

In Ann Arbor, from a humble start in her basement, the steadily increasing numbers led to the creation of Chinmaya Avantika in July 2000. The present strength of the center is more than one thousand BV students. And classes are conducted in seven Michigan locations — Ann Arbor, Canton, Novi, Troy, Toledo, West Bloomfield, and Lansing — by more than eighty trained teachers.

Every year in February, the centre observes a very special day. Families from all seven locations come together at Ann Arbor, to celebrate with grandeur the Indian Republic Day. It is a mark of reverence to India, the land of this life transforming knowledge that is their strength. It is also respectful to their ancestors, which helps them: "to serve as an army courageous and disciplined." A truly splendid spectacle to warm the hearts of all the participants!

A Piece of Kerala

During Gurudev's marathon, month long *Vivekacūḍāmaṇi* camp in 1982, in Grand Rapids, about one hundred kids from Ann Arbor presented the "Śaṅkarācārya" play. Gurudev quietly entered the hall from the back, where the kids were waiting, all dressed up, to go on the stage. And what did he see? Ten Śaṅkarācāryas and thirty to forty sannyāsīs and the rest dressed in Kerala style dresses! Gurudev was overjoyed and started dancing to the chant of, "This is my kind of place!!!"

...During a conversation with Shraddha, Ācārya Vilasini Balakrishnan traced the common history behind the growth of BV, from its very early days in the U.S....

In the late 1970s and early 1980s, BVs started in people's living rooms or basements in several cities in the U.S. The classes catered to all ages — children from six to-seventeen-years old. The whole experience was so joyful! The twelve-year olds helped to look after the younger ones, making the class like one big family. Gurudev's advice regarding teaching a single class of children spanning a wide age group was that we should always address the youngest, so that everyone understands.

▲ ĀCĀRYA VILASINI

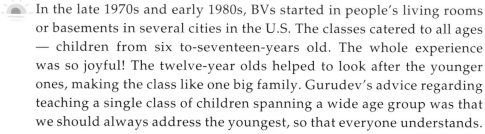

As more and more people heard about BV throughout the U.S., interest grew rapidly. Professionals moving from India to the U.S., wishing to keep their roots strong and their religion alive, looked to Chinmaya Mission to provide satsaṅga and cultural education. As the Indian diaspora grew, so did Chinmaya Mission. The Mission also attracted many Westerners to the Vedānta Study Groups, and some of them had their children join the BVs.

In some cities, the demand for BV grew to the point where bigger facilities had to be rented. Once a critical mass of BV attendance was reached, classes started taking shape according to the grades of the children, and a systematic curriculum was developed for teachers to plan their lessons.

Then the idea of finding a large facility with several classrooms for BV took birth. The first BV to start that trend was in Los Altos, California, run by Ācārya Uma Jeyarasasingam. The scene in the rented elementary school in 1980 was reminiscent of India — a tropical landscape, balmy weather, and happy children running around in salwar-kameez and kurtas, at home with the sounds of Sanskrit chanting.

...Shraddha noted in her journal, "In retrospect, it is interesting to find a unifying pattern in how the Mission centers grew in the U.S. Everywhere, one person accepted the mantle of responsibility. He or she then formed a team, which helped increase the activities and brought more people into the fold.

It is impossible to cover the detailed history of each of the BV centers in the U.S., neither is it feasible to document the stupendous work being done by thousands of volunteers in dozens of centers. The number of volunteer hours that have been individually and collectively devoted to raise the BV program to its present remarkable levels in North America is indeed mind-boggling.

Many volunteers are parents who have seen the benefit of the program in their children's lives. They accept nothing by way of compensation except the satisfaction of molding generation after generation of well-behaved, caring, poised, and self-confident children."

Still, it was Shraddha's mission to try to glean the brief histories of at least a few major BVs in the Tri-state area, as well as San Jose, Los Angeles, Houston, Washington D.C., and Chicago, and showcase the common and special features adopted by the American BVs.

Shraddha had reached out to them with her questions: How did they begin? How did Pujya Gurudev guide some of the initiators of the program? The representative centers each had their unique spark, and yet, the same founding inspiration....

The Tri-State Area — New York, New Jersey and Pennsylvania

When considering the Tri-State BV, it is best to think of it as three streams, that started as a trickle, meandered, grew at their own pace and swelled to become the nourishing, wide-spread river it is today.

▲ SWAMI SHANTANANDA PERFORMS PŪJĀ

▲ RAISING FUNDS FOR CORD

The early stream started in NY City after Br. Krishnamoorthy moved to New York from Mumbai. BVs followed from the jñāna yajñas by Pujya Gurudev from 1972-75 in New York and surrounding suburbs. Facing the various challenges of a large city that stream found its strength after the setting up of the Mission's New York Center in 2007 with over 150 children.

The second stream started in the early 80s further south in the Philadelphia area of Pennsylvania with sevaks like Kusum Patel, Rameshbhai and Binduben Choksi. In the mid 80s, they were joined by Subrah Cheruvu and others from Central New Jersey, and Jahnavikaben in Pennsylvania.

Pujya Gurudev was very pleased with the progress he saw when he conducted jñāna yajñas in Princeton and Philadelphia in 1991. He directed the sevaks to acquire 'our own' property. He strengthened the members' hesitant resolve by appointing Swami Shantananda to the new Tri-State Center in Langhorne, Pennsylvania in 1992. The centre was later re-named Chinmaya Kedar by Pujya Guruji.

In 1994 Swami Siddhananda took charge of Chinmaya Publications West, and further energized BV in Pennsylvania, which now serves over 400 children extending services as far away as Delaware. Kedar Utsav, the annual cultural program, is celebrated with grand flair.

THE FUTURE OF TRI-STATE ▲

The New Jersey BV stream began in homes and basements in the mid 80s and blossomed with the impetus provided by Swami Shantananda. Currently the center serves over 1000 children. The backbone of its smooth functioning is a team of over hundred sevaks, organized by Ameet Bhatt, Sivaprasad Pandyaram, and many others.

A unique aspect of BV in New Jersey is the pioneering Toddler (parent-child) and Pre-kindergarten program. Starting 2005, Sanskrit learning has been incorporated in all BV classes including the toddlers. The programs' success can be gauged by the fact that even the middle and high school age kids have been motivated to perform dramas in Sanskrit. With the construction of Chinmaya Vrindavan spread over seven acres of rural Cranbury in Central New Jersey, this river is all set to flow: "Thy grace and blessings to the world around us".

The latest outpost of the Tri-State movement has been in Fairfield, Connecticut.

SAN JOSE

The story of this bustling center began with Uma Jeyarasasingam's daughter, Gayathri. Ācārya Uma recalls:

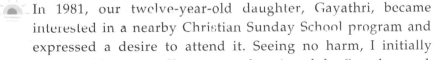

ĀCĀRYA UMA ▲

In 1981, our twelve-year-old daughter, Gayathri, became interested in a nearby Christian Sunday School program and expressed a desire to attend it. Seeing no harm, I initially permitted her to go. She apparently enjoyed the first class and wanted to attend it every week. I had no valid reason not to allow her but was getting concerned about it. I postponed the Sunday school issue for a while. It was my good fortune that Gurudev was visiting us. I sought his guidance as soon as he arrived. Here is what transpired...

"Swamiji, I am in a real dilemma and don't know how to handle it. Gayathri wants to attend the Christian Sunday School."

"Start your own," he answered.

"Start what, Swamiji?" I asked.

"Sunday School," he answered.

"We don't have Sunday School, Swamiji," I said.

"We shall call it 'BV.' Conduct classes every Sunday for children just like we do in India. You teach them Hindu culture for an hour with arts and crafts, bhajans, and prayers," suggested Pujya Gurudev.

I confessed my utter ignorance on the subject and the method of instruction. Besides, I felt that I lacked communication skills and organizational skills.

Swamiji looked at me with great pity. His compassion took over, and he spent the next seven days instructing me on how I should proceed, step by step. That's how it all began way back then in 1981.

With just eight children and some parents to help, the Bay Area BV was born. Within a few months, the enrollment had increased to a comfortable number. Besides the core spiritual quotient, several Indian languages were also taught. In recent years, Vedic Math, also known as Cognitive Math, has been introduced. BV in this region nourishes more than 2,100 children at the time of this writing in three different locations in the area — San Jose, Fremont, and San Ramon.

▲ SANDWICH SEVĀ

▲ TUG-OF-WAR IS HARD WORK

A child in Grade one wrote: Thank you, Gurudev, for having thought of us even before we were born and making this BV available for us.

Ācārya Uma: When I hear these things from these children, who have never had the opportunity to meet Gurudev, I strongly believe that he has already met them.

Los Angeles

The Los Angeles chapter began in much the same way as did San Jose.

When Ācārya Mahadevan and his wife Viji moved from Wayland, Massachusetts, to California, one predominant thought lingered in their minds: "How do we ensure that our daughter Shobha, while growing up in the U.S., gets the essence of our rich Indian heritage and its cultural and spiritual roots?"

Viji Mahadevan recalls:

The answer to this challenge came promptly from the Master himself, who, knowing that I was trying to do some sevā said: "Why don't you start a BV in Los Angeles?"

Thus, what started out as a small bhajan and śloka class at our home in Whittier, California, in June 1982, with six to eight children, has today expanded to become the BV home of over thirteen hundred children. Who would have thought this possible? When Pujya Gurudev himself had given his blessing, why should it not happen? The Master knows all!!

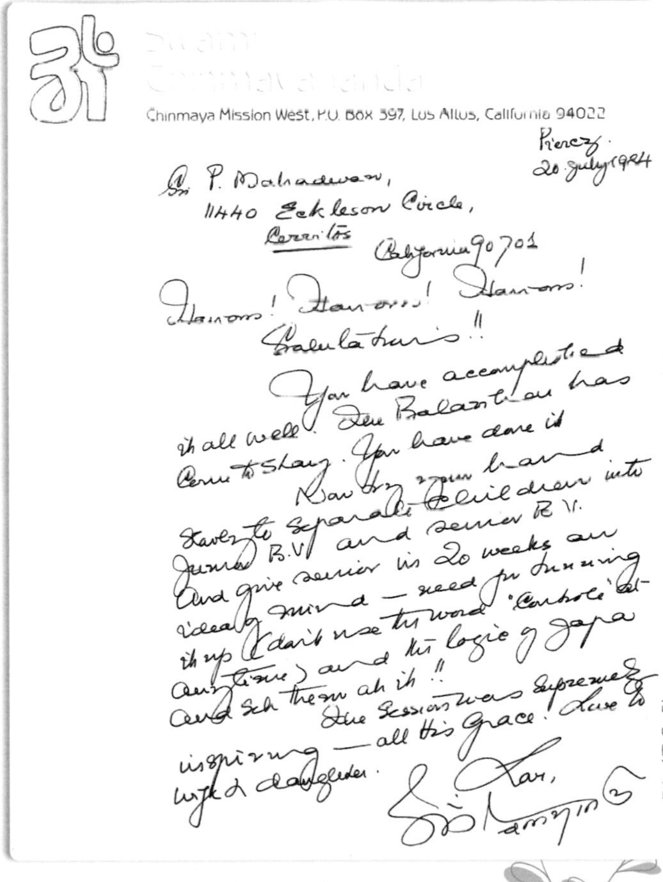
Swami Chinmayananda
Chinmaya Mission West, P.O. Box 397, Los Altos, California 94022

[illegible]
20 July 1984

Sri P. Mahadevan,
11440 Eckleson Circle,
Cerritos
California 90701

Hari Om! Hari Om! Hari Om!
Salutations!!

You have accomplished it all well. The Balavihar has come to stay. You have done it. Now try your hand: Start to separate children into Junior B.V. and senior B.V. and give senior in 20 weeks an idea of mind — need for training it up (don't use the word 'control' at any time) and the logic of japa and teach them all it!! The session was supremely inspiring — all His grace. Love to wife & daughter.

Love,
Swami Chinmayananda

In March 1983, when the Mahadevan family made the city of Cerritos, California their home; more families flocked to the BV program. Adult classes for parents were conducted, alongside the children's classes.

1996 saw the inauguration of Chinmaya Kasi, in Anaheim near Disneyland by Guruji Swami Tejomayananda. The Mayor of Anaheim, present at the inauguration of Kasi, aptly observed, "This BV is in an ideal place, close to Disneyland, the home of so many children!"

▲ BV GRADUATES WITH SWAMI ISHWARANANDA AND ĀCĀRYA MAHADEVAN

BVs conducted in homes in the vicinity of Anaheim joined Kasi, and the numbers continued to swell. A satellite center of BV flourished at Chinmaya Mithila with Swami Ishwarananda as the Resident Ācārya. Later language classes in Hindi, Gujarati, Tamil, and Telugu were added. While the children attended BV, parents attended Vedānta classes by Swami Ishwarananda and Ācārya Mahadevan.

The constant growth in numbers, activities, and accompanying parking problems, made the search for a bigger place imperative. In January 2010, Lord Kaśi Viśvanātha from the Kasi Center, and the Rāma Parīvāra from Chinmaya Mithila traveled ceremoniously to Chinmaya Rameshwaram, their new abode. In the first decades of the twenty-first century, a total of 900 children attended two parallel BV sessions at Chinmaya Rameshwaram.

Houston

The story of BV Houston began close to Gurudev's heart. In 1980, when Gurudev was flown to Houston, Texas, for his triple bypass surgery, he said, "Everything has a reason and a deep purpose. But for this unexpected turn of events, Chinmaya Mission would not have so easily become established here in this great, growing city of Houston."

ĀCĀRYAS GAURANGBHAI AND DARSHANABEN NANVATY ▲

In 1981, on his next visit to Houston, Gurudev encouraged the birth of informal study groups with a cryptic assurance, "Someone will be coming soon." True to his word, Gaurangbhai and Darshanaben Nanavaty arrived in Houston, after graduating from the two-and-a-half-year Vedānta Course conducted at Piercy, California. Their move was mainly for professional reasons and they had no intention to teach Vedānta. But Providence was to transform their purpose, true to Gurudev's promise!

Chinmaya Mission gained a voice in Houston. The *Gītā* classes began with just two families. As a natural extension, two children came to study under Darshanaben — that marked the quiet beginning of BV Houston in January 1983. Darshanaben had found her calling. Her ability to convey the message of the scriptures, in memorable ways, attracted children of all ages.

Tarun Mital, one of her first two students, recalls those early days, "For the first few months, it was just me and another girl. Gradually, many children came and teachers joined. Darshana Aunty taught the whole BV for the first three years. With much dedication she worked hard on all aspects."

At the time of this writing, in 2012, the numbers have grown from two to eight hundred. The fragrance of dedication brought a committed team of teachers that grew from few to more than seventy-five in 2012.

The thriving BV spirit moved to a permanent home in 1987, when a seven-and-a-half-acre property became its place of residence. Gurudev christened the land 'Chinmaya Prabha,' assuring Darshanaben that the place will reflect the glory of Chinmaya!

▲ CM HOUSTON CELEBRATES DIVĀLĪ

The property has since transformed into a sprawling facility of 4,000 sq. ft. to house the beautiful Saraswati Nilayam and sixteen classrooms. Along with the children, the structure holds an expanding network of BV teachers, as well as teachers of bhajans, slokathon, and Indian languages.

WITH 100,000 BLESSINGS

At the International Camp at Frostburg, Maryland (July 5–13, 1991), Darshanaben and her team of BV teachers trained the children to present a play, "P.O. Box, Mr. God" to Gurudev.

During that camp, Gurudev had met with the CMW Board of Directors to decide about the use of certain funds amounting to $100,000. Suggestions were made about sharing the funds among the many centers in the U.S. Then, on the last day of that camp, after the banquet, Gurudev announced his decision: "I am going to give this cheque to the center that does good work. Darshana, come!"

It was a moment of overwhelming disbelief. Gurudev's gift came right in time for the expansion plans at Chinmaya Prabha!

Washington D.C.

Ācārya Vilasini broached the subject of beginning a BV in Maryland to Sreedevi Kumar in 1987, and so BV found roots in the Washington, D.C. area. At first, Sreedevi was unsure about taking the plunge, but a few months later, she decided to volunteer. Like all fresh recruits, she was equipped with neither the knowledge nor the materials to teach.

Ācārya Vilasini happily filled in the gaps in the knowledge and also provided the resource materials. Wonders never ceased. Dr. and Krishnaveni Sriram in Potomac came forward to volunteer their large basement for the classes. Due to the selfless collective effort, success was ensured with a huge turnout on the very first day of the BV class!

Kusum Patel, who was running a successful BV in Philadelphia, drove all the way to Washington to provide additional support to the fledgling class. Sreedevi's amazement grew. She said, "I could see Kusum's commitment toward the Mission and it inspired me even more." Similarly inspired, Dr. J. K. Naidu of Fairfax, started the first BV in his house.

After the arrival of Swami Dheerananda in 1989, the center expanded rapidly and to absorb this growth, the Chinmayam Spiritual Center was built and inaugurated in 2002. First Brni. Arpita, and then, from 1999, Ācārya Vilasini served as the Regional BV Director. Ācārya Vilasini developed the curriculum and later took an active role in training teachers to support the program.

Another larger center is under construction for BV and Mission programs in nearby Chantilly, Virginia. Additionally, Richmond, Frederick, and Salisbury (the suburbs in the Washington, D.C. area) also have growing BVs.

Under the inspiration of Swami Dheerananda, the Chinmaya Mission Washington Regional Center (CMWRC) has grown from a modest membership base of a few families in the late 1980s to around 700 families and 900 children by 2010.

A special feature of the Washington center is the graduation ritual called the Tilak Ceremony. A brain child of BV sevaks, Chetana and Nagaraj Neerchal and Mangala Rao, the Tilak Ceremony is a special event for the Maryland, Virginia and Frederick chapters of BV. It is a well-planned, thought provoking day, designed to make an impact and leave a lasting impression.

▲ RECEIVING THE BLESSING

The graduation ceremony of high school seniors (twelfth graders) is a meaningful milestone in the BV journey, a celebration of accomplishments and aspirations, a thanksgiving and an occasion to reaffirm the CM pledge.

To the sound of the conch blowing, the graduation procession headed by the Ācāryas enters the Chinmayam Auditorium followed by the seniors — bright in their best Indian attire. This young, auspicious procession is greeted by family, friends and teachers. It is a poignant moment in the lives of the graduates and the atmosphere is charged with emotional memories.

The seniors receive the blessings of Swami Dheerananda, Ācārya Vilasini and the entire Chinmaya family. The ceremony ends with a prayer and pledge and a memorable group picture on the front steps of Chinmayam.

Summer Camps at Washington

Nanik Lahori suggested the idea of a summer camp for children back in 1990, while considering camp options for his daughter. The timing was perfect because, a year earlier, Swami Dheerananda had moved to Maryland from India. And so, the first ten-week summer camp started in Maryland with twenty kids and a few adult volunteers. Though kids have the option of signing up for a minimum of two weeks, most attend all ten weeks.

Some of the themes selected for the camps include, 'Care and Share', 'Live to Give', 'We Can, We Must, We Will', and 'God Is in Everyone'. Children enrich their minds by exploring diverse topics ranging from Sanskrit, Hinduism, bhajans, ślokas to Vedic Math, yoga, dance, arts and crafts, calligraphy, robotics, sports and swimming, all within the context of the theme selected for the year. The highlight of each day is the session of soulful meditation and the singing of the Chinmaya ārtī at the close.

Children over thirteen years are given an opportunity to serve as youth volunteers. These exuberant youngsters are the backbone of the camp's operation. They play with the younger kids during sports, provide first-aid, assist in the classroom, plan activities, organize the food, and clean the facility.

To accommodate growing numbers the camp was split into two camps, one in Maryland, and the other in Virginia. As each camp draws to a close, the campers go their own ways with fond memories of learning, participation, and eager anticipation of the camp in the following year!

Chicago

The yajña by Pujya Gurudev's in 1977, inspired BV programs to start in people's homes. Ācārya Vilasini stayed back after the yajña to train the band of enthusiastic founding sevaks — Shanker and Soumini Pillai, Ashok and Nirmita Dholakia, Shanta Nair, and Ramesh and Kamala Gupta. These initial classes provided the base and the impetus for the growth of Chinmaya Mission Chicago.

▲ SWAMI SHARANANANDA BLESSES THE PARTICIPANTS

In 1986, a beautiful seven-acre property to house the Badri center was purchased. Thereafter, there was a sudden surge in BV registrations. Later, in 1991, Gurudev posted Uncle Mani from Mumbai as the Ācārya. He worked with great enthusiasm and in his two-year stint laid a strong foundation for BV. Swami Sharanananda (then Br. Sharan) followed Uncle Mani as the Ācārya, and he has guided the BV activities ever since.

The growth of the Indian community in the northern suburbs of Chicago, culminated in the inauguration of the Yamunotri center by Guruji in 2009. Under Swami Sharanananda's guidance Chinmaya Mission Chicago supports several satellite programs in Illinois, Indiana and Iowa. His regular visits ensure that these auxiliary programs, serving a total of close to 2,000 children, maintain their strength and vigor.

Apart from the regular BV activities, the Stuti Vandana program is special to the center and its satellites. The program encourages children to memorize key scriptural verses and win medals as they learn the chanting and meaning of the Sanskrit verses. On completion, each child is awarded a plaque with Pujya Gurudev's signature on it.

More than 500 children attend classes at Badri, and another 500 children convene at Yamunotri — the two Chinmaya Mission centers in Chicago.

The stories of these highlighted centers have their parallels in the stories of many other great BV centers all across the U.S. Through one center sharing its experiences with other centers, one sevak with another, one child with others, the story of this amazing movement continues blazing a trail.

Challenges to Overcome

The BV trail often passes through rough terrain. Lakshmi Sukumar, a sevikā since 1988, instrumental in setting up BV in San Diego, explains the challenges that had to be overcome:

▲ LAKSHMI SUKUMAR ENGAGES HER CLASS

- Parents have to understand the vision of the Mission and the vital role of BV in the formative years of children. Often, BV classes are compromised when schoolwork, sports, music, or dance classes conflict.
- Sevaks need to realize that continuous study and growth are a vital part of sevā. There can be no short cuts or use of quick methods.
- BV children of present times have great difficulty sitting still even for a few minutes. Many of them do not have an opportunity to experience silence outside the BV or camp environment. Thus, disciplining is a greater challenge.
- The ancient wisdom of the scriptures has to be linked to modern themes and many stories have to be interpreted in ways that children of this electronic age can relate to.

Canada

The BVs in Canada are close cousins of the U.S. centers and the BV family there has been steadily growing in the recent years. There are six main regions with active BV involvement; located at Calgary, the Halton Region, Niagara, Ottawa, Toronto and Vancouver.

Again, the inspiration drawn from Gurudev and Guruji is sustained by a dedicated teaching team, involved parents and enthusiastic children. The children learn the scriptures, are trained in Indian music and dance, and also learn to serve through CM Canada's strong partnership with CORD.

...As Shraddha concluded her narration of the journey of BV in the U.S.A., some special words wafted through Shanti's mind. Following a quiet moment with devotees after a camp in Switzerland, Gurudev had said: "I have given you a big bouquet of roses. When you go back home, you will take each flower out and inhale its fragrance. Nay, each petal will exude its fragrance and fill your life!"

Bala Perspectives

One three-year-old from New Jersey, adores Śrī Rāma and must watch or listen to the *Rāmāyaṇa* everyday. For him each member of the family is a character from the *Rāmāyaṇa*; his brother is Lakṣhmaṇa. One day he ran to his mother and said, "Amma, I won't be Rāmā anymore. I want to be Shatrugna." Seeing his mother's surprise, he added with concern, "If I am Rāma and my brother is Lakshmanā, we must have two different mothers (Kauśalyā and Sumitrā). I don't want that. I want both of us to have you as our Amma!"

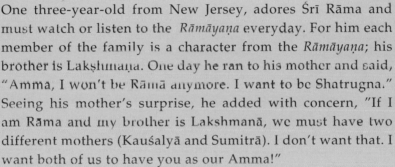

• *Varun Khanna* – twenty three years old, born and brought up in the U.S., with a post-graduate degree in Sanskrit from Cambridge is an exceptional person. His father read Gurudev's commentary of the *Gītā* to his mother while Varun was still in her womb. With this prenatal education, it is no wonder that he joined BV and later Yuva Kendra.

At university, Varun wished to do something different. He left for India to study Ayurveda, moving to a gurukul in Bangalore to learn Sanskrit – naturally, the way babies do. Varun says, "Sanskrit is logical, beautiful, and easy to grasp. Children have turned away from this ancient language because they are not introduced to the correct methodology."

Varun was exposed to Vedic chants along with their meanings. He found learning Sanskrit stimulating - a whole new world opened up for him, he noticed a transformation within! He concluded that the only change was in his understanding. Now, he viewed the world through the lens of Sanskrit as opposed to English or Hindi.

He discovered that the whole universe is made up of vibrations. Omkāra is the substratum of the entire universe and from that springs forth the whole creation. By diving deeper into Sanskrit, we know the true value of things and realize that all the vibrations come from one vibration, infinite in value.

After six months, Varun left India, empowered as a teacher for Samskrita Bharati in the States. He graduated in Neuro science and Mathematics and then proceeded to study the scriptures, and is currently pursuing a Doctorate in Sanskrit at the Cambridge University. His subject: Consciousness in the Upaniṣads according to Swami Chinmayananda with special reference to Śaṅkara.

With great intensity and conviction he speaks of his goal of working towards global peace. Varun says, "The concept of dharma and oneness are sorely absent. The East requires the efficiency of the Western methodology, whereas the West needs the spirituality of Eastern philosophy. Varun is confident that this synthesis would lead to universal harmony!"

Part 5

The Impact

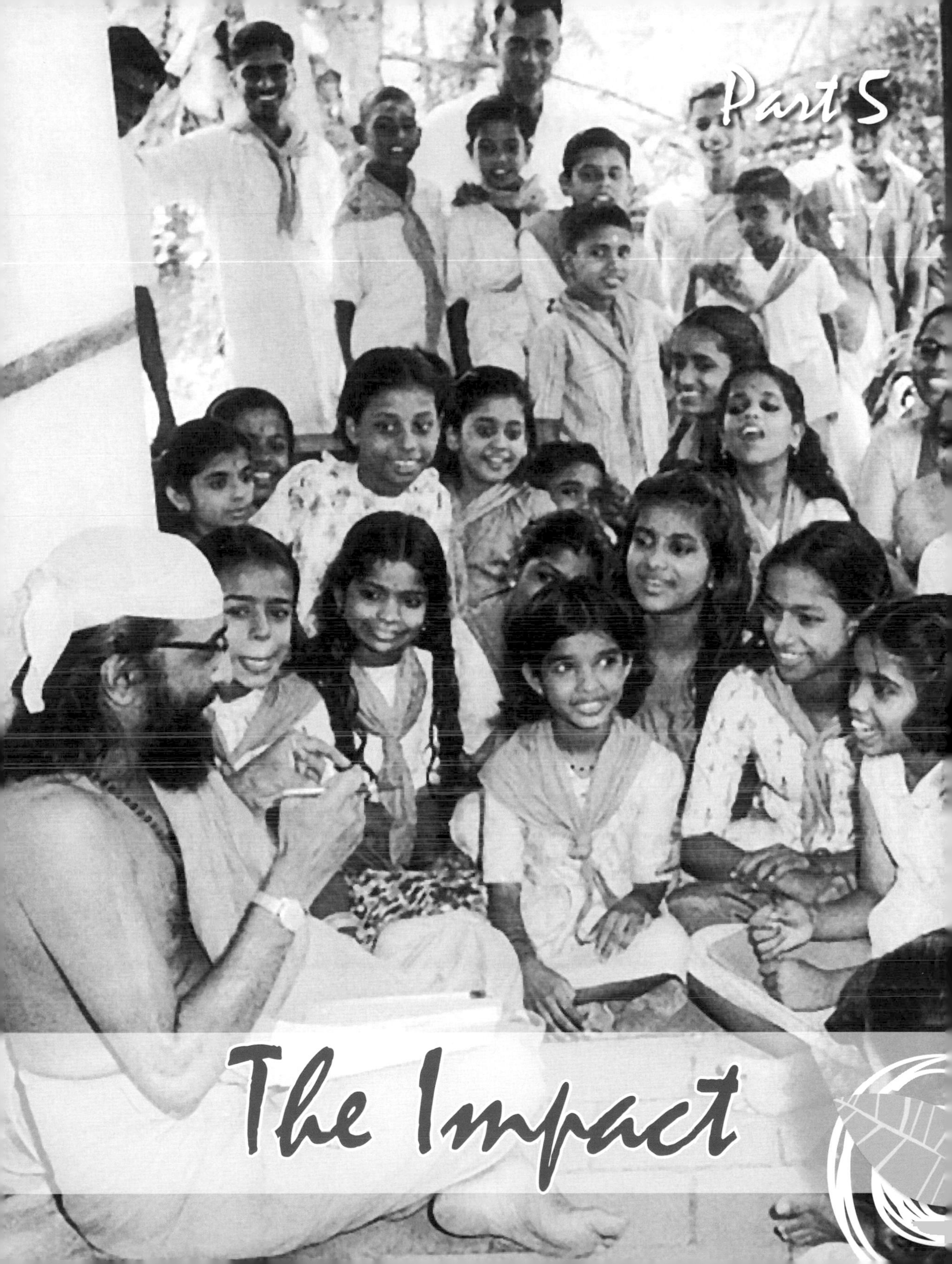

Part 5

The Impact

XVII

Peaking in Perfection

Reviewing life is like walking backward, tracing the footprints in time, watching the play of light and shadow and the high points and dips, replaying life's defining moments in the theater of the mind.

The sense of wonder is most intensely defined in the happy and carefree days of childhood. For the curious little child, the world is an open playground where everything must be explored. Maximum learning takes place in these early years. Lessons learned and experiences gathered in childhood settle deep in the psyche, to lay the foundation for the edifice of the personality.

Thus, impressions gathered in Bala Vihar (BV) play a significant role in casting the mold of the individual. Several Ācaryas of Chinmaya Mission, who grew up in this tradition, are tangible proof of this premise. Their fundamental values, garnered from early training in the halls of BV, have become their intrinsic strength. These define who they are and cement the vision they have. Fearlessness, perseverance, dedication, devotion, sacrifice, love for the scriptures, and, above all, love for Gurudev keep the fires of motivation blazing.

...On her travels, Shanti met Ācāryas who were blessed with parents who understood the potency of Gurudev's teaching and its relevance to their lives. So powerful was the force of Gurudev's personality that, in some cases, even extended families were pulled into the expanding orb of the Mission. Even in Shanti's case her husband Gautam, both their children, Vivek and Radhika and in turn, their children, were all a part of Chinmaya Mission.

Of these Ācāryas, some blossomed through a direct connection with Gurudev, and some transformed through association with other Ācāryas. Shanti recorded glimpses of their childhood and thought-provoking stories of the influences that molded their lives. Wanting to share this inspiration with the growing generation, she instinctively turned to her teenage granddaughter Kirti, Radhika's child. The grandmother and granddaughter bonded really well.

Shanti discovered that, as children, these Ācāryas had unwittingly gravitated toward Gurudev, drawn by his love and charisma....

How Gurudev Kindled Love!

Sridhar *now* **Swami Dheerananda**: One day, when Sridhar was five, his mother told him that the Lord would be visiting them that day. Sridhar dearly loved his mother and implicitly trusted her word. So, when Gurudev walked into the house, he had no doubt — he was convinced that this was God!

This laid the foundation for his life, and the vibrations of the devoutly religious family surrounding him helped cement his conviction. The home reverberated with the sounds of mantra chanting and melodious bhajans. His parents and grandmother regaled him with fascinating stories from the *Rāmāyaṇa*, *Mahābhārata*, and the *Pañcatantra*.

In 1983, after completing his undergraduate education, Sridhar was led by destiny to a weeklong yajña conducted by Gurudev in Salem, Tamil Nadu. Gurudev's words aroused Sridhar's curiosity and nudged him to take the first tentative step in the quest of his own true identity. His seeking culminated in the donning of ochre robes.

May 8, 1993, was a memorable day for Br. Sudheer (Sridhar). At Gurudev's birthday celebrations, Gurudev invited the young

GURUDEV WITH SWAMI DHEERANANDA ▲

brahmachari to cut the birthday cake along with him. As Br. Sudheer curled his fingers around the handle of the knife, Gurudev covered it firmly with his own hand and, together, they sliced the cake. A few days later, Gurudev initiated Br. Sudheer into sannyās and Swami Dheerananda was born.

Reminiscing, Swami Dheerananda says, "The memory of Gurudev's powerful hand holding mine while cutting his birthday cake is a constant reminder that he lovingly takes care of me, firmly committing my BMI for his work!"

..."This is the power of love made manifest, my dear," said Shanti. "Gurudev effortlessly attracted these young people. And now they, in turn, are nurturing the children of today to be the leaders of tomorrow."....

Gurudev, My Father

When young teens were experimenting with the latest in fashion or keeping up with tidbits of gossip, Anusha, aged thirteen, was determining her future. She decided she wanted "to live, serve, and be in the Chinmaya Mission." For a person so young, a momentous decision indeed. But she knew her calling and is currently enrolled in the 15th Vedānta course at the Powai ashram.

Devastated by the loss of her father early in life, she was advised to see her father in Gurudev. From that day on, her sense of loss vanished. She had found her eternal father.

While pursuing a postgraduate degree in Management she discovered, "The focus was on how to manage others, whereas, the first lesson I learned from Pujya Gurudev was: *'You change and the world will change.'* The Management Program focused outside, never within."

Fascinated by Gurudev's early stints as a freedom fighter and journalist, her mind wondered, "What suddenly changed him from a common man into a Mahatma?" This single thought had enough impetus for her to be transformed!

— G. Anusha, CM Siddipet

Raju *now* **Swami Mitrananda**: Little Raju's earliest memory of Pujya Gurudev centers on a picture of Gurudev, which he saw on the BV altar as a three-year-old. Looking back, he says, "It was the most wonderful thing that BV did for me. His picture was established in the depth of my mind even before I met him. That early impression had a very strong influence."

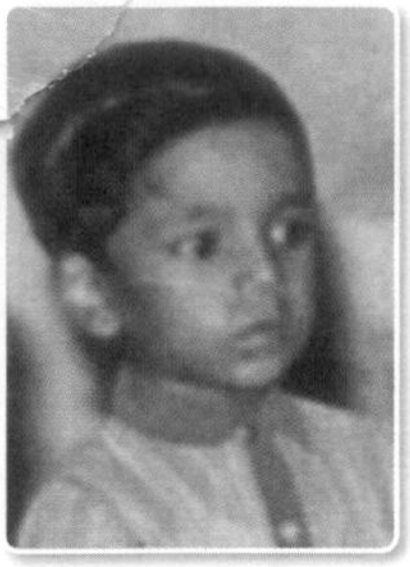
▲ RAJU

Raju's fond memories cluster around Gurudev's visits to Chennai. Gurudev, with his animated expressions and sound effects, brought many stories to life amid the BV children. On one such visit, Gurudev narrated the tale of the two birds drying up the ocean. For Raju, that has remained the most unforgettable story.

He could vividly recollect: Gurudev's eyes glowed as he described Garuḍa's golden wings, with arms outstretched to show their unimaginable expanse. Raju's eyes grew rounder by the minute as he listened in wonder and joy. Without his knowing, while his mind focused on the wings, the moral quietly slipped in to settle in his heart.

...Kirti's eyes also opened wide in wonder, more so because she had met and heard Swami Mitrananda speak at the Delhi center. She had really enjoyed the session and also the interaction thereafter....

The message in that story became indelibly etched in Raju's mind, and still acts as a beacon on his path: 'Keep Going. Don't Quit.'

This is the biggest lesson I learned at BV. It is difficult for me to quit because 'don't give up' is so firmly embedded in my mind. Once a goal is set, however elusive, whatever the setbacks, pain, and hardship — just keep working for it.

...Though Kirti was making no comments at this point, her body language was expressive enough. Shanti could sense that the message had found its target....

Lasting Saṁskāra

BV teachings certainly influence the choices made in life. For some, the link is direct and definite, for others it may be indirect and circuitous. In the case of K. S. Prakash, the former was true.

PRAKASH AT THE MASTER'S FEET ▲

K. S. Prakash *now* **Swami Chidrupananda**: From the second grade onward, holding onto his father's hand, K. S. Prakash was a regular at Gurudev's talks in Hyderabad. He was introduced to the world of spirituality at an age when most of his contemporaries were engaged in playing with marbles. He was fortunate to belong to a family of philosophers, steeped in spirituality, and deeply devoted to Gurudev.

Prakash was in a great hurry to leave behind the drudgery of a mundane existence and dedicate his life to serving his Guru. But Gurudev had other plans for him. He commanded, "Stay where you are — study and work hard."

Gurudev wished to ensure that Prakash would discharge his responsibilities as the first-born in the family. His father having already passed on, his mother needed his support. There was no question of going against Gurudev's wishes.

..."Nānī, Gurudev took care of not just his devotees. He made sure that their families were also taken care of," observed Kirti.

Shanti agreed, "That is correct, Kirti. The hallmark of the Chinmaya Mission ethos, is the emphasis on the family unit. We are constantly reminded that we must at all times be loving and respectful to all members of the family – not just the immediate family but also the extended world family**....**

SWAMI CHIDRUPANANDA ▲ SPEAKS FROM STRENGTH

So Prakash stayed home, completed his studies, and made sure his younger siblings were settled. He had now earned the right to surrender his life to the work of his Guru.

... Said Shanti, "On my trip to Mumbai, I met up with some students from the 15th batch of the Vedānta course, who began their association with Chinmaya Mission through BV. The thinking and the motivation that culminated in their pledging two years of their life to the dedicated study of Vedānta were diverse. The common running thread was: the conviction that this knowledge is special; this knowledge can transform; this knowledge must be shared**....**

▲ RAHUL AND PRIYA

Rahul Maini and **Priya Kumar:** They met at a youth camp and decided to tie the knot. Two years later, they took another decision and walked through the gates of Sandeepany Sadhanlaya, Mumbai. Following an inner calling, they chose to relocate half way across the world, to study Vedānta. Says Rahul, "India is completely different from the world in which we were born and reared. And the Powai ashram is at least 75% different from the rest of India!"

Reared in the BV tradition, in the U.S., Rahul became an active participant in the activities of CHYK West. A camp, under the leadership of Achārya Vivek, proved to be a life-turning experience. "For the first time I heard Vedānta from someone who competently, coherently and eloquently spoke about it in the same language as my own."

Priya's entire life has also revolved around BV. She says, "For youth growing in the U.S., in a non-Indian environment, BV has imparted the strength to be proud of our heritage. Being different from everybody else it is important for children of the Indian diaspora to have a sense of self-esteem."

After graduating from college, she began teaching the Tenth and Twelfth Grades in BV thinking that it would be a cakewalk. But to her dismay, "I discovered serious gaps in my knowledge. The easy flow was missing. The realization that I did not know enough of the basics of Vedānta was a huge eye-opener. To be a competent teacher I needed to know much more. This was the motivation that brought us to Powai, Mumbai."

As they grew, they learnt more about the Vedānta course - trickles of information, turned into a waterfall. Fortunately, both Priya and Rahul felt that this was the best juncture in their lives to study Vedānta seriously. Rahul says, "To pass up an opportunity to do something like this seemed almost sinful. It took some guts to take the plunge, but it seems to be the correct decision."

Priya and Rahul are not sure of what the future holds; for now, their focus is on the study of Vedānta. Of one thing they are certain: going forward they want to serve the Mission and concentrate on the youth by being role models for them!

CHAITANYA ▲

Chaitanya: As a student, Chaitanya was faced with the prospect of supporting a family that was going through a financial downturn. Realizing the futility of making big money as an employee, he opted for the export business.

However, very soon he understood that small-time exporters do not have easy choices, and the path to quick success often meant compromising with instilled value systems. This led to a inner conflict.

Br. Shailesh (now Swami Siddheshananda) advised him to start a business based on values that could be sustained in the long run. This changed Chaitanya's thought patterns, and a desire arose in him to aim for the highest. He then embarked on a daring exploration — the possibility of enrolling for the Vedānta course in Powai.

In the face of strong resistance from his family, he somehow held onto his resolve. Chaitanya says, "I am not sure how this happened, but my family now supports my decision and is proud of the path I have chosen. When we dedicate our life to the Lord's work. He makes sure that all our responsibilities are taken care of!"

SUSHANT BHIDE ▲

Sushant Bhide: In contrast, Chaitanya's classmate, Sushant, had total support from his mother when he announced his decision to enroll for the Vedānta course. An only child, he had listened to discourses by Ācāryas of the Mission since he was three years old.

His mother Savita says, "Even as a young child, Sushant was never a passive spectator. He would listen carefully, absorb, and then ask pertinent questions. I am proud of the way my son has turned out, and I am happy that he has joined the Vedānta course."

On his arrival at the Powai ashram, he called home and announced, "I have reached my destination. I am comfortably settled and look forward to doing what I am here for!"

Nadessen Apavou: Born and reared in the Reunion Islands, Nadessen is a French speaking citizen of the islands. For him the journey to Sandeepany Sadhanalaya, Powai has been a daring adventure.

His mother is an active member of the Mission and so Nadessen's involvement with BV began early in life. He says, "I have been in the Mission since birth. Initially I had to be pushed to attend the BV camps but once there I remember being very happy. When I was young the

▲ NADESSEN APAVOU

BV activities in the Reunion Islands were not too structured but despite that they left a deep impression."

During a stressful time at University he says, "I fell back on Gurudev's books. They spell stability for me. Now in Powai, the connection with him has been further cemented through his videos."

For Nadessen grappling with a foreign language, "The big issue is to be able to assimilate what I am here to assimilate. In the future I hope to continue to pass on Gurudev's message to the children of tomorrow!"

... Shanti said, "Interestingly Vivek Gupta completed the Vedānta course at Sandeepany Sadhanalaya and then opted to work for the Mission, but not as a brahmachārī in yellow clothes. That is why he is known as Ācārya Vivek.

This is yet another instance of Gurudev's openness. Guruji also carries forward the tradition of accepting each individual as he or she is and the importance of the family. When Vivek married, Chinmaya Mission added one more person to its ranks of committed workers — his wife, Sheela."**....**

▲ ĀCĀRYA VIVEK

Vivek Gupta: Ācārya Vivek does not see a direct connection between the influence of BV and his decision to become an Ācārya for the Mission. However, he admits that BV led him to a Family Camp, which in turn, stirred in him a desire to serve at CORD, Sidhbari.

Says Ācārya Vivek: "At Sidhbari, I was exposed to the Mission's Vedāntic training for the first time. This seed remained and inspired me to join the Vedānta Course in Mumbai, after which I became what I am today."

Soon after his arrival in Sidhbari in 1999, to serve at the CORD facility, Vivek was gripped with loneliness. He was away from home in unfamiliar surroundings: "More than anything, I wanted to pack my bags and head home, to the known and secure."

Fortunately memory came to his rescue and his mind chanted Pujya Gurudev's words: *"This Too Shall Pass!"*

Courage grew, and with it the conviction that, given time, he would be comfortable with the situation. He stayed, and when he completed his seven weeks of sevā, he was so relaxed and felt so at home that he did not want to leave!

For Ācārya Vivek, the world is an open learning university under the blue skies. The story of Lord Dattātreya and His twenty-four Gurus, heard at BV, is the torchlight that illuminates his path. Alert to the underlying messages that come his way, he readily imbibes the knowledge they contain. He gratefully acknowledges: "This story taught me to be a student of life, ever ready to learn from all."

Ācārya Vivek believes that the inculcation of Vedāntic teachings, early in life, is the most appealing aspect of BV. He says, "This knowledge grounds one among the ever-changing objects, beings, and situations that constitute 'Life.' By the practice of this subtle technique of living, we come to live the potent and powerful motto of BV — Keep Smiling!"

BR. KEDAR ▲

Chetan Shigaonkar *now* **Br. Kedar**: Chetan joined BV in sixth grade and followed the Chinmaya route to Yuva Kendra. He believes that though not the sole reason for his being an Ācārya, the saṁskāras imbided in BV have helped in his inner journey.

A humorous approach and an easy demeanor draw the child brigade to Br. Kedar. He declares: "I like to take BV classes because, temperamentally, I am comfortable with children and they are also happy to be with me. The summer camps are my happiest times because there is the complete joy of bonding with the children."

He believes that the children should be accepted as they are. Acceptance opens the doors to love and understanding. The children reciprocate fully and are receptive to the teachings and so transformation happens.

AT A BV CAMP SURROUNDED BY HAPPY CAMPERS ▼

The Chinmaya Bond

Sidhu: Currently pursuing the 15th Vedānta course at Sandeepany Sadhanalaya, Mumbai, Sidhu confides: "The only organization I have ever been associated with is the Chinmaya Mission! For me, school and BV began simultaneously. After joining CHYK, I worked at Chinmaya International Foundation (Kerala), and the only interview I ever appeared for was the one in connection with the Vedānta course. My whole life has revolved around the Mission."

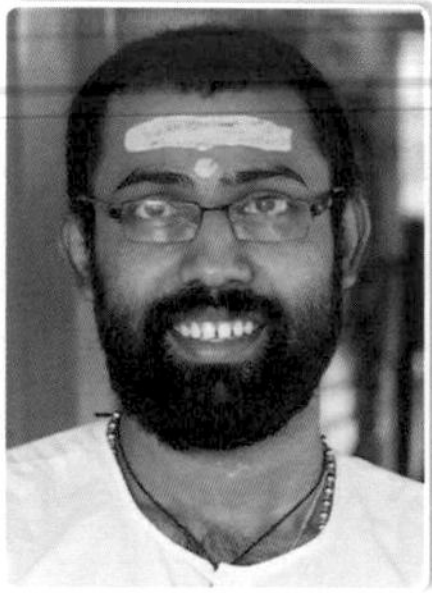

▲ SIDHU

Gurudev visited Sidhu's village in Kerala. As a four-year old this is his earliest memory of the Master. Later the connection with Gurudev was strengthened by an anecdote he heard in class six:

The story goes that Gurudev directed a devotee who was to catch a flight to postpone his trip until the next day. The devotee was unwilling to change his plans but relented on Gurudev's insistence. The next day's newspapers stunned the country with news of the plane's crash. All aboard the ill-fated aircraft had perished. The devotee went around proclaiming that Gurudev had saved his life. When questioned by a reporter, Gurudev dismissed any foreknowledge of the tragedy and said, "Had I known, would I not have saved 359 lives?" Sidhu was impressed that Gurudev did not wish to deceive the public with self-proclaimed miracles — and a lifelong devotion was born!

Jay Tarkas *now* **Swami Swatmananda:** In the life of Jay Tarkas, his grandfather Yashwant Tarkas played the pivotal role of mentor. Jay's grandfather was actively involved in CM Chennai, and Jay, his siblings and cousins all benefitted from exposure to the BV classes conducted in their home.

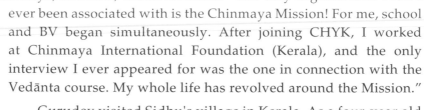

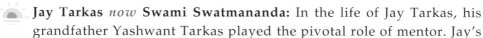

▲ SWAMI SWATMANANDA

But for Jay where did the turning point come? He admits, "Perhaps the very first turn was made in 1991 in Sidhbari." An inspired Jay wrote a camp report which greatly pleased Gurudev and he forwarded it to *Tapovan Prasad* for publication.

Then during a subsequent camp in Kodaikanal, he learnt of the beauty of Indian culture and the derelict straits it was in.

A powerful promise arose in his mind. He resolved, "to work for the resurrection of this ancient and highly evolved culture!"

..."Just like I gained from the BV class you ran in your home," interjected Kirti. "You were my role model, Nānī. No, you actually still are!"....

TEACHING WHAT HE LIKES BEST ▲

A privileged child, Jay often had the opportunity to chant for Gurudev and, later, for Guruji. Jay's familiarity with Sanskrit and the chanting of Vedic mantras helped him greatly in his studies in the Vedānta course.

My Friend Gopal

Ganesh's elder sister attended BV regularly and implored her younger sibling to join on his own. But this was an exercise in futility. For Ganesh, Sunday afternoons were prime playtime. So why would he do anything other than play?

GANESH ALL SET ▲ FOR SCHOOL

Then, one fateful day, his sister decided for him, and he found himself going with his sister to a BV class led by Brni. Smriti (now Swamini Vimalananda).

At BV Ganesh 'met' Gopal and this became the turning point.

The widow in the tale told her little boy, "Son, whenever you are scared, call out loudly with love for your elder brother, Gopal. He will come to you and never let you down."

The boy in the story implicitly believed his mother and was rewarded with the companionship of Lord Kṛṣṇa as Gopal Bhaiyā!

That day our Ganesh discovered an unusual friend. He learned that the Lord could be contacted by merely calling out to Him — "Gopal, Gopal!"

And when Ganesh called with complete faith, a miracle happened: he felt as if Gopal was by his side!

Ganesh *now* **Br. Atharvana:** A product of the BV system, Ganesh gathered gemstones from his learning — like confidence in public speaking, the artistry of poetry, and the value of self-discipline. Now as Br. Atharvana, an Ācārya of the Mission, he carries effortlessly the

▲ BR. ATHARVANA

responsibility of the CM Ahmedabad center because of his deep faith in his childhood friend Gopal.

To work full time as a brahmachārī was not a conscious decision that Br. Atharvana made one fine day. It emerged through an evolving process. Despite youthful distractions, the strong childhood saṁskāras helped to mold his personality. He realized, "This is what I want to do in life. This is where I belong."

... Kirti looked thoughtful, as if trying to fit pieces of a jigsaw puzzle in her mind. Then she said, "Is this the same Ganesh Bhaiyā who had once helped conduct a Summer Camp in Delhi?"

"Yes," said Shanti. "You are right! I had completely forgotten about that. I am glad you reminded me. That was before he joined the Vedānta course in Powai. He was then wearing white clothes. He is now a brahmacārī wearing yellow robes."**....**

Youthful Role Models

... Kirti responded, "Nānī, have you noticed that nearly all of these Ācāryas interact easily with the younger members of the Chinmaya family, perhaps as a spinoff from their childhood experiences? They know how BV or Yuva Kendra children feel and are able to give them what they need. In one way or another, they have a serious commitment to BV and Yuva Kendra."**....**

Swami Mitrananda: Clearly Swami Mitrananda's greatest interest lies in training the youth. He has served the All India Yuva Kendra in many capacities and continues to serve as its Director. The Youth Empowerment Program (YEP) is part of the impressive list of projects he has promoted. Saluting Gurudev's foresight, he believes that by recognizing this innate urge for self-transformation, Gurudev created platforms and infrastructure for future generations, making the process a whole lot easier. YEP was started as a platform for young people wanting to serve.

Refusing to take credit for the achievements of the program, Swami Mitrananda says, "It is a success because the participants have a passion for the cause."

Swami Chidrupananda: In his past, when the young man was still known as Prakash, Gurudev once commanded him: "Take Care of the Youth!" That was enough for Prakash. He knew in which direction his future lay. Engaged in setting lofty goals for the youthful cadres, he never missed an opportunity to interact with them. At the time of this writing, he is the Director AICHYK (All India Chinmaya Yuva Kendra), North Zone.

Swami Swatmananda: Surrounded by youngsters, Swami Swatmananda can often be seen at the Powai ashram, meticulously planning or rehearsing for some forthcoming event. Every year for three months, along with Swami Mitrananda, he trains the volunteers of the Youth Empowerment Program (YEP).

YEPSTERS WITH SWAMIS MITRANANDA AND SWATMANANDA ▲

... Kirti was a keen and attentive listener – a trait imbibed through BV. As always, even now, she was listening carefully, absorbing and assessing. She knew about YEP and had often thought of dedicating a year of her life to the service of the Mission. She now shared her inner plans with her grandmother.

"Nānī," said Kirti, "YEP has always fascinated me and I have often considered signing up for it, at some point. Do you think it is a good idea?"

Shanti responded, "Yes Kirti, this program provides a perfect platform for sevā. The years of youth are most suited for imbibing the value of service, for then there are many more years of useful contribution available to the individual.

Young people associated with this program have made significant, selfless contributions to the world. Ganesh's life could serve as a case study."**....**

Spotlight on Bala Vihar

Ganesh: His mantras are: "I am CM" and "Keep smiling." His spiritual travels began as a BV child. As a Chinmaya youth he was motivated by YEP and belongs to the first batch of Yuva Veers (alumni of the Youth Empowerment Program). Years of working actively in the Mission then led him to join the Powai ashram for the serious study of Vedānta.

▲ GANESH

For Ganesh, the persona of Gurudev epitomises the gamut of values he wishes to emulate. Punctuality, work ethics, frugal living, excellence at all levels, unselfish service and patriotism are qualities he has tried to imbibe. His greatest wealth is the realisation that it is important to understand the scriptures, follow the Guru-śiṣya paramparā and spread this knowledge to the maximum number of people.

Ganesh claims that the love he received molded him into the person he is today. He remembers it as being special, genuine, and undemanding. This exposure makes sharing effortless, more so with children. In the last ten years, he has helped with over hundred children's camps! His motivation expresses as: "The love in their hearts, the shine in their eyes and the warmth of their hugs."

Passionately devoted to BV, he feels that this is an important aspect of the Chinmaya Mission. Its teachings, necessary to building strong communities and nations, are especially relevant for a demographically young country like India. He says: "Our focus should be on the young - in accordance with their backgrounds. Children from villages and towns have to be dealt with differently. The former have more love but lack information, whereas the latter are inundated with information but need more love."

Having served in the villages of Tamil Nadu and Andhra Pradesh, he knows, "Children respond differently according to the area, time and circumstance. So ideally, teaching modules should cater to all these needs. As opposed to cities, the potential for conducting BV camps and other activities in villages is tremendous.

Ganesh says: "If we focus on transforming the lives of children, their parents will automatically be attracted; by impacting one life, many more will follow. To begin with, Gurudev made a difference in a few lives, and then millions followed. The key is to touch the hearts of people. That is what BV is all about - to bring the light of life to the child!"

Knowledge Through Osmosis

The transfer of knowledge takes place in diverse ways — through conventional or unorthodox situations. We learn in the classroom, in the home, and also on the playing field. Children learn whether they are seated on the lap of a grandparent, having a serious but innocent exchange of views with friends, or when confronted by the challenges of life.

GURUDEV WITH THE PRAKASAM FAMILY ▲

The four children of Śrī and Smt. C. G. Prakasam were indeed very fortunate. They never attended a formal BV class but nonetheless received the same training. Of the four siblings, Swami Advayananda and Brni. Shruti now serve the Mission as Ācāryas. In the photograph alongside, they are seated at Gurudev's feet.

...Shanti told Kirti how she had met Brni. Shruti at a camp in Kolwan and was amazed at how Saraswathy and her siblings had effortlessly assimilated the knowledge of the Vedas — a testimony to the power of satsaṅga! The transfer of knowledge had happened subconsciously by spending time in yajñaśālās and divine company....

Saraswathy *now* **Brni. Shruti:** Along with the other children, Saraswathy was exposed to the scriptures at a very young age. Brni. Shruti says: "Almost every other day an Ācārya from the Mission would be at our home for bhikṣā. They used this time productively by teaching us to chant. Very soon, we memorized the various Upaniṣads: Kena, Muṇḍaka, Māṇḍūkya, and Kaivalya. And also learned several other popularly chanted Vedic mantras and hymns. The next logical step was learning Sanskrit, which also happened naturally."

Brni. Shruti simply summed up their extraordinary journey by saying, "The Study Group classes of Chinmaya Mission and our association with the Ācāryas became our BV classes!"

Listen to My Children Chant!

At a camp in Sidhbari, Pujya Gurudev once asked the devotees gathered there: "How many of you have listened to Kenopaniṣad from me?" Many hands went up.

Then he asked: "How many of you have listened to Kaivalya Upaniṣad from me?" Again many hands were raised.

"How many of you know Kaivalya Upaniṣad by heart?" All hands came down.

With pride in his voice and a beaming countenance, he announced, "Now, listen to my children chant Kaivalya Upaniṣad!"

..."The power of her memory must be very strong to be able to chant verbatim so many Upaniṣads," said Kirti

"Yes," replied her grandmother. Memory is like any other instrument or limb of the body. If it is trained properly, it gives good service for a lifetime. Gurudev is remembered for his razor-sharp memory. Swami Tapovan Maharaj, his Guru, agreed to teach him on one condition — every lesson would be taught just once and he had to retain whatever had been taught! Gurudev kept his side of the bargain and we all know the result!"....

Ambalavanan *now* **Swami Advayananda:** Śrī Prakasam, Swami Advayananda's father played an important role in the lives of all his children and this grooming led to Ambalavanan's decision to join the Vedānta course.

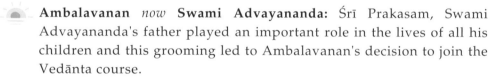

▲ GRACE FLOWS TO AMBALAVANAN

Swami Advayananda says: "My father took a close interest in our learning. When I was in the seventh grade, instead of sending me on the school trip, he took me to something better — a jñāna yajña at Chinmaya Gardens, Coimbatore. This was my first exposure to Gurudev at a camp.

I was the youngest person at the camp and I took notes the entire time. Even then, at that age, Gurudev's words made complete sense.

'You are not the body, you are apart from the body,' said Gurudev. This powerful statement left a strong and lasting impression.

▲ SWAMI ADVAYANANDA

Gurudev's personality was a tremendous, magnetic force and exerted a pull. But, it was when I was in the eleventh grade, at Gurudev's camp in Sidhbari, that I recognized my desire to join the āśrama and study Vedānta. This was the decisive moment, the final call!"

The experience extraordinaire of the Prakasam siblings establishes that exposure to the timelessness of Vedānta can never start too early.

Swami Advayananda observes: "We should not assume that young children will not understand. They may not comprehend the in-depth meaning, but they will imbibe what is necessary in their own way. The seeds, having been sown, will sprout when the situation is conducive. So, give them the exposure."

• A THOUSAND-MILE JOURNEY BEGINS WITH THE FIRST STEP •

...Shanti concluded, "Kirti, the next time we meet, remind me to tell you the stories about the experiences of sevaks. It is equally fascinating to watch the evolution of parents into sevaks. Many committed sevaks followed this route. Drawn to BV because of their children, they have stayed to become the backbone of this program."....

Bala Perspectives

Hello, My Dear Friend God. A friend in need is a friend indeed. So you must take care of me, your poor friend on earth. Give my regards to your wife and love to children. – a BV child

XVIII

Gratitude Flows

Love for the goal fosters the desire to serve. Service deepens understanding. When understanding matures into wisdom, life is filled with an eagerness to give back.

The majority of active BV sevaks currently working to make the program flourish were parents who came with an initial desire to expose their children to a rare teaching, but without complete knowledge of its depth or its beauty.

Then some of those parents realized that their children would benefit more by their own involvement in BV. Also, they became aware of how they, too, would evolve by teaching in the program. So, they joined hands with the Mission and stayed to become the life breath of the movement — privileged to bring to life Gurudev's vision for the future.

...It was obvious to Shanti that the roots of BV were made strong by the ever-growing gratitude of the various people involved in the program. She shared with her granddaughter the countless lifelines of the BV program — the sevaks and parents who came, believed, and then strived to give back.

Shanti recollected how Guruji had outlined the process of a sevak's involvement at the BV sevaks' camp held in Chinmaya Vibhooti (May 2009). He had remarked....

When we start a class, the sevaks and children also come. Somebody takes the lead, and others follow. So the first role of a BVsevak is of an initiator. Try it! Second, to facilitate the learning process, the sevak becomes a facilitator. Organization at various levels is required to make smooth progress of the class possible. To be successful, sevaks must be endowed with the qualities of fortitude (dhṛiti), enthusiasm (utsāha), and patience (samanvitaḥ).

When the process sometimes loses momentum, a sevak also has to act as an accelerator to quicken the pace. An accelerator is a motivator, whose presence helps bring movement to the slackening class. This is the third role that a BV sevak is called upon to play.

Finally, when the children are happy and have learned what we set out to teach them, the goal is accomplished. There should be an overall sense of achievement for all concerned, not for the sevak alone. Then the sevak becomes an accomplished person. It is of paramount importance that the sevak does not lose sight of the fact that, at the personal level, he or she remains a devotee of the Lord and worships Him through this process of sevā.

...Shanti could relate to the journey of the sevak that had both enriched and exhausted many aspects of her inner self. She recalled Gurudev's words of inspiration from an address to BV sevaks in Bengaluru, copied from the notes of Uma B. Nagenddra, a senior sevikā who was present at that speech....

Gurudev had remarked:

- Politicians of a country work, keeping the next five years in mind. Diplomats work, keeping the next ten years in mind. Statesmen work, keeping the next twenty-five years in mind. And all of you BV sevikās, whether you know it or not, are working like statesmen. You are molding the next generation! It takes twenty-five years to see the result of the work you are doing today. When your child comes back to you after twenty-five years as a young adult, and declares that the values instilled by you helped him or her to grow to the present status, you will be able to see the fulfillment of your work.

GURUDEV WITH BENGALURU SEVAKS IN 1991 ▲

...Beginning with just a few, Shanti had witnessed the phenomenal growth of an army of sevaks from the ranks of the parents. Many a parent-turned-sevak spoke or wrote enthusiastically about how teaching BV had enriched their lives....

BV and Study Groups have a symbiotic relationship. Sometimes, parents develop a stronger connection with the Study Group because their children are attending BV. In other cases, parents exposed to Study Groups realize that BV provides a balanced, growth forum for their children.

Ritual to Existential

Once our first born entered BV it soon became a Sunday ritual in our home. As we moved through the annual cycle of festivals, my son would come home with Kṛṣṇa's peacock feather or his little clay Gaṇeśa. He learned to dance the garba at Navarātri and to light a diya for Divālī. With each celebration, his repertoire of stories grew and, through them, he grew, too.

▲ THE NATESANS

When his little sister was born, her introduction to BV began as we both waited outside the class. Before long, it was time for her also to start BV. She lisped her way through the ślokas and built a little circle of 'sakhīs' (girl friends).

Soon I decided to volunteer as a sevak. Only then did I realize the true value of this program. It makes children think; it makes children question. As the questions progressed to the more existential issues, I learned that it is the teacher who becomes the learner.

— Sivagami Natesan, CM Austin

Like many parents, Anita and Satyadev Dodia were overwhelmed when they realized how much their children had gained from BV. They were inspired to give back by actively being a part of the program. Three members of the Dodia family currently serve as BV teachers! Anita observed, "Many times in class the children come up with analogies that make me think outside the box. It is very instructive." — Anita Dodia CM Austin

◀ THE DODIA FAMILY

THE TEACHING TEACHES

...Shanti said to Shraddha, "Sometimes sevaks mistakenly believe that they are doing the children a service. The ego pitches in with, 'I am teaching these children.' Gurudev was quick to clear such misconceptions."....

He admonished Premila Modi in Hyderabad: "You are not teaching them; you are learning from them." Immediately, she realized, "Through teaching comes personal growth."

...BV sevaks agreed wholeheartedly that they received more than what they gave at every class. This sentiment was voiced consistently and severally....

BRENT COY WITH HIS STUDENTS ▲

I was drawn to teaching because I enjoyed being around children. Also, I quickly realized that the best way for me to learn about Hinduism was to teach it to others. With their wonderful curiosity and keen sense of observation, the children keep me alert and humble.

This particular incident captures the ongoing learning perfectly. One day, a young boy in my class asked, "Brent Uncle, are you a Hindu?" Some what caught off guard, I started answering his question with a lengthy answer full of philosophic nuances. "Well, I wasn't born in India, but I try to follow the Hindu philosophy, rituals, and so on."

The boy shook his head in exasperation and asked again, "Brent Uncle! Yes or no? Are you a Hindu?"

Realizing my mistake, I simply stated, "Yes, I am a Hindu."

A simple question taught me many important principles. When working with children, teach to their level of understanding; don't confuse the main issue with unnecessary details. Be secure in who you are and in your beliefs. It raises the higher notion of "Who am I?" a favorite question of the great Master, Ramana Maharishi. Much can be learned from teaching and maintaining our own childlike curiosity.

— Brent Coy, CM Ann Arbor

It is not just about what you teach the children; it is also about what the children teach you. — Preeti Pathak, CM Kolkata

The most important teaching that comes from children is 'Nothing is impossible.' — Ganesh, CM Chennai

I took a year off from teaching, thinking I should focus more on my sādhanā and use the time to attend classes instead of conducting them. That year, I hardly attended lectures and classes. Then wisdom dawned and I realized that teaching at BV is my sādhanā.

— Sharanya Rao, CM Austin

...The advantages of increased involvement in the Mission became apparent to the parent-sevaks. In her informal chat sessions with sevaks worldwide, Shraddha gathered that they were happy to be spiritually linked to the enormous, global Chinmaya family. The sense of belonging, of connecting with like-minded individuals, is an unsought boon....

As we attended the Sunday classes, we started to like the discourses and made good friends. In no time, it became very apparent that our Mission is more about growing together, about courage and strength, and about being a family bound to each other with love and respect, praying together, attending satsaṅgas together, and looking at ways for spiritual growth. — Anil Kishore, CM Washington

...Shanti said, "Shraddha, I came across many instances that showcase how BV achieves effortlessly what parents take pains to inculcate! This is the power of external reinforcement. See how these two little girls absorbed the learning."....

Prasana and Rohini Iyengar's two young girls began to question the practice of daily prayer at home.

Rohini said, "Making them do something because 'I do it...' wasn't going to work. We were unable to provide a comprehensible reason for them to follow." The girls were enrolled for BV and as a by-product, the parents joined Vedānta classes. The results came fast. Through BV's introduction of "Gaṇeśa says..."and Kṛṣṇa stories, God made a subtle, yet overt, appearance. At dinner, four months or so after her first BV class, the older sibling admonished her younger sister, "Don't waste your food, Kṛṣṇa won't be happy…"

The parents were taken aback, because they had never used that line of reasoning at home before. It was conclusive proof of the role that BV had played in their daughter's perspective.

— Rohini Iyengar, CM San Jose

THE IYENGARS ▲

The ABCD of Prayer

Prayer is a common practice that children are frequently asked to follow, for which parents are seldom able to offer explanations, as they themselves lack the necessary knowledge.

To fill this knowledge gap, CM Sydney organized a gurukula-style residential camp for children ages eight to fifteen years (April 1994). The aim of the camp was to create awareness about the ritual of prayer. Pravina Rachakonda, the key organizer of the camp recollected the impact:

Initally, the task was daunting because my husband and I had to be foster parents to about twenty campers for a week.

The children were taught to propitiate the various dieties, to recite and memorize hymns and ślokas, to understand their meaning, and to prepare the altar for pūjās.Very soon they delighted us by intoning the ślokas in the correct meter and with the right pronunciation. They not only enjoyed the repetition but also liked leading the chanting sessions. Projects relating to what they had learned reinforced the learning.

Children being children, it was not all smooth sailing. The challenge was to motivate the quiet ones and to deal with the pranksters. There was even the danger of a bushfire when one of the boys showed off his newfound knowledge to make fire from sunlight using a lens!

At the convocation on the last day of the camp, parents were pleasantly surprised by their children's performance and the knowledge they had acquired in just a few days. The camp resulted in a win-win situation. The children left better equipped to perform their daily prayers and the sevaks were grateful for the opportunity to serve.

— Pravina Rachakonda, CM Sydney

Service Any Place, Any Time

Traveling around the world, with her diplomat husband, Kumkum Bhatia was embraced by the large CM family. With the inspiration and loving guidance of Guruji and other Swamins, she encouraged and actively helped BVs in Toronto, Nairobi and Johannesburg, and started new ones in Yangon and Mexico City.

Kumkum recollects, 'With fifty children attending the BV classes, the walls of historic India House in Yangon would reverberate with the chanting of Hanumān Cālīsā! Each class was a wonderful learning experience. Once, when the little ones were asked why Lord Viṣṇu was blue in colour, a bright-eyed girl responded promptly: "Because God is asking us to look after the environment!"

▲ KUMKUM BHATIA

BV classes would culminate in joyous Divālī celebrations when the children would present a skit on the *Rāmāyaṇa* at the Embassy auditorium. "Somehow, all the girls wanted to be monkeys, while the boys insisted on being in Rāvaṇa's army! It was exhilarating to see even the most shy and introvert children perform their roles to perfection," adds Kumkum.

Cricket was a passion, which the children enjoyed after class in the sprawling lawns of the ambassador's residence. During an intense, action-packed match between India and Pakistan, Kumkum was certain that no one would turn up for the class. But not a single child was absent. Surprised though pleased, she asked them, "Didn't you want to watch the match?" Pat came the reply in unison, "Yes, but this is more important!"

In some places the BV classes stopped after Kumkum left, but she is keenly aware of their value and positive impact, "Saplings planted with care and love produce flowers that are a joy forever."

— Kumkum Bhatia, CM Delhi

...At one point, Shraddha voiced a nagging doubt. She asked Shanti, "Ma, how is it that despite the study of Vedānta and the sādhanā of teaching in BV, misgivings about rightful duties still surface?"Shanti replied, "It is to clear these that a Guru is required. Gurudev in a single sentence could clear the mists of doubt. His crisp message to members of CM Washington is a beauty!"....

Straighten The Record!

...Arvind Bhagwat, vividly remembers how Gurudev once dealt with the doubts of his sevaks. In just a few words Gurudev deftly delivered a profound teaching....

GURUDEV WITH THE BHAGWATS ▲

In the early days of BV, the Mission had just acquired its own property in the Washington, D.C. area, and there were about fifty children enrolled in the program. Coincidentally, around the same time (fall of 1989–1990) the Ramakrishna Mission (RKM) Washington chapter also began their activities, which focused more on adults. On one occasion, RKM scheduled its two-day retreat and requested CM Washington to help by conducting activities for their children.

We did not know exactly how to respond to this atypical request. And so we sent a letter to Pujya Gurudev in India seeking his permission to do this 'favor.' Three weeks passed and the RKM organizers were anxious for a confirmation, while we awaited Gurudev's response. The year being 1989, we had none of the modern technology that would let us communicate instantly.

A day before the camp was scheduled to begin, Gurudev's telegram arrived from Melbourne. It read: *"Grab the opportunity to serve the Lord!"*

Our confused minds thought we were doing a favor to RKM, but Gurudev set the record straight and taught us to take it as an opportunity to serve. His message was clear — it is not 'they,' but the Lord we are serving. It is a privilege to serve the Lord. Grab every opportunity on the way! — Arvind Bhagwat, CM Washington D.C.

...On another occasion, Jyoti Raj, during a Skype session with Shraddha, shared the story of how she was assailed by doubt, even after so many years of being in the Mission. She turned to Guruji for reassurance....

Jyoti asked: "Guruji, while working as a sevak, have I neglected my family in any way? Have I in any way not served my own children properly? I know these are foolish thoughts but...."

There was no ambiguity in Guruji's rejoinder,"You are doing His work and He will do your work."

Hearing those words, Jyoti's doubts vanished. She learned to believe fully in the great work that had been entrusted to her.

...Shanti thoughtfully observed: "As we evolve, the impurities of our mind surface as fears and reservations. This shows that the conviction is not a hundred percent and must be remedied, because anything less will not help us achieve the goal of Self-realization."

On the spiritual path implicit faith in the words of the scriptures and the Guru are the prerequisites to progress. Having found the right teacher the student must remain steadfast and obey all instructions....

The Unwilling Teacher

For each one the Master has a plan, which is revealed step by step. In this every player plays a role distinct from that of any other. In her growing years as a BV child and later as a young adult, Padma Jaishinghani was being molded for what was to come.

At Gurudev's insistence Padma studied for her B. Ed. degree but before the exams, she went to pieces. She was taken to Gurudev. He just held her hand and said, "You just go and sit for the examination. I will write for you." She emerged with a 1st class degree. And this young lady who told her examiners, "I don't want to be a teacher but am destined to be a teacher," became a teacher!

Today the Chinmaya Nursery School, in Mumbai, has Padma in the driving seat. In one of her interactions with Gurudev, Padma recalls him telling her, "Don't you ever say you are going to leave my school. If you do I will drop you in the Arabian Sea!"

THE HIGHEST INSPIRATION

Over the years, multitudes have given unstintingly of their time and energy to the BV movement. Their commitment, enthusiasm, and perseverance are truly heroic. The nobler the motivation, the more inspired are the actions. A prolific writer, Gurudev's letters helped to set lofty standards and elevated goals for his devotees. Some excerpts....

To Bharati Sukhatankar: It is only when the inspiration springs from a point higher than the subtle intellect, when it floods out from spiritual beauty and vitality that the work becomes a blessing to the generations afterwards.

The body inspiration of the wrestlers, the mental inspiration of poets, the intellect inspiration of the politicians, the greater intellect inspiration of scientists, and the subtle intellect inspiration of artists are all great. But the greatest of them all is the one whose inspiration is from the Self, the Infinite. Such a one is an A+ wrestler, an A+ poet, an A+ politician, an A+ scientist, and an A+ artist.

To Bharati Sukhatankar: When you decide to serve them as their ideal you are also caught up with an ideal to live by. Every time you are morose, quarrelsome, bad tempered, dejected, egoistic, vainful, disobedient, foul-mouthed, you start catching yourself napping. An ideal of others cannot afford it. This is the sweet tragedy of those who live in society and grow to be an ideal for a few. Look at my trouble!! Would you dare share it with me? I have already sown seeds of admiration in the children.

To Manisha Khemlani: Give my love to the children and give each a bear Hug from me. I love them. Surely bring them all to Versova during the session there.

Very happy to hear that you are happy in your work. Remember Lord of the body is He in your heart and let him thro' you give relief and remove all discomfort of your patients.

GURUDEV WITH MANISHA ▲

To Miss M. Ranjini Shastri: Please judge my children lovingly. They are just children. But judge the group leaders harshly — they have to keep a very high spiritual beauty.

Thy own self

Hooked to the Ideal

... Gurudev sowed the seeds, which his army of inspired sevaks have nurtured, giving selflessly of their time and effort. Shanti realized that only a higher altar can keep the levels of motivation elevated over long periods of time**....**

▲ ARUNA NATARAJ

Since we moved to the San Francisco Bay Area in 1998, I have been teaching BV and have missed just two classes in all these years. This is because I witness a miracle every Sunday. I always plan my class but then end up saying much more that was totally unplanned. Incidents from life, jokes and riddles all effortlessly enhance the original story. There is a feeling that someone else is speaking through me. This leaves me fulfilled and I love witnessing this wonder every week. — Aruna Nataraj, CM San Jose

During the first couple of years of my exposure to Vedāntic lectures, I was quite indifferent. Later when my enthusiasm for Vedānta and Chinmaya Mission Study Groups was evident, Ācārya Sharada Kumar asked me to be a substitute teacher and shortly after came the opportunity to become a regular teacher. I still vividly remember the hours I spent practicing with tape-recorded ślokas, trying to get the Sanskrit pronunciation right.

▲ JOHN WIERSBA

To keep my attitude infused with love, before each class, I mentally recite and visualize Guruji's prayer, "BV is my temple, Children are my God, Teaching is my worship, Vision of God is my reward." — John Wiersba, CM Ann Arbor

The One as Many

... Through the varied experiences of fellow BV sevaks, Shraddha understood that, gradually and inevitably, sevā brings a complete transformation in the relationship of the sevak with the family, with the world and most importantly, with God**....**

Just as a thermostat aids in controlling the temperature of the room, Gurudev's teachings help me to delve within and adjust my inner equipment. I have learned that the only change that is needed in this world is my attitude alone.

— Anupama Bathala, CM Princeton

GURUJI WITH THE BATHALAS ▲

The one resounding message of BV is devotion to God — make Him the underwriter of your life. Gurudev's message has been a great source of strength and inspiration over the years: "Surrender and serve. Discover the joy of service by placing at His feet not your achievements but only the sense thereof. It costs you nothing but brings you everything."

— Ashok Grandhee, CM Ann Arbor

GURUJI WITH ASHOK GRANDHEE ▲

Through the experience of BV, I learned that God manifests in special ways. He surfaces as inspiration, as the innocence of the children whom He cares for through me, as my mentor and nourisher who takes care of everything despite my many shortcomings, and as a strict teacher who punishes harshly when the ego rears its ugly head.

My relationship with God has certainly improved, and, so too, my outlook toward worshiping Him. I try to remain in constant awareness of His presence.

— Shalini Prasad, CM Bengaluru

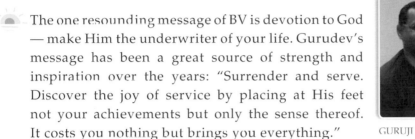

SHALINI PRASAD ▲

God, Dear God!

BV has increased my faith in God and decreased my fear of God.

— Shobha Ravishankar, CM Houston

BV has strengthened my belief in a loving, caring, supreme power we call God. I need to get in touch with Him many times during the day to feel strong, calm, and centered. — Vanita Venugopal, CM Washington

God suddenly became all the kids, families, and parents. He wasn't just sitting in my pūjā room only! — Bhavya Trivedi, CM Tampa

By constantly discussing the nature and virtues of Bhagavān my own sense of appreciating His glory has increased. There is acceptance that we are not isolated beings but part of an intelligently put together creation. By praying to the Higher, we can establish an intimate relationship with the Supreme who resides in our very own heart. My greatest growth in BV has been the subconscious increase in the level of sevā bhāva (spirit of service). — Shankar Edamadaka, CM Princeton

'Children are like God' — I must have heard my grandmother say that a billion times. Now I have begun to see what she meant. — Suman Rao

Those A-ha! Moments

...Both Shanti and Shraddha enjoyed teaching the youngest in BV. Children from four to seven years of age repay their teachers with huge dividends in the form of their laughter, joy, and infectious love of life. They are a veritable delight. Their innocence and freshness of outlook often lead to startling new perspectives for their teachers....

The confidence of the five-year-olds and the enthusiasm with which they come to class on Sunday mornings are to be marveled at! The three years I have been a kindergarten teacher for the BV program have been the most important years in my search for eternal happiness.

I was expecting to have a lot of fun with a bunch of naughty kids. I saw naughty Kṛṣṇa, hyper Hanumān, righteous Rāma, good Gaṇeśa, wise Brahma, super Śiva, notorious Nārada, shy Sītā, and all manifestations of God in my class! When I taught *Bala Ramayana*, the kids in my class knew the story in such detail that I had nothing to teach. We used to have many 'discussions' and, at one point it struck home — there I was sitting with God and just not seeing Him!

— Suman Rao

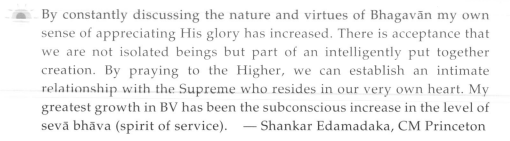

The kindergarteners are a pure delight! In one class, we were all seated in a circle on the floor discussing the different ways we react in a toy store when a parent tells us we cannot have a toy we want. Said one child, "I scream, cry, and drop to the ground, and my mother usually buys me the toy." Another said, "I keep on asking for the toy till my father gives up and buys it for me." And a third child said, "I know my mother will not buy it for me, so I don't ask."

Then the subject changed to the ways we could teach ourselves to react in this situation. One boy said, without any hesitation, "We can learn to wait for it."

It is such 'Eureka' moments that make being a sevak fulfilling.

— Sivagami Natesan, CM Austin

ARUNDHATI AFTER CONCLUDING A PŪJĀ ▲

I was teaching 'Understanding Hinduism' in my BV class of ten- to thirteen-year-olds. The topic was Brahman; the discussion turned to the infinite nature of Brahman. It soon became intense, as the kids churned over the concept of Bigger than the Biggest, and Smaller than the Smallest!

"What about supernovas, black holes, and expanding space-time?"

They challenged each other and grappled with the contradictions, till suddenly one kid piped up, "Oh! Now I get it!"

"What did you get?" I asked.

"Now I understand. When Yaśhodā Mā thought Kṛṣṇa had eaten mud, she made Him open his mouth. And all at once in His open mouth, she saw the entire universe and the movement of the stars! All the universes exist in Kṛṣṇa who is Brahman!"

This revelation of the power of the Purāṇic stories struck me like lightning. As a toddler, he must have heard that Kṛṣṇa story, the deep impact of which emerged long after it was told. Just one story became the springboard to catapult a child's imagination into the realms of subtle Vedāntic concepts. — Arundhati Sundar, CM Singapore

Sheela Srinivasan, a lawyer by profession and a Bharatanatyam dancer by interest, is an active Mission worker. Married to Ācārya Vivek of CM Niagara, she shares his vision and deep commitment. As a devoted wife, she willingly supports him, as she puts it, "In any way I can

▲ SWAMI SHARANANANDA WITH SHEELA AND VIVEK

— taking care of his transportation needs, helping with administrative matters, or just making sure that he is well-fed!"

Sheela teaches Bharatanatyam at the ashram in Niagara Falls. She loves teaching the little ones, but she confesses: I was apprehensive about teaching the youngest group of BV students (four-to seven-year-olds). I did not want to taint their impressionable young minds with a forced understanding of theology and rituals.

Their thoughtful questions never cease to amaze me, and their excitement is contagious. I always leave feeling inspired. They encourage me to be more creative and to invest more time in making the class the highlight of their week.

Evolve through Self-Study

Pujya Gurudev and Guruji have often reiterated that, for a sevak to be effective as a teacher, it is essential to engage in self-study, svādhyāya. Only this clarifies concepts and finally subdues the 'whys' and the 'whats' of the mind.

Satsaṇga in the form of group discussions, lecture sessions or even just meeting with Ācāryas helps to deepen the commitment of the seekers and are necessary to keep alive their interest in the goal.

I started attending *Gītā* classes with Ācārya Sharada Kumar and was inspired by her love for God and Pujya Gurudev. My interest increased and I spent time thinking up new ways to introduce my BV class to the mystery of God and His glories.

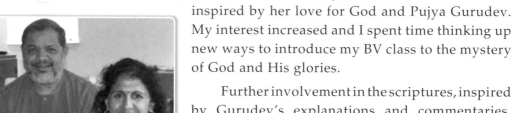

▲ GURUJI WITH SEEMA JANI

Further involvement in the scriptures, inspired by Gurudev's explanations and commentaries, has increased my thirst to be firmly embedded in the Knowledge.

— Seema Jani, CM Atlanta

Run to Give Back

...Shanti asked Shraddha, "Were you able to get the story about the impressive Project Om Run? If I remember correctly it was flagged off by an inspired BV sevak looking for a way to actively give back!"....

Sanjay Bombawal's introduction to the Mission came about through his son's enrollment in BV San Jose. From there, the call of the spirit led him to attend the Sunday talks by Br. Prabodh.

With time came the realization that Br. Prabodh walked in the great lineage of teachers nurtured by Pujya Gurudev. What impressed him even more was the spirit of service and selflessness of the Mission workers. This realization made him yearn to give back, and through this compelling urge 'Project Om Run' was born.

Om Run has become a very successful once-a-year-fundraising event, which involves the BV students and families of all three Bay Area centers. It is a day of fun, food, and activities for kids. The highlights are the five-kilometer and ten-kilometer races and the walkathon.

...In 2010, over 2,000 participated in the event, and at this writing, the event has raised US $ 112,827.65 in funds....

TIME TO RUN ▼

In 2011, it was decided to make the occasion even more colorful by adding Holi as one of the events. Unfortunately, the weather turned inclement, going from bad to worse. To the complete amazement of the park wardens, where the function was held, Uma Jeyarasasingam started reciting the Hanumān Cālīsā. She was joined by hordes of kids and parents and, in a matter of minutes with Śrī Hanumān's blessings, the conditions threatening heavy downpour turned to cloudy but dry weather!

Recalls Sanjay, "During the first year, it was hard to recruit volunteers. However, the following year, people took pride in helping and there was a sense of ownership. This, in turn, led to tight friendships and bonds across the three centers, increasing commitments to the Mission. Its impact has exceeded my wildest dreams."

A Universal Blessing

...Shraddha read an email from a BV sevikā, which, to her, summarized the experiences and emotions of countless families touched by the special brand of love offered by Gurudev and Guruji ....

They say that BV is a garden for children to bloom and grow. But as a parent and as a sevikā at BV for more than fifteen years, I believe that BV is a mystical garden where a soul grows toward fulfillment.

While a child learns to wonder, the parent learns to introspect.

The family learns to respect and revere, within and without.

The volunteers learn to work together as an offering to a future generation, and the teachers learn to reach beyond themselves to embody the teaching they share.

Our story is not unique. Our daughter started BV when she was only two years old. Wide-eyed, she would listen to the Ācārya, absorbing the stories

SEVAKS OF CM HOUSTON WITH ĀCĀRYA DARSHANABEN ▼

and the chanting of the *Gītā*. With each year, her love for the scriptures grew deeper. To our son, who was born while our daughter was already in BV, it is like a second home. Even before he could identify his friends, he could spot Gurudev's face in a picture. Now, at ages sixteen and twelve, both our children believe they are truly a part of the worldwide Chinmaya family, and they love the *Gītā*, Gurudev, and Guruji!

Our children, though growing up in the West, have their souls nurtured in Vedānta. It is as if Gurudev beautifully orchestrates every step we take, and Guruji's guidance in our lives reaffirms Gurudev's presence.

— A BV sevak

WHILE CELEBRATING THE INDIAN REPUBLIC DAY, CM ANN ARBOR COMES TOGETHER ▲ TO THANK ALL THEIR TEACHERS IN A GREAT SHOW OF STRENGTH.

...Each story Shraddha and Shanti shared was unique, influencing both the teacher and the taught. Sevaks told of the joy of selfless giving, an unfolding of dormant talents and abilities, leading to a total blossoming of the personality. Children exposed to Vedānta, reinforced by huge deposits of inner wealth, felt prepared to fearlessly face the challenges of life. In and through all the grateful praise for BV, Shanti and Shraddha found a shining connecting thread Gurudev's vision to unearth the beauty inherent in each jiva!....

Bala Perspectives

Dear God, Are boys better than girls? I know you are one, but try to be fair. – a BV child

XIX

The Legacy Blesses

THE PRIMARY REASON TO ATTEND BALA VIHAR IS TO PREPARE ONESELF TO LEAD A SUCCESSFUL AND HAPPY LIFE AND TO MAKE OTHERS HAPPY.

| SWAMI TEJOMAYANANDA |

The heartfelt gratitude of everyone connected with Bala Vihar (BV) came pouring in from all parts of the globe — the children, their parents, their teachers, and all associated sevaks. Among these, the loudest cheer emerged from the ranks of the BV children, who outnumbered the other categories in sheer numbers.

... Shanti and Shraddha heard the voices of BV children from different centers across the world — precious testimonials to the dedication of the sevaks; to the love of their parents; and to the sheer grandeur of the BV vision of Pujya Gurudev! The children's expression of grateful thanks was evocative of love for the Chinmaya name. They were proud to be the privileged recipients of sacred wisdom.

Shanti and Shraddha had spent close to eighteen months understanding the BV phenomenon. As the project drew to a close, they decided it was time to celebrate with the family. They wanted to share glimpses of their experiences, both humbling and inspiring, they wanted their loved ones to partake of their joy.

Shanti invited Vivek, her son, and Radhika, her daughter, along with their families to an early dinner. At the dining table conversation went into reminisce mode and light banter. The family wanted to know if any of their anecdotes had found a place in the archives. It was then that Shanti remembered the conversation with Vivek just before he moved away from the parental home.

Shanti: Before leaving home at least learn one thing from me.

Vivek: What else do you want to teach me? Haven't you taught me everything you wanted to?

Shanti: The Guru Stotram, so the blessings of the Guru are always with you.

Vivek: But Ma, I know that. I learnt it at BV from Bharati Aunty.

Shanti: That was over twenty years ago and I have not heard you chant it. (He attended BV for a short time as a five year old and Shanti had never heard him chant the stotra in so many years.) Are you sure, son? Let me hear you!

Shanti was thrilled beyond words when she heard her son chant the Guru Stotram from beginning to end. She only had to support him with the first word of each śloka. Now she was fully convinced that her son would fare well protected by the Guru's grace!

GURUDEV BLESSES A SEVAK ▲

Later, the family settled themselves in comfort, eager to hear the presentation planned by Shanti and Shraddha. Shraddha began the verbal slideshow with a disclaimer.

"There is no way we can share all the thoughts and stories that came from these blessed children exposed to BV. The comments of each one are inspiring and thought provoking. The collection we present are, at best, a representative sample." With a smile, she added, "Feel free to voice your thoughts anytime."

"So let's begin," said Gautam, Shanti's husband; he fully supported Shanti and was the strength behind her commitment to BV.

Shraddha began, "Well, I thought I would begin with one heartstring puller, adorable and enviable altogether!" ....

The Comfort of Love

My earliest memories are that of a sleepy three-year-old, rubbing her eyes, clutching onto her favorite doll with one hand, tugging her pyjamas with the other, and making a beeline for the most comfortable place to be.... the room of Br. Vivek (now Guruji Swami Tejomayananda). I did not know what intruding meant, and neither did I care. All I wanted was the warmth of selfless love!

And I got it. As I walked in, I was securely wrapped in a big hug. Content thereafter, I was happy to leave Guruji to his work, while I sat somewhere in the vicinity of his feet, playing and dreaming the dreams of a three-year-old.

Could there be a better BV? I literally grew at Guruji's feet. On hindsight, I am awestruck at my good fortune and thank my grandmother, Smt. Kamala Bhargava, whose home in Lucknow functioned as a CM center for many years. It was her devotion that drew Guruji, who lived in that area for a few years.

Even now, in my mind, after all these years, I am that confident three-year-old sure of being accepted as I am. Thank you, Nānī, and thank you Guruji! — Rajika Thareja, CM Lucknow

Vivek: Lucky kid! The exposure to the warm comfort of selfless love is so necessary for children to grow up as whole and complete adults.

Shanti: Specially for children growing up in a land that has a value system different from that practiced in the home. That's why BV is a safety net for the children of the Indian diaspora. It is the lifeline, which removes confusions and connects them to the cultural heritage of their ancestors.

▲ MYTHILI IYER

BV centers, particularly those outside India, function as forums for interactions with a large, diverse community that shares the same values and respect for Indian culture. From the adult sevaks who teach, man the bookstalls, clean the ashram, and organize celebrations; to my peers who attend classes with me, there is a never-ending supply of interesting people.

— Mythili Iyer, CM Princeton

The more generations we are away from India, the harder it is to keep the connection alive. BV offers valuable solutions, and holistic perspectives to stay connected with our roots.

— Srivatsa Marthi, CM Ottawa

Lack of knowledge about Hinduism is responsible for many teens converting to other religions. The values that I learned in BV have changed my character and overall outlook on life. The advantage of being exposed to it at a very young age is that you will never forget its essential teachings, and you can proudly call yourself a true Hindu! — Kris Dadlani, CM Jakarta

◀ KRIS DADLANI

True understanding through BV has helped me to practice Hinduism and also be comfortable within the American culture.

— Tanmay Satam, CM Ann Arbor

Radhika: No wonder BV is a haven for Indian children raised abroad.

Shanti: Yes, and whether in India or a foreign country, BV is a happening, welcoming place. Listen:

My BV journey began when I was four years old, in Mumbai. Subsequently the family moved to Kolkata and then to Delhi. The transfer to Kolkata initially filled me with apprehension, but, in the very first class, I experienced familiarity and a sense of homecoming!

The story repeated itself when we moved to Delhi. Again, one summer I happened to be in Mumbai, and like a homing pigeon, gravitated toward the Summer BV Camp at the Powai ashram. Though among strangers, I had an underlying feeling of ease, a sense of being at home.

Through BV, I was introduced to Guruji, who was and continues to be a source of never-ending encouragement in my academic journey and in my Bharatnatyam dance career.

No matter where I traveled, BV has introduced me to like-minded people and convinced me that my beliefs are not wrong, even though I may belong to a minority! How can I not be grateful for this knowledge that gives me the confidence to adjust easily to new situations and gives me an edge over many of contemporaries?

— Nitya Kishore, CM Delhi

NITYA KISHORE ▲

Friends for Life

Shraddha: Where there is acceptance, friendships blossom. Children spoke about the enduring, lifelong friendships forged through BV and in the expanse of the Chinmaya family:

Travel to a different part of the world, just walk into a Mission center, and say, "Hari Om." In an instant, you are connected to family — the Chinmaya family!

— Deepa Balakrishnan, CM Bengaluru

The Sidhbabi Bug

Jujhar Singh, a senior executive producer and anchor with NewsX, was 14 in June 1983, when he went for his first camp in Sidhbari. He was looking at it like a holiday. But he recalls how the excitement soon turned to grave disappointment! His mother, Anjali Singh, and sister Nanki, and he were accommodated in the small, cramped, covered verandah of a cottage. The bathroom was shared with another family.

Jujhar says: "There were dozens of flies in the verandah room. And of course, we were expected to get up early in the mornings! In frustration, I asked my mother: 'Where have you brought us??'"

But within one day, the magic started. We discovered several friendly, young people. Medha Mehta (now Swamini Vimalananda) played 'Monopoly' with us. Pramodini Acharya (now Pramodini Rao) sang beautiful bhajans for me.

And then there was Br. Vivek Chaitanya (now Swami Tejomayananda). His talks on the *Rāmāyaṇa* floored me. The narration of Śivaji's wedding procession was the most gripping and funny story I had ever heard.

We would also meet Gurudev in his kutiyā. Each time, we were received with bear hugs! Then one day, I was asked to play the role of Gurudev in a skit being put up for camp delegates. Gurudev laughed and laughed as I appeared on stage dressed in white robes, a false beard, a BMI chart and crossed my legs exactly as Gurudev would do. He laughed even more — and the audience gasped — when at the end of the skit, I walked towards and into Gurudev's own kutiyā! Later, Gurudev remarked: 'He could have taken orange clothes from me!'"

▲ JUJHAR PLAYS GURUDEV

Jujhar remembers the 'fantastic' seven days in Sidhbari. He says he had never had so much fun before! There was a positive atmosphere all around. He and his sister made many friends. He recalls: "The talks by Gurudev and Guruji were brilliant. And on the last day, in great anguish, the boy who had complained to his mother 'Where have you brought us' — now asked her: 'Can't we stay here for another six months!?'" The Sidhbari bug had bitten. — Jujhar Singh, CM Delhi

The family I inherited, thanks to Chinmaya Mission, is amazing. My vision of the concept of family grew. It started from my center and now expands worldwide. — Puja Sabnani, CM Miami

We have a whole family here. We have a couple of hundred siblings, parents, grandparents, and cousins. — Anjali Madhok, CM Twin Cities

Wake-up Call

Shanti: To forge friendships we must first get to BV, and the hard part is waking up every Sunday morning for the class. Perhaps most BV children hear this jingle every Sunday, "Chalo betā jāgo (Come on kids, it's time to rise and shine)!" But for some it was different:

NANDINI KISHORE ▲

BV on Sunday was a way of life. No reminders, no complaints about waking up early, and no question of giving up BV due to the heavy school workload!

— Nandini Kishore, CM Washington D.C.

To wake up on Sunday mornings, especially when my friends are sleeping, is hard. I argue with Dad and test his patience, but once there, I forget all the trouble of getting ready. Even on the Sundays when there is no BV, I check with my parents, "Is it not time for BV?"

– a BV child

Shanti: All said and done, after graduating from BV, children are unanimous in their expression of gratitude to their parents; they acknowledge the worth of their persistence. Some like Shiva Sharma, CM Los Angeles, would be driven as far as sixty miles each way.

They Do Listen

Shraddha: Children almost unanimously agreed that they appreciated the benefits of BV learning the most when they moved away from the safety of home and parental support:

At BV, I learned the art of listening and absorbing information. In life, we encounter differing individuals, ideas, and establishments. Regardless of one's beliefs, it is important to listen, question, and understand why views differ. — Aditya Pandyaram, CM Princeton

"While it may seem that some of the kids in BV are not listening, they are. When that knowledge is needed, it will come and be of help to them." Vineet Bhagwat's conviction is backed by experience. Vineet holds a Doctorate in Finance from the Kellogg School of Management.

Despite such academic excellence, he had his moments of doubt. At the end of his first year as a Ph. D. student, he was required to take a qualifying exam. With his mind in turmoil, he wondered, "What if I fail? I will be asked to leave. Oh, the shame!"

Suddenly, a śloka from the *Gītā* flashed in his mind —

karmaṇyevādhikāraste mā phaleṣu kadācana

(your right is to work only, never to its fruits — 2.47)

▲ VINEET GETS THE HUG OF LIFE

Instantly, he knew, "All I can do is study. That is in my hand. I cannot control the questions. I just need to study without worrying about success or failure." His spiritual training from BV came to his rescue and turned a potentially dismal situation into a winner!

To Vineet, "The bottom line of Vedānta is the finitude of the experienced world. This is actually inspirational because the goal is not in the end result, but in striving to reach there!"

— Vineet Bhagwat, CM Washington D.C.

▲ AVNI MEHTA (LEFT) WITH SIBLINGS

My appreciation for BV increased exponentially after I moved to college. The realization dawned on me that it was time to incorporate those teachings into my life and also share them with others, who were struggling like me. So I did, and in the process vastly improved my own understanding of the scriptures!

— Avni Mehta, CM Los Angeles

Vedānta Made Easy

Geeta Menon, an alumna of BV Chennai, heads a movement that transforms ordinary people into the extraordinary — the Chinmaya Institute of Management (CIM), Chennai. Gurudev envisaged CIM as an institution that would train corporate personnel based on the principles of Vedānta.

CIM Chennai also trains college students. Geared to the questioning mind of the undergraduates, the teaching modules are carefully created by the CIM team using activities, videos, Power Point presentations, and apt examples from the *Bhagavad-gītā*, the Upaniṣads, and everyday life.

GEETA MENON ▲

On the role of her early BV training in her life, Geeta is convinced, "The ability to face challenges and tests of life is far enhanced. As a child, you learn fast and it becomes a part of your personality. Nobody can take it away, and you cannot even throw it away!"

Mantras Are Lifelines

Shanti: We all have our favorite key words or mantras that help in crucial moments. It is all about using the right mantra in the right place, at the right time:

During a bleak phase, Raghuveer Akula learned that even the darkest clouds have a silver lining — that even a hopeless situation potentially holds the seeds to a bright future. His story:

A few years ago, I held a dream job as a video-game programmer. I had it all, until one morning when my boss informed me that seventy-five percent of the staff was being laid off, and I was one of them. I was shocked. How could I be kicked out after four years of dedicated service?

Then I remembered WOW, the acronym for With or Without. WOW means one can be happy with or without a particular object, person, action, or situation. What I learned at BV came to my rescue. My unemployment was a blessing in disguise. It allowed me to think deeper about where my happiness lay. The focus shifted to other meaningful activities and, eventually, I was inspired to join the Yuva Veer course. A devastating event transformed into a positive situation. I understand that, with right thinking, we have the infinite potential to achieve anything we want. — Raghuveer Akula, CM Houston

"Listen more and Learn more" — Gurudev's mantra, imbibed as a child, has stayed with me. It nudges my mind to march into a world of expanding ideas, thoughts, and actions. — Meera, CM Bengaluru

I am better equipped to handle life-and-death situations, which are an integral part of the profession of medicine, by viewing the situation as part of a larger picture. BV reminds me to 'Be an instrument in His hands.'
— Amita Kathuria, CM Orlando

At the end of a yajña in Pune, Gurudev gave a picture to Keshav. Written across it was the mantra he has used successfully thereafter: *'Never say you can't. Do it and win over life!'*

Having understood the power of the mantra, Keshav named his company 'Mantra'; today it is an established name in the world of consultancy and human resources-related training.

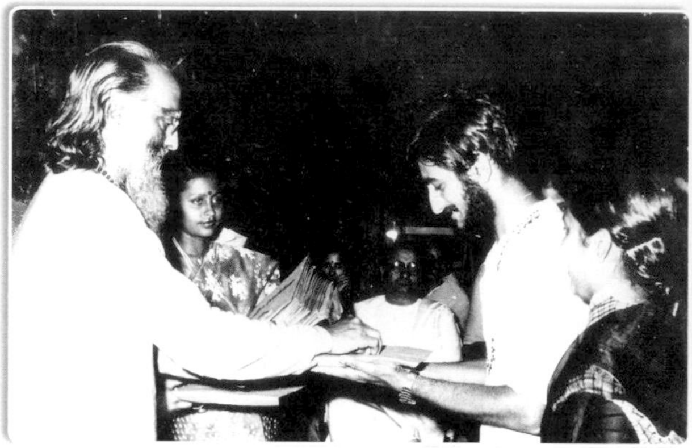

▲ GURUDEV WITH KESHAV

A smiling Keshav remarks, "Nobody would have believed that I could have built a business around the values and skills I learned and make it profitable for myself."

When he conceptualized the idea of starting Mantra, Keshav wrote to Gurudev. Promptly came the reply, "Great idea, but when you train these executives in five-star hotels, think of my teachers." Keshav's human resources skills are readily on call for assisting the Chinmaya Vidyalayas whenever required.
— M. Keshav, CM Chennai

BV teaches us to view the world from a different perspective. It becomes easier to detach from a situation and view it from a broader point of view. This helps in understanding why something happened and how best to move forward.
— Kaushik Bhatia, CM Chicago

Shanti: Gurudev's letters are legendary, you know how many thousands he wrote. Despite his hectic travel schedule he meticulously replied to every letter he received; even his short notes carried a message. We found some letters where he has addressed the concerns, of his young devotees and some were just an open expression of his love:

To Puja Krishnani, anxious about public speaking Gurudev wrote:

"Remember that the Lord is always with you and He alone is the audience... Relax and talk to the 'Crowd' as though you are talking to your little sister!!... This is after all only 1.5 minutes – may be only 5-7 sentences!"

To the children of Manisha Khemlani's BV class Gurudev wrote:

Thank you dear children I got your Raksha Bandhan wrist-lets. I appreciate your love and faith in me. With these wrist-lets, I am trying to tie each one of you to your Gopal Bhaiya.

May He bless you all.

▲ GURUDEV WITH TWO-YEAR-OLD RAGHUVEER AKULA

Raghuveer Akula has fond memories of privileged interactions with Gurudev. He remarks, "Pujya Gurudev was always smiling and full of energy; his storytelling sessions unforgettable. He engaged us in minute details by acting like the characters in the story.

His love for children was boundless. In his presence everyone felt loved. Stamped in my memory is a BV moment from a camp where all the children were singing enthusiastically and loudly for Gurudev:

khāte bhī rāma kaho! pīte bhī rama kaho!
bolte bhī rāma kaho, rāma rāma rāma!"

(Chant Śrī Rāma while eating, Chant Śrī Rāma while drinking! Keep repeating His name, Rāma.... Rāma.... Rāma!).

Gurudev joined the chorus and began to dance in joy!

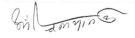

WITH GURUDEV AFTER A PLAY IN SIDHBARI ▲

BV helped Gayatri Krishnamurty explore her true potential. Unequivocally, she declares: "The sevaks are like gardeners for whom every plant, whether a flowering plant or cactus, is beautiful and worth nurturing. I owe my grounding to BV."

Gayatri enjoyed participating in competitions, more because of the numerous prizes and accolades that came her way. Her greatest achievement was winning third place in the All India *Gītā* Chanting Competition in 1993 at Adi Sankara Nilayam, proof enough that effort and dedication will reap its rewards.

Even today, at the age of thirty-five, Gayatri says: "I still think of myself as a BV child. BV is where I have belonged the most, and still belong to. The one place where I feel truly at home is with a bunch of children, chanting ślokas, telling stories, and playing games!"

— Gayatri Krishnamurty, CM Kolkata

Vivek: BV teachings have a way of enveloping a family. Even our family is proof of that!

Shanti: Gurudev built Chinmaya Mission on a model, where the family is the core unit. He knew that the dedication of one member of the family ensures that others follow.

▲ UJWALA ACHARYA

Belonging to a Mission family from Mumbai, Ujwala Acharya had no option but to attend BV, as her parents, Shyamala and Vijay, were first students and then teachers in the program. Her aunt is Pramodini Rao. She heard her first discourse seated on her grandfather's lap!

An outstanding student, talented singer, designer, and artist, Ujwala has received numerous accolades. However, perhaps her greatest achievement has been the difference she made in the life of a classmate by befriending her when she needed it the most. Expressing heartfelt gratitude her friend wrote:

Dear Ujwala,

I am writing this letter to tell you what a difference you have made in my life.

In school I was always everybody's target. You supported me and taught me to smile. You told me that no one is a failure and because of that I got a distinction in SSC.

My parents were thinking of getting me married right after school. But because I did well in my exams, they let me go ahead with my study. Today I have an MBA and am working in a multinational firm. Thank you for making that big change in my life, for standing by me.

Lots of Love,

Uma

Values Redefine Workplaces

Vivek: Now tell us about how BV children have made a difference in the workplace? How did it influence their career choice in the first place?

Shraddha looked through their collection and found the stories that Vivek wanted to hear:

The Śivarātrī celebrations of 1987 at the Powai Ashram changed the course of Radhakrishnan Pillai's life. From then on, he was a regular at BV and all Mission functions.

An entrepreneur by nature, under Guruji's guidance he began a tourism company. The business flourished, but he was not satisfied. His mind envisioned a company managed through the tenets of an indigenous model as opposed to a business plan based on Western philosophy. This powerful desire resulted in an in-depth study of Kautilya's Arthaśastra (a voluminous text that covers every aspect of the ethics of business, management, and politics) at the Chinmaya International Foundation, Kerala.

Little did Radhakrishnan know that his expertise on (Kautilya) Chanakya's business model would catapult him into the limelight. Today, a much sought-after management consultant with disarming humility, Radhakrishnan says:

RADHAKRISHNAN ▲ PILLAI

"My achievements can be attributed 120 percent to my BV values and ideals, the grace of my Guru, and the knowledge of Kautilya's Arthaśastra. The training in BV gave me the ability to understand the nuances and depths of this great text."

His experience teaches: "To succeed in any field, a spiritual base is essential. With a spiritual base, you can succeed in any field!" — Radhakrishnan Pillai, CM Mumbai

GURUJI WITH PUJA ▲

It took a while to understand that gratitude and appreciation are not necessary for the work we do. Doing the work perfectly is its own reward.

These lessons influenced my choice of the hospitality industry as a career; the guest does not need to know who did the work, as long as it gets done.

— Puja Sabnani, CM Miami

Step by Step

▲ ANIL SACHDEV

Anil Sachdev and his siblings were trained in the BV tradition by their mother. His exposure to Vedānta and the *Bhagavad-gītā* began at the impressionable age of thirteen.

Anil's memories of the many treasured interactions with Gurudev include the time when he was asked, "So young man! What do you want to do when you grow up?"

Out tumbled his dreams. He said, "I want to serve my country, to develop something which will help it become economically strong again, using our heritage and wisdom based on your teachings."

His mother expressed concern at this talk of big plans. Gurudev laughed and said, "Amma, your son knows what he is doing. This is the right way to serve the country."

With Gurudev's blessings, Anil's dreams have come true step by step — from being an employee at TELCO to founding two successful management consulting organizations and finally setting up SOIL (School of Inspired Leadership) to train leaders structured by a vision of the scriptures.

In 2010, the Planning Commission of India appointed him as a consultant, and from then on, he began to work for his country. He is a member of a think tank to develop a vision for India that would form the basis for the next five-year plan.

Of this fantastic journey, Anil says, "When we follow a great cause with deep love, leadership qualities automatically surface. A great leader is always a great follower; the power of the leader comes from the cause with which he is in love, something bigger than himself."

— Anil Sachdev, CM Delhi

Anjali Thakkar, a first-year medical student at Harvard, remembers the thrill of leading the assembly in reciting the Chinmaya Mission pledge in a BV class. The pledge is ingrained in her memory. It was the seed for who she is today and for what she hopes to become tomorrow.

ANJALI THAKKAR ▲

As a ten-year-old, Anjali entered the Chinmaya essay contest pondering over the goal of life — Who Am I? She says, "The essay came naturally; I described my hobbies, enthusiastically explaining what I loved most about each one. Needless to say, I did not win..."

Many years later, Anjali encountered the same topic under vastly changed circumstances. In 2011, she was being interviewed for the prestigious Harry S. Truman Scholarship — only sixty are selected out of seven hundred candidates. Countless hours had been spent refining interview skills. Her nervousness peaked as the chairperson asked her: "Can you tell us about who you are?"

Suddenly, all anxiety and tension dissipated because she had answered this question as a ten-year-old. Anjali smiled, "I shared the vignette about the Chinmaya essay contest, segueing into the impact that BV has played in my life. Since my days of reciting the Chinmaya Mission pledge during assemblies, its meaning has lingered and materialized in my mind. The common thread defining my experience has become one of service, inspired by the values that the Chinmaya family instilled." She convinced the judges about her passion to enter public service and was selected.

When asked to share a cultural prayer before the awards ceremony, she recited the Chinmaya pledge. Anjali again experienced, "the thrilling chills that I felt fifteen years ago during the BV assembly. But this time, it held new meaning to me, reaffirming my goal of combining my love of science with my call to service!"

Anjali's calling to serve began in KG. She collected the academic award monies for first place — through KG to grade six — and then anonymously donated the entire amount to the Chinmaya Mission New Building Fund. At her araṅgeṭram, instead of gifts, she requested contributions to two noble charities. Anjali fully lives the pledge of "Producing more than what we consume and giving more than what we take."

— CM San Jose

Good leaders must listen to different viewpoints. Decisions that emerge after collating the diverse views of all stakeholders are invaluable to the growth and well-being of any organization. — Meera, CM Bengaluru

Groomed by Nirmala Chellam, Nand Kishore was a reticent ninth-grade student, till he began teaching at BV. His gain was the blossoming of confidence and leadership qualities. Even today, the leader in Kishore continues to lead — at work and in the Mission.

Not withstanding frequent transfers in his career, Nand Kishore's association with Chinmaya Mission has continued uninterrupted for over forty years. Despite a demanding travel schedule, he ensures that the youth classes over the weekend continue uninterrupted. The saṁskāra of regularity, implanted in BV, continues to unfold in this committed sevak.

Says Kishore: "The only common thread in my life has been the Mission, and the roots for my growth were sown the day I joined BV!"

— Nand Kishore, CM Mumbai

God Is One

Gautam: How did children respond on the subject of God?

Shanti: They had some interesting viewpoints and experiences to share.

My concept of God underwent a radical change when I heard Pujya Gurudev's sonorous voice enunciate, "Śrī bhagavānuvāca." And then in English, he continued, "Lord Kṛṣṇa said, Allah said, Buddha said, and Jesus said!" I was left with the undeniable truth that indeed they are all one. — Kavitha Shreeharsha, CM Bay Area

My relationship with God is like that of two good friends. When I'm feeling down or stressed out, I chant His name, which allows me to calm my mind and refocus on the tasks at hand.

BV introduced me to the concept that each person is nothing but a nicely packaged form of Consciousness. This view helps to remove the barriers of race, gender and nationality and aids in empathizing with people regardless of their background.

— Bhavana Shivakumar, CM Ann Arbor

◀ BHAVANA SHIVAKUMAR

God is a power that exists whether or not we believe in Him. He is the strength of a believer, whereas an atheist depends on no one other than himself. Unflinching faith and belief in a higher power equips us to cope with the vicissitudes that life may present.

— Srijit Nair, CM Bengaluru

The concept of God presented to me through BV was one of kindness and mercy. The stories and thrilling tales from our rich and diverse culture foster love for God and encourage children to make the right choices in life. — An Alumnus, CM Muscat

Paths to the Universal

Shraddha: With questions about God come thoughts about our purpose in the world. Children who went through BV have turned what they learned into a passion, a purpose in unique or tough circumstances.

The spiritual journey is lifelong and often arduous. It is something that each one must embark on individually. On the way, you will doubt yourself and question the scriptures. Your resolve will be tested and your intellect will be challenged. At such junctures, Chinmaya BV gives the tools to success. In the final analysis, we all have different aptitudes for spiritual knowledge, and every being has a different way of connecting to the Supreme. Chinmaya Mission allowed me to understand this and be truly tolerant of others.

— Ramesh Cheruvu, CM Beaumont

Akshay Bhise, just eighteen years old, has an unusual passion. His mission in life is wildlife conservation, more particularly the rescue of snakes.

AKSHAY WITH A 'FRIEND' ▲

Akshay explains, "Snakes, birds, and other animals are displaced from their natural habitats with the felling of trees. They have to move away, but often have a desire to revisit their earlier homes. So they retrace their paths and end up in the middle of a city. Some reptiles enter homes and frighten the inmates, whose natural instinct is to kill the reptile."

Akshay is part of a group of youngsters who protect such creatures. When alerted to the sighting of a snake, one member rushes to the rescue. Snakes are collected in gunny bags and transported to safer and natural havens.

Akshay said, "I feel that I have to go because a friend is in need of help. I have no second thoughts." He attributes his love of animals to his BV training in the value of universal love. He learned to be compassionate in dealing with all living beings. During meditation sessions, his mind used to conjure up the image of Śiva with snakes around his neck. Slowly, this love for his kuladevatā (family deity) developed into a passion and has now become a life mission.

— Akshay Bhise, CM Goa

Shraddha: What we have shared this evening is just a drop in an ocean. We will close with the words of a protégé of Nirmala Chellam's. Mahesh Shetty's reflections on the journey of a BV child:

Life is a series of photographs — stack them together and flip them ever so slowly. Your whole life is animated and passes by in minutes and images — parents, siblings, friends, relatives, school, college, countries, marriage, kids, jobs, triumphs, and disappointments. As I mentally animate my life's journey, I find it interspersed with the word C-H-I-N-M-A-Y-A.

▲ MAHESH SHETTY

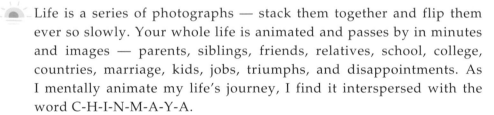

Time dims photographs and memories and I cannot exactly remember when I went to my first Chinmaya class. I was in the third grade when we moved to another house and, soon after, on Sundays, my siblings and I were enrolled in BV.

When I close my eyes, I can still recall the taste of the prasāda. If prasāda is a metaphor for God's blessings, then I must confess that I have had more than my fair share!

In India you are a Hindu through osmosis — from morning bhajans, treks to the local temple, savories associated with festivals, piety on the faces of parents murmuring their prayers, the annual pūjā at the business place, random crowds piling on to each other for a crack at the dahī-pot during Janmāṣṭamī, incredible idols during Gaṇeśa caturthī, and friends religiously begging forgiveness by clutching their ears and performing sit-ups at the local temple.

Without ever knowing it consciously, it seems that we all know the stories of our Gods. You utter God's name several times just by calling out your friends names — Murali, Kanha, Mohan, Narayan, or you extol Mother Nature and happiness in Ravi, Prakash, Jyoti, Vinay, Santosh, and so on!

The BV classes, subconsciously, connected the dots and made a spiritual person out of me, imbued me with the belief in a greater power that guides and watches over us. Even early on, I discarded the concept that God could ever punish someone.

The prayers and bhajans I learned in Chinmaya BV were not an attempt to make a list of wants. It was an opportunity to calm the mind and sift through the clamor of thoughts and ideas that drown out tranquility. Through this, I learned to objectively observe my thoughts and discover the Divinity within. This idea that we can be one with God has never ceased to amaze me.

Nirmala Aunty, Acharya Uncle, Subramaniam Uncle and my older peers — Mohan, Uday, Vijay, Kishore, Shobhana — are all examples of people who provide selfless service with a smile. Their desire to educate the younger generation to make something of their heritage and to convert the information all around us to something more tangible inspired me to do the same. Many years later, as a parent, I took my kids to Chinmaya BV, and in the spirit of service also became a teacher.

I am proud to be a Chinmaya BV alumnus, grateful to be a Chinmaya BV parent, and enormously blessed to be a Chinmaya BV teacher!

— Mahesh Shetty, CM Mumbai

...There was silence in the room as each one absorbed the magnitude of what had been said. Speaking into the quiet Vivek, Shanti's son, said slowly, "If this is just a sample, how magnificent would the whole be? We are blessed to be part of an amazing movement, speeding away to a glorious future."....

Bala Perspectives

A sevikā from San Jose was telling little children about Lord Gaṇeśa, when a four-year old boy asked: "Excuse me teacher, but is Lord Gaṇeśa from the U.S.A.?"

Bridge to the Future

On the solid foundation of a tried and tested philosophy, the Ācāryas, devotees, volunteers, and well-wishers of Chinmaya Mission are working together to build the Bala Vihar (BV) movement. The guiding inspiration still comes from the all-encompassing vision, which Pujya Gurudev, Swami Chinmayananda bequeathed to the coming generations:

- To make the future leaders of society conscious of the world's great spiritual and cultural values, Chinmaya Mission has an activity to educate children and teenagers through Bala Vihars and Yuva Kendras. These programs give children a spiritual orientation of character right through the most pliable stages of their growth.

It all started out as an experiment; it is even now an experiment, and I am sure it will ever continue to be an endless process of experimentation. It should be so. The human mind is never the same; it transforms with every change in the whim of the subjective person and with every breeze of change in the outer society around. To train such a fluttering human mind that is constantly exposed to the crisscross currents of change in a community is indeed a constant experimentation.

This is an experiment; it should continue as an experiment, making the necessary adjustments from time to time to protect the growing minds of our students from the malicious whims of change in the values of the society.

> We must succeed. This is our experiment. We shall not fail the nation and the silent demand of the innocent children growing under our care to make a cultural history of the morrow.

...Shanti felt that in the closing pages of this tribute to Gurudev's vision for the children of the world, it would be well to reiterate his thoughts, so that they stay with us long after the book rests on the bookshelf of the reader.

Taking off from where Shraddha had halted, Shanti began to speak....

Gurudev sums it all up in these words:

- The Bala Vihar and Yuva Kendra try to create self-confidence in the youth in order for them to serve and rightly act in cheerfulness, to generate in them a true affection in all their contacts, and to inculcate in them personal discipline and a true spirit of leadership. We train their capacity to express themselves and to assert their individuality. They gain a healthy resistance against the temptations of the world. These programs also aim to detect, cultivate, and improve the dormant faculties of children.

  We hope the Bala Vihars and Yuva Kendras will get the hearty cooperation of all teachers and parents. Our humble request is only, 'Help us to help our children.' We seek your cooperation to give our growing children a healthier intellectual and physical climate wherein they can grow with noble ideals, healthy emotions, and physical discipline.

...From its first faltering steps as a start-up movement in the second half of the twentieth century, the BV movement has now grown immensely and is equipped to take on the challenges of the twenty-first century. What we see now is something Gurudev had envisioned even before the first class started. The experiment he began continues to flourish in the laboratory of the world for the benefit of unborn generations. Gurudev said....

- It must be well-recognized that never has humanity ever grown in any direction in any period of history without the play of a few intelligent men of vision and a mission — be it in politics, sociology, science, spirituality, or culture. We, the elders — parents, teachers, elder brothers and sisters —have the responsibility to provide for our children this much of education that they may come into the fields of life with full confidence in themselves and a right knowledge of the world and the life therein.

If one does not know the rules of the game and what is expected of himself, he cannot truly be a player in that given game, nor can he be expected to play in a team spirit. When such an individual does not know what the rules of life are, and what exactly the game of striving in this world is, he must necessarily be a nuisance, and we should not expect him either to play the game of national endeavor or to contribute to the team spirit for world unity.

..."Here is an interesting testimonial," said Shanti, "a cynic congratulating Gurudev! One can imagine Gurudev's shoulders shaking as he enjoyed a merry laugh while reading this letter."....

Gurudev quoted from the gentleman's letter:

In this general chaos of today, Chinmaya Mission must be congratulated for still keeping up their enviable optimism that they can, through their Bala Vihars, re-orientate the future generation.

The simple and unpretentious efforts that have been started by the Chinmaya Mission in organizing BVs in the private home of the very sevikās and sevaks themselves, though apparently may seem to be of no significance at all, I foresee them as history-making schemes for the world. In these workshops, we are conceiving and molding the leaders of tomorrow and, as such, a great and onerous responsibility rests upon the shoulders of the BV workers.

And now supporting the shoulders of the thousands of BV workers and carrying the responsibility of Chinmaya Mission worldwide are the steady and strong shoulders of Pujya Guruji Swami Tejomayananda.

Radhika: Now tell us what Guruji said about the future of BV? What is his vision?

Shanti's mind relived those precious, quiet moments with Guruji in his kuṭiyā (dwelling place) at Chinmaya Vibhooti. Notwithstanding the grandeur of the vision or the project, in his pragmatic style, he remains rooted in the present. Without any preamble he came to the point and spoke his thoughts....

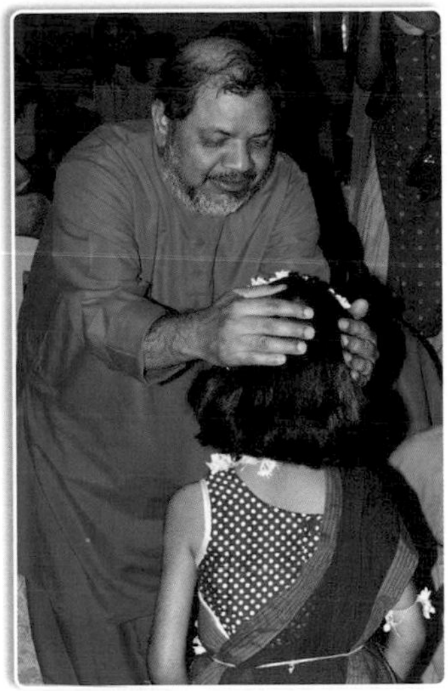

I have no special vision for the future. I only know that we should continue to do what we are supposed to and the future opens up. I never visualized the way the Mission has grown. Despite the changing society and situations, the aims and objectives of BV will not change. We must hold onto its vision. The methodologies used to impart the teaching may have to undergo changes to suit the needs of the hour.

The main focus should be on continuing the work; the results will come. Look at the growth of the BV movement. First the classes began. Then the *Balvihar* magazine came into being. Now we have the children's website. Then again look at how the face of the children's literature has changed. The books for children are now illustrated and in color. Our job is to do the right thing and to continue doing it. Let us remember, 'Leaders don't do different things; they do things differently.'

What he left unsaid, but is evident to all seekers of spirituality, is that the work gets done, and is done to perfection when it is offered at a higher altar. All of Guruji's actions, great or small, are undertaken in the spirit of selfless service in the name of Pujya Gurudev and the Lord. This pure love for the Guru and the Lord is his greatest strength.

...Shanti then related a coversation that took place between Guruji and Deepa Rai (a sevikā from CM San Jose), in his kuṭiyā at Chinmaya Vibhooti....

Guruji pointed to a picture of Śrī Rāma adorning one of the walls in his room. He asked rhetorically, "See this picture? You know what this little animal here is? This is a squirrel. I like him the best because I feel like I am a squirrel." He paused and looked at Deepa again.

She recalls, "I was stunned when he said this, looking directly at me. This is the exact metaphor I use over and over again with my BV students whenever any activities come up that require all of us to participate. It is a running theme with us every year. I could not believe it!"

Guruji referred to the story of how the bridge to Lanka was built:

Lord Rāma had given the monkeys the task of building a strong bridge across the ocean to Lanka. Monkey after monkey set to work carrying huge stones and boulders to the seaside. Thousands of them worked ceaselessly, and Lord Rāma was pleased. Then the Lord noticed a small brown squirrel rushing up and down from the hills to the shore carrying little pebbles in her mouth.

The monkeys also saw the squirrel and grew angry. "Get out of our way," the monkeys yelled. "You are too small. You are not needed."

The little squirrel looked up and said, "I am helping to build the bridge to save Mother Sītā."

The monkeys, holding their sides, roared with laughter. They even mocked the little squirrel. They said, "We have never heard anything so foolish in our entire lives."

The squirrel answered, "My heart weeps for Mother Sītā and I want to be of assistance. I cannot carry rocks or stones. I can only lift small pebbles, so that is what I will do."

The monkeys asked the squirrel to move away, but she continued with her self-assigned task of piling up the small pebbles. Finally, one monkey, in irritation, lifted the little animal and threw her into the air.

The squirrel cried out, "Rāma!"

No sincere call to the Lord goes unanswered. In an instant, the squirrel was safely in the palm of the Lord. It was just at that moment that the monkeys realized that they needed the little pebbles to place between the larger stones to keep the bridge from falling!

Śrī Rāma admonished the monkeys "Never despise the weak or the deeds of those who are not as strong as you. Each serves according to his strength and capacities and each is needed to make this bridge."

With his hand, the Lord stroked the squirrel's back and drew three lines down its fur. To this day, the little squirrels wear these stripes of honor on their rich furry backs, bestowed on them by the Lord Himself.

It is not the magnitude of the service but the devotion behind the service that purifies our minds. That is how the strongest bridge across the sea was built.

The BV movement is a bridge to the future. Over the years, the movement has grown by the committed offerings of thousands of children, parents, and sevaks. A few centers grew to become the large boulders. The thousands of classes the world over, that run out of the homes of sevaks, catering to, in some cases, only a few children are the pebbles. Both the big and small centers have contributed to the combined strength of this bridge of BV. Thousands have helped to build it, so that millions more can walk across the ocean of saṁsāra to reach the shores of bliss!

...Shanti's heart was full as she offered this labor of love at the feet of Lord Śrī Rāma and Pujya Gurudev, thanking all those she met in the process of this enriching experience. All along, Guruji's inspiring words continued to ring in her ears:

The main objective of Bala Vihar is to connect children to Bhagavān. Children should blossom in such a way that they turn to Him not just in need or during difficulties; they should be connected to the Lord at every point in time!

THE FARTHER I GO

THE NEARER I WILL BE TO EACH ONE OF YOU!

| Swami Chinmayananda |

Glossary

A	*Ācārya*	teacher; also in this book, initiated disciples — Brahmachari or Swami of Chinmaya Mission
	āśrama	residence or center of a spiritual teacher, often including lodgings for students
	Aśvalāyana	Ṛṣī spoken of in the Kaivalya Upaniṣad
	Airavatha	king of elephants; mount of the Hindu god Indra
	āratī	ritual worship performed by waving a flame of light
	asura	demon
B	*Bālakṛṣṇa*	Kṛṣṇa as a child
	Bhagavad-gītā	"Song of God." A major scriptural poem in eighteen chapters contained in the Mahābhārata
	Bhagavān	God, Lord
	Bhāgavata	(also, Śrīmad Bhāgavatam) one of the most important Purāṇas describing the life and times of Lord Kṛṣṇa, authored by Sage Veda Vyāsa
	bhajans	a musical rendering of hymns
	bhakta	devotee of the Lord
	bhakti	devotion
	bhikṣā	offering of food, especially to a renunciate
	brahmacārī	one who lives a student life, pursuing the knowledge of the infinite Self (Brahman)
	Brahmavidyā	knowledge of the infinite Self (Brahman)
C	*Carnatic*	referring to music commonly associated with the southern part of India
D	*Daśaharā*	Hindu festival celebrating the victory of Lord Rāma over the demon king Ravaṇa
	Daśāvatāra	the ten famous incarnations of Lord Viṣṇu
	dharma	essential nature of a thing; duty; righteousness

	Dhruva	a great child devotee of Lord Viṣṇu
	Dhyāna śloka	verse which helps in meditation
	Devarṣi Nārada	divine sage, celestial musician, and traveling monk spreading devotion toward the Lord
	Divālī	a major Hindu festival, the festival of lights celebrating the victory of good over evil
G	*Gaṇeśa*	Lord revered as the remover of obstacles
	Gāyatrī Mantra	a sacred Vedic mantra invoking Lord Sun, who also symbolizes God, Truth, the Self
	gopis	devotees of Lord Kṛṣṇa, exemplifying the most intense love for the Divine
	Guru	teacher; usually used to denote a spiritual teacher
	Gurukula	ancient Indian residential school wherein students lived in proximity of the Guru
	Gurustotram	Sanskrit verses in praise of the Guru
	Guru-śiṣya paramparā	the lineage of Guru and disciple
	Guru Pūrṇimā	festival dedicated to the worship of the Guru; birthday of Sage Veda Vyāsa, the teacher of all teachers
H	*Hiraṇyakaśyapu*	demon king; father of Prahlāda
	Holī	Hindu Spring and harvest festival of colors
I	*Indra*	king of gods and ruler of the heavens; the Hindu god of thunder and rain
	Iśvara	Lord
J	*Jagadīśvara*	Lord of the world
	japa mālā	string of 108 beads used for continuous chanting of the Lord's name or a mantra
	Janmāṣṭamī	Hindu festival celebrating the incarnation of Lord Kṛṣṇa
	jñāna	knowledge
	jñāna yajñās	Knowledge Sacrifice, a series of lectures on Vedāntā; sacrificing one's ignorance in the fire of knowledge.
K	*kamaṇḍalū*	a vessel used by ascetics for carrying water
	karmaphala	the results, or fruits, of action
	Kṛṣṇa	a beloved incarnation of Lord Viṣṇu
L	*likhita japa*	repeated writing of the Lord's name or mantra

	loka	universe or any particular division of it
	Lord Brahmā	Lord expressing as the Creator
	Lord Śiva	Lord expressing as the Destroyer
M	*Mahābhārata*	longest historic epic poem (in 100,000 verses) composed by Sage Veda Vyāsa
	Mahāsamādhī	end of the physical being of a spiritual Master
	Mahāmṛtyuñjaya mantra	well-known Vedic prayer for Lord Śiva
	mananam	contemplation, reflection
	manasa pūjā	mental worship
	mātṛ pūjā	worship of mother
N	*Navayogīs*	the nine yogis mentioned in the Bhāgavata
P	*Pañcatantra*	collection of animal fables providing instruction on human values
	Prahlāda	a great child devotee of Lord Viṣṇu, son of Hiraṇyakaśyapu
	prāṇāyāma	breath-control exercises advocated in yoga
	prasāda	anything that is first offered to a deity or saint and then distributed as a blessing
	pūjā	ritualistic worship
	Purāṇas	the eighteen Purānas, consisting of ancient scriptures in the form of stories of the Lord and His devotees
R	*Rādhā*	beloved of Lord Kṛṣṇa, symbolizing bliss, devotion, and surrender
	Rāmāyaṇa	epic depicting the life of Lord Rāma, composed by Sage Valmiki
	Ṛṣī	'Seer' or sage to whom the Vedas were originally revealed
	Rāvaṇa	demon king of the epic Rāmāyaṇa
S	*sādhanā*	spiritual practices
	Sage Vālmīki	the first poet of Sanskrit literature; author of the epic Rāmāyaṇa
	Saint Tulsidas	poet-saint, reformer, and philosopher; author of the epic Rāmacharitmānas
	saṁskāra	inclination; impression; innate tendency
	saṁskāra pradhāna	emphasis on inculcating noble values and right disposition in life
	Sant Gyaneshwar	thirteenth century saint, poet, and philosopher from Maharashtra

	sannyāsī	renunciate
	Sanātana Dharma	"Eternal Way" — the Hindu spiritual tradition
	Sarasvatī Devi	Hindu goddess of knowledge, music, arts, and science
	sāttvic	one of the three thought textures (guṇas) that characterize qualities of the human personality; sāttvic expresses as knowledge, purity, and serenity
	satsaṇga	company of the wise and pure
	sevā	service done in a spirit of selflessness
	sevak/sevikā	one who is serving
	Śivarātrī	Hindu festival celebrating the auspicious night dedicated to Lord Śiva
	śraddhā	complete faith and trust in the words of the scriptures and the Guru
	Śrī	title of respect used before the name of a deity, a holy book, or a man
	śravaṇa	listening to scriptures from the Guru
	stotras	hymns
	subhāṣita	wise sayings and instructions in Sanskrit literature, presented in a pithy style
	svādhyāya	regular chanting or study of the scriptures
T	*tamburā*	stringed musical instrument; used as a drone
	tapas	austerity
U	*Upaniṣad*	portion of Vedas that pertain to knowledge of the Self
	upāsanā	spiritual practice; worship
V	*vāsanās*	habitual tendencies; impressions gained from past inclinations or tendencies dictated by past actions
	Vedānta	the Upaniṣadic section of each of the Vedas, dealing with the knowledge of the supreme Reality
	Vedic	relating to the Vedas, which are the basic scriptures of Hinduism
Y	*yajña*	worship; cooperative activities that integrate